DATA WRANGLING
Using Pandas, SQL, and Java

DATA WRANGLING
Using Pandas, SQL, and Java

Oswald Campesato

MERCURY LEARNING AND INFORMATION
Dulles, Virginia
Boston, Massachusetts
New Delhi

Publisher: David Pallai

MERCURY LEARNING AND INFORMATION
22841 Quicksilver Drive
Dulles, VA 20166
info@merclearning.com
www.merclearning.com
1-800-232-0223

O. Campesato. *Data Wrangling Using Pandas, SQL, and Java.*
ISBN: 978-1-68392-904-8

Library of Congress Control Number: 2022945211
222324321   Printed on acid-free paper in the United States of America.

Our titles are available for adoption, license, or bulk purchase by institutions, corporations, etc. For additional information, please contact the Customer Service Dept. at 800-232-0223(toll free).

All of our titles are available in digital format at *academiccourseware.com* and other digital vendors. *Companion files for this title are available by writing to the publisher at info@merclearning.com.* The sole obligation of MERCURY LEARNING AND INFORMATION to the purchaser is to replace the book, based on defective materials or faulty workmanship, but not based on the operation or functionality of the product.

I'd like to dedicate this book to my parents —
may this bring joy and happiness into their lives.

CONTENTS

PREFACE

WHAT IS THE VALUE PROPOSITION FOR THIS BOOK?

This book contains a fast-paced introduction to as much relevant information about managing data that can be reasonably included in a book of this size. However, you will be exposed to a variety of features of NumPy and Pandas, how to create databases and tables in MySQL, and how to perform many data cleaning tasks and data wrangling.

Some topics are presented in a cursory manner, which is for two main reasons. First, it's important that you be exposed to these concepts. In some cases, you will find topics that might pique your interest, and hence motivate you to learn more about them through self-study; in other cases, you will probably be satisfied with a brief introduction. In other words, you decide whether to delve into more detail regarding the topics in this book.

Second, a full treatment of all the topics that are covered in this book would significantly increase its size, and few people have the time to read technical tomes.

THE TARGET AUDIENCE

This book is intended primarily for people who plan to become data scientists as well as anyone who needs to perform data cleaning tasks. This book is also intended to reach an international audience of readers with highly diverse backgrounds in various age groups. Hence, this book uses standard English rather than colloquial expressions that might be confusing to those readers. People learn by different types of imitation, which includes reading, writing, or hearing new material. This book takes these points into consideration to provide a comfortable and meaningful learning experience for the intended readers.

WHAT WILL I LEARN FROM THIS BOOK?

The first chapter briefly introduces Python, followed by Chapter 2, which delves into processing different data types in a dataset, along with normalization, standardization, and handling missing data. You will learn about outliers and how to detect them via z-scores and quantile transformation. Then you will learn about SMOTE for handling imbalanced datasets.

Chapter 3 introduces Pandas, which is a powerful Python library that enables you to read the contents of CSV files (and other text files) into data frames (somewhat analogous to Excel spreadsheets), where you can programmatically slice-and-dice the data to conform to your requirements.

Since large quantities of data are stored in the form structured data in relational databases, Chapter 4 introduces you to SQL concepts and how to perform basic operations in MySQL, such as working with databases.

Chapter 5 contains Java-based code samples for creating and accessing data in a MySQL database. Chapter 6 introduces you to data cleaning, along with various techniques for handling different scenarios, such as missing data and outliers.

The seventh chapter of this book explains *data wrangling*, and contains Python scripts and awk-based shell scripts to solve various tasks. Finally, there is an appendix for awk, which will assist you in understanding the awk-based scripts in Chapter 7.

WHY ARE THE CODE SAMPLES PRIMARILY IN PYTHON?

Most of the code samples are short (usually less than one page and sometimes less than half a page), and if need be, you can easily and quickly copy/paste the code into a new Jupyter notebook. For the Python code samples that reference a CSV file, you need an additional code snippet in the corresponding Jupyter notebook to access the CSV file. Moreover, the code samples execute quickly, so you won't need to avail yourself of the free GPU that is provided in Google Colaboratory.

If you do decide to use Google Colaboratory, you can easily copy/paste the Python code into a notebook, and use the upload feature to upload existing Jupyter notebooks. Keep in mind the following point: if the Python code references a CSV file, make sure that you include the appropriate code snippet (as explained in Chapter 1) to access the CSV file in the corresponding Jupyter notebook in Google Colaboratory.

DO I NEED TO LEARN THE THEORY PORTIONS OF THIS BOOK?

Once again, the answer depends on the extent to which you plan to become involved in data analytics. For example, if you plan to study machine learning, then you will probably learn how to create and train a model, which is a task that is performed after data cleaning tasks. In general, you will probably need to learn everything that you encounter in this book if you are planning to become a machine learning engineer.

GETTING THE MOST FROM THIS BOOK

Some programmers learn well from prose, others learn well from sample code (and lots of it), which means that there's no single style that can be used for everyone.

Moreover, some programmers want to run the code first, see what it does, and then return to the code to delve into the details (and others use the opposite approach).

Consequently, there are various types of code samples in this book: some are short, some are long, and other code samples "build" from earlier code samples.

WHAT DO I NEED TO KNOW FOR THIS BOOK?

Current knowledge of Python 3.x is the most helpful skill. Knowledge of other programming languages (such as Java) can also be helpful because of the exposure to programming concepts and constructs. The less technical knowledge that you have, the more diligence will be required to understand the various topics that are covered.

If you want to be sure that you can grasp the material in this book, glance through some of the code samples to get an idea of how much is familiar to you and how much is new for you.

DOES THIS BOOK CONTAIN PRODUCTION-LEVEL CODE SAMPLES?

The primary purpose of the code samples in this book is to show you Python-based libraries for solving a variety of data-related tasks in conjunction with acquiring a rudimentary understanding of statistical concepts. Clarity has a higher priority than writing more compact code that is more difficult to understand (and possibly more prone to bugs). If you decide to use any of the code in this book in a production website, you should subject that code to the same rigorous analysis as the other parts of your code base.

WHAT ARE THE NON-TECHNICAL PREREQUISITES FOR THIS BOOK?

Although the answer to this question is more difficult to quantify, it's very important to have strong desire to learn about data cleaning and wrangling, along with the motivation and discipline to read and understand the code samples.

HOW DO I SET UP A COMMAND SHELL?

If you are a Mac user, there are three ways to do so. The first method is to use `Finder` to navigate to `Applications > Utilities` and then double click on the `Utilities` application. Next, if you already have a command shell available, you can launch a new command shell by typing the following command:

```
open /Applications/Utilities/Terminal.app
```

A second method for Mac users is to open a new command shell on a MacBook from a command shell that is already visible simply by clicking `command+n` in that command shell, and your Mac will launch another command shell.

If you are a PC user, you can install Cygwin (open source: *https://cygwin.com/*), which simulates bash commands, or use another toolkit such as MKS (a commercial product). Please read the online documentation that describes the download and installation process. Note that custom aliases are not automatically set if they are defined in a file other than the main start-up file (such as .bash_login).

COMPANION FILES

All the code samples and figures in this book may be obtained by writing to the publisher at info@merclearning.com.

WHAT ARE THE "NEXT STEPS" AFTER FINISHING THIS BOOK?

The answer to this question varies widely, mainly because the answer depends heavily on your objectives. If you are interested primarily in NLP, then you can learn more advanced concepts, such as attention, transformers, and the BERT-related models.

If you are primarily interested in machine learning, there are some subfields of machine learning, such as deep learning and reinforcement learning (and deep reinforcement learning) that might appeal to you. Fortunately, there are many resources available, and you can perform an Internet search for those resources. One other point: the aspects of machine learning for you to learn depend on who you are. The needs of a machine learning engineer, data scientist, manager, student, or software developer are all different.

## CHAPTER 1

INTRODUCTION TO PYTHON

This chapter contains an introduction to Python, with information about useful tools for installing Python modules, basic Python constructs, and how to work with some data types in Python.

The first part of this chapter covers how to install Python, some Python environment variables, and how to use the Python interpreter. You will see Python code samples and how to save Python code in text files that you can launch from the command line. The second part of this chapter shows you how to work with simple data types, such as numbers, fractions, and strings. The final part of this chapter discusses exceptions and how to use them in Python scripts.

NOTE *The Python scripts in this book are for Python 3.*

TOOLS FOR PYTHON

The Anaconda Python distribution is available for Windows, Linux, and Mac:

http://continuum.io/downloads

Anaconda is well-suited for modules such as NumPy (discussed in Chapter 3) and SciPy (not discussed in this book). If you are a Windows user, Anaconda appears to be a better alternative (and also works well for Mac and Linux).

easy_install and pip

Both `easy_install` and `pip` are easy to use when you need to install Python modules. Whenever you need to install a Python module (and there are many in this book), use either `easy_install` or `pip` with the following syntax:

```
easy_install <module-name>
pip install <module-name>
```

NOTE *Python-based modules are easier to install, whereas modules with code written in C are usually faster but more difficult in terms of installation.*

virtualenv

The `virtualenv` tool enables you to create isolated Python environments, and its home page is available online:

http://www.virtualenv.org/en/latest/virtualenv.html

`virtualenv` addresses the problem of preserving the correct dependencies and versions (and indirectly permissions) for different applications. If you are a Python novice you might not need `virtualenv` right now, but keep this tool in mind.

IPython

Another useful tool is `IPython` (which won a Jolt award), and its home page is available online:

http://ipython.org/install.html

Type `ipython` to invoke `IPython` from the command line:

```
ipython
```

The preceding command displays the following output:

```
Python 3.8.6 (default, Oct  8 2020, 14:06:32)
Type 'copyright', 'credits' or 'license' for more information
IPython 7.18.1 -- An enhanced Interactive Python. Type '?' for help.

In [1]:
```

Type a question mark ("?") at the prompt and you will see some useful information, a portion of which is here:

```
IPython -- An enhanced Interactive Python
==========================================

IPython offers a fully compatible replacement for the standard Python
interpreter, with convenient shell features, special commands, command
history mechanism and output results caching.
At your system command line, type 'ipython -h' to see the command line
options available. This document only describes interactive features.

GETTING HELP
------------

Within IPython you have various way to access help:

?           -> Introduction and overview of IPython's features (this
               screen).
object?     -> Details about 'object'.
object??    -> More detailed, verbose information about 'object'.
%quickref   -> Quick reference of all IPython specific syntax and magics.
help        -> Access Python's own help system.

If you are in terminal IPython you can quit this screen by pressing 'q'.
```

Finally, type `quit` at the command prompt and you will exit the `ipython` shell.

The next section shows you how to check whether Python is installed on your machine and where you can download Python.

PYTHON INSTALLATION

Before you download anything, check if you have Python already installed on your machine (which is likely if you have a Macbook or a Linux machine) by typing the following command in a command shell:

```
python -V
```

The output for the Macbook used in this book is here:

```
Python 3.8.6
```

NOTE *Install Python 3.8.6 (or as close as possible to this version) on your machine so that you will have the same version of Python that was used to test the Python scripts in this book.*

If you need to install Python on your machine, navigate to the Python home page and select the "Downloads" link or navigate directly to this website:

http://www.python.org/download/

In addition, PythonWin is available for Windows, and its home page is as follows:

http://www.cgl.ucsf.edu/Outreach/pc204/pythonwin.html

Use any text editor that can create, edit, and save Python scripts and save them as plain text files (don't use Microsoft Word).

After you have Python installed and configured on your machine, you are ready to work with the Python scripts in this book.

SETTING THE PATH ENVIRONMENT VARIABLE (WINDOWS ONLY)

The PATH environment variable specifies a list of directories that are searched whenever you specify an executable program from the command line. A good guide to setting up your environment so that the Python executable is always available in every command shell is to follow the instructions here:

http://www.blog.pythonlibrary.org/2011/11/24/python-101-setting-up-python-on-windows/

LAUNCHING PYTHON ON YOUR MACHINE

There are three different ways to launch Python:

• Use the Python Interactive Interpreter.
• Launch Python scripts from the command line.
• Use an IDE.

The next section shows you how to launch the Python interpreter from the command line. Later in this chapter, you will learn how to launch Python scripts from the command line and also about Python IDEs.

The emphasis in this book is to launch Python scripts from the command line or to enter code in the Python interpreter.

The Python Interactive Interpreter

Launch the Python interactive interpreter from the command line by opening a command shell and typing the following command:

```
python
```

You will see the following prompt (or something similar):

```
Python 3.8.6 (default, Oct  8 2020, 14:06:32)
[Clang 12.0.0 (clang-1200.0.32.2)] on darwin
Type "help", "copyright", "credits" or "license" for more information.
>>>
```

Now type the expression 2 + 7 at the prompt:

```
>>> 2 + 7
```

Python displays the following result:

```
9
>>>
```

Press ctrl-d to exit the Python shell.

You can launch any Python script from the command line by preceding it with the word "python." For example, if you have a Python script myscript.py that contains Python commands, launch the script as follows:

```
python myscript.py
```

As a simple illustration, suppose that the Python script myscript.py contains the following Python code:

```
print('Hello World from Python')
print('2 + 7 = ', 2+7)
```

When you launch the preceding Python script you will see the following output:

```
Hello World from Python
2 + 7 =  9
```

PYTHON IDENTIFIERS

A Python identifier is the name of a variable, function, class, module, or other Python object, and a valid identifier conforms to the following rules:

- starts with a letter A to Z or a to z or an underscore (_)
- zero or more letters, underscores, and digits (0 to 9)

NOTE *Python identifiers cannot contain characters such as @, $, and %.*

Python is a case-sensitive language, so Abc and abc are different identifiers in Python. In addition, Python has the following naming conventions:

- Class names start with an uppercase letter and all other identifiers with a lowercase letter.
- An initial underscore is used for private identifiers.
- Two initial underscores are used for strongly private identifiers.

A Python identifier with two initial underscore and two trailing underscore characters indicates a language-defined special name.

LINES, INDENTATION, AND MULTI-LINES

Unlike other programming languages (such as Java or Objective-C), Python uses indentation instead of curly braces for code blocks. Indentation must be consistent in a code block, as shown here:

```
if True:
    print("ABC")
    print("DEF")
else:
    print("ABC")
    print("DEF")
```

Multi-line statements in Python can terminate with a new line or the backslash ("\") character, as shown here:

```
total = x1 + \
        x2 + \
        x3
```

Obviously, you can place x1, x2, and x3 on the same line, so there is no reason to use three separate lines; however, this functionality is available in case you need to add a set of variables that do not fit on a single line.

You can specify multiple statements in one line by using a semicolon (";") to separate each statement, as shown here:

```
a=10; b=5; print(a); print(a+b)
```

The output of the preceding code snippet is here:

```
10
15
```

NOTE *The use of semi-colons and the continuation character are discouraged in Python.*

QUOTATION AND COMMENTS

Python allows single ('), double ("), and triple (' " or """) quotes for string literals, provided that they match at the beginning and the end of the string. You can use triple quotes for strings that span multiple lines. The following examples are legal Python strings:

```
word = 'word'
line = "This is a sentence."
para = """This is a paragraph. This paragraph contains
more than one sentence."""
```

A string literal that begins with the letter "r" (for "raw") treats everything as a literal character and "escapes" the meaning of meta characters, as shown here:

```
a1 = r'\n'
a2 = r'\r'
a3 = r'\t'
print('a1:',a1,'a2:',a2,'a3:',a3)
```

The output of the preceding code block is here:

```
a1: \n a2: \r a3: \t
```

You can embed a single quote in a pair of double quotes (and vice versa) to display a single quote or a double quote. Another way to accomplish the same result is to precede a single or double quote with a backslash (\) character. The following code block illustrates these techniques:

```
b1 = "'"
b2 = '"'
b3 = '\''
b4 = "\""
print('b1:',b1,'b2:',b2)
print('b3:',b3,'b4:',b4)
```

The output of the preceding code block is here:

```
b1: ' b2: "
b3: ' b4: "
```

A hash sign (#) that is not inside a string literal is the character that indicates the beginning of a comment. Moreover, all characters after the # and up to the physical line end are part of the comment (and ignored by the Python interpreter). Consider the following code block:

```
#!/usr/bin/python
# First comment
print("Hello, Python!")   # second comment
```

This will produce following result:

```
Hello, Python!
```

A comment may be on the same line after a statement or expression:

```
name = "Tom Jones" # This is also comment
```

You can comment multiple lines as follows:

```
# This is comment one
# This is comment two
# This is comment three
```

A blank line in Python is a line containing only whitespace, a comment, or both.

SAVING YOUR CODE IN A MODULE

Earlier you saw how to launch the Python interpreter from the command line and then enter Python commands. However, everything that you type in the Python interpreter is only valid for the current session: if you exit the interpreter and then launch the interpreter again, your previous definitions are no longer valid. Fortunately, Python enables you to store code in a text file, as discussed in the next section.

A *module* in Python is a text file that contains Python statements. In the previous section, you saw how the Python interpreter enables you to test code snippets whose definitions are valid for the current session. If you want to retain the code snippets and other definitions, place them in a text file so that you can execute that code outside of the Python interpreter.

The outermost statements in a Python are executed from top to bottom when the module is imported for the first time, which will then set up its variables and functions.

A Python module can be run directly from the command line, as shown here:

```
python first.py
```

As an illustration, place the following two statements in a text file called first.py:

```
x = 3
print(x)
```

Type the following command:

```
Python first.py
```

The output from the preceding command is 3, which is the same as executing the preceding code from the Python interpreter.

When a Python module is run directly, the special variable __name__ is set to __main__. You will often see the following type of code in a Python module:

```
if __name__ == '__main__':
    # do something here
    print('Running directly')
```

The preceding code snippet enables Python to determine if a module was launched from the command line or imported into another Python module.

SOME STANDARD MODULES

The Python Standard Library provides many modules that can simplify your own Python scripts. A list of the Standard Library modules is available online:

http://www.python.org/doc/

Some of the most important Python modules include cgi, math, os, pickle, random, re, socket, sys, time, and urllib.

The code samples in this book use the modules math, os, random, re, socket, sys, time, and urllib. You need to import these modules to use them in your code. For example, the following code block shows you how to import four standard Python modules:

```
import datetime
import re
import sys
import time
```

The code samples in this book import one or more of the preceding modules, as well as other Python modules.

THE HELP() AND DIR() FUNCTIONS

An Internet search for Python-related topics usually returns a number of links with useful information. Alternatively, you can check the official Python documentation site: *docs.python.org*.

In addition, Python provides the help() and dir() functions, which are accessible from the Python interpreter. The help() function displays documentation strings, whereas the dir() function displays defined symbols. For example, if you type help(sys), you will see documentation for the sys module, whereas dir(sys) displays a list of the defined symbols.

Type the following command in the Python interpreter to display the string-related methods in Python:

```
>>> dir(str)
```

The preceding command generates the following output:

```
['__add__', '__class__', '__contains__', '__delattr__', '__doc__',
'__eq__', '__format__', '__ge__', '__getattribute__', '__getitem__',
'__getnewargs__', '__getslice__', '__gt__', '__hash__', '__init__', '__
le__', '__len__', '__lt__', '__mod__', '__mul__', '__ne__', '__new__',
'__reduce__', '__reduce_ex__', '__repr__', '__rmod__', '__rmul__', '__
setattr__', '__sizeof__', '__str__', '__subclasshook__', '_formatter_
field_name_split', '_formatter_parser', 'capitalize', 'center', 'count',
'decode', 'encode', 'endswith', 'expandtabs', 'find', 'format', 'index',
'isalnum', 'isalpha', 'isdigit', 'islower', 'isspace', 'istitle',
'isupper', 'join', 'ljust', 'lower', 'lstrip', 'partition', 'replace',
'rfind', 'rindex', 'rjust', 'rpartition', 'rsplit', 'rstrip', 'split',
'splitlines', 'startswith', 'strip', 'swapcase', 'title', 'translate',
'upper', 'zfill']
```

The preceding list gives you a consolidated "dump" of built-in functions (including some that are discussed later in this chapter). Although the max() function obviously returns the maximum value of its arguments, the purpose of other functions, such as filter() or map(), is not immediately apparent (unless you have used them in other programming languages). The preceding list provides a starting point for finding out more about various Python built-in functions that are not discussed in this chapter.

Note that while dir() does not list the names of built-in functions and variables, you can obtain this information from the standard module __builtin__ that is automatically imported under the name __builtins__:

```
>>> dir(__builtins__)
```

The following command shows you how to get more information about a function:

```
help(str.lower)
```

The output from the preceding command is here:

```
Help on method_descriptor:

lower(...)
    S.lower() -> string

    Return a copy of the string S converted to lowercase.
(END)
```

Check the online documentation and experiment with help() and dir() when you need additional information about a particular function or module.

COMPILE TIME AND RUNTIME CODE CHECKING

Python performs some compile-time checking, but most checks are *deferred* until code execution. Consequently, if your Python code references a user-defined function that does not exist, the code will compile successfully. In fact, the code will fail with an exception *only* when the code execution path references the non-existent function.

As a simple example, consider the following Python function `myFunc` that references the non-existent function called `DoesNotExist`:

```
def myFunc(x):
    if x == 3:
        print(DoesNotExist(x))
    else:
        print('x: ',x)
```

The preceding code will only fail when the `myFunc` function is passed the value 3, after which Python raises an error.

Now that you understand some basic concepts (such as how to use the Python interpreter) and how to launch your custom Python modules, the next section discusses primitive data types.

SIMPLE DATA TYPES

Python supports primitive data types, such as numbers (integers, floating point numbers, and exponential numbers), strings, and dates. Python also supports more complex data types, such as lists (or arrays), tuples, and dictionaries. The next several sections discuss some of the Python primitive data types, along with code snippets that show you how to perform various operations on those data types.

WORKING WITH NUMBERS

Python provides arithmetic operations for manipulating numbers a straightforward manner that is similar to other programming languages. The following examples involve arithmetic operations on integers:

```
>>> 2+2
4
>>> 4/3
1
>>> 3*8
24
```

The following example assigns numbers to two variables and computes their product:

```
>>> x = 4
>>> y = 7
>>> x * y
28
```

The following examples demonstrate arithmetic operations involving integers:

```
>>> 2+2
4
>>> 4/3
1
>>> 3*8
24
```

Notice that division (/) of two integers is actually truncation in which only the integer result is retained. The following example converts a floating point number into exponential form:

```
>>> fnum = 0.00012345689000007
>>> "%.14e"%fnum
'1.23456890000070e-04'
```

You can use the int() function and the float() function to convert strings to numbers:

```
word1 = "123"
word2 = "456.78"
var1 = int(word1)
var2 = float(word2)
print("var1: ",var1," var2: ",var2)
```

The output from the preceding code block is here:

```
var1:  123   var2:  456.78
```

Alternatively, you can use the eval() function:

```
word1 = "123"
word2 = "456.78"
var1 = eval(word1)
var2 = eval(word2)
print("var1: ",var1," var2: ",var2)
```

If you attempt to convert a string that is not a valid integer or a floating point number, Python raises an exception, so it's advisable to place your code in a try/except block (discussed later in this chapter).

Working with Other Bases

Numbers in Python are in base 10 (the default), but you can easily convert numbers to other bases. For example, the following code block initializes the variable x with the value 1234, and then displays that number in base 2, 8, and 16, respectively:

```
>>> x = 1234
>>> bin(x) '0b10011010010'
>>> oct(x) '0o2322'
>>> hex(x) '0x4d2'
```

Use the format() function if you want to suppress the 0b, 0o, or 0x prefixes, as shown here:

```
>>> format(x, 'b') '10011010010'
>>> format(x, 'o') '2322'
>>> format(x, 'x') '4d2'
```

Negative integers are displayed with a negative sign:

```
>>> x = -1234
>>> format(x, 'b') '-10011010010'
>>> format(x, 'x') '-4d2'
```

The chr() Function

The Python `chr()` function takes a positive integer as a parameter and converts it to its corresponding alphabetic value (if one exists). The letters `A` through `Z` have decimal representations of `65` through `91` (which correspond to hexadecimals `41` through `5b`), and the lowercase letters a through z have decimal representations of `97` through `122` (hexadecimals `61` through `7b`). Here is an example of using the `chr()` function to print an uppercase `A`:

```
>>> x=chr(65)
>>> x
'A'
```

The following code block prints the ASCII values for a range of integers:

```
result = ""
for x in range(65,90):
  print(x, chr(x))
  result = result+chr(x)+' '
print("result: ",result)
```

You can represent a range of characters with the following line:

```
for x in range(65,90):
```

However, the following equivalent code snippet is more intuitive:

```
for x in range(ord('A'), ord('Z')):
```

If you want to display the result for lowercase letters, change the preceding range from `(65,91)` to either of the following statements:

```
for x in range(65,90):
for x in range(ord('a'), ord('z')):
```

The round() Function in Python

The Python `round()` function enables you to round decimal values to the nearest precision:

```
>>> round(1.23, 1)
1.2
>>> round(-3.42,1)
-3.4
```

Formatting Numbers in Python

Python allows you to specify the number of decimal places of precision to use when printing decimal numbers, as shown here:

```
>>> x = 1.23456
>>> format(x, '0.2f')
'1.23'
>>> format(x, '0.3f')
'1.235'
```

```
>>> 'value is {:0.3f}'.format(x) 'value is 1.235'
>>> from decimal import Decimal
>>> a = Decimal('4.2')
>>> b = Decimal('2.1')
>>> a + b
Decimal('6.3')
>>> print(a + b)
6.3
>>> (a + b) == Decimal('6.3')
True
>>> x = 1234.56789
>>> # Two decimal places of accuracy
>>> format(x, '0.2f')
'1234.57'
>>> # Right justified in 10 chars, one-digit accuracy
>>> format(x, '>10.1f')
' 1234.6'
>>> # Left justified
>>> format(x, '<10.1f') '1234.6 '
>>> # Centered
>>> format(x, '^10.1f') ' 1234.6 '
>>> # Inclusion of thousands separator
>>> format(x, ',')
'1,234.56789'
>>> format(x, '0,.1f')
'1,234.6'
```

WORKING WITH FRACTIONS

Python supports the `Fraction()` function (defined in the `fractions` module), which accepts two integers that represent the numerator and the denominator (which must be non-zero) of a fraction. Several example of defining and manipulating fractions in Python are shown here:

```
>>> from fractions import Fraction
>>> a = Fraction(5, 4)
>>> b = Fraction(7, 16)
>>> print(a + b)
27/16
>>> print(a * b) 35/64
>>> # Getting numerator/denominator
>>> c = a * b
>>> c.numerator
35
>>> c.denominator 64
>>> # Converting to a float >>> float(c)
0.546875
>>> # Limiting the denominator of a value
>>> print(c.limit_denominator(8))
4
>>> # Converting a float to a fraction >>> x = 3.75
>>> y = Fraction(*x.as_integer_ratio())
>>> y
Fraction(15, 4)
```

Before delving into Python code samples that work with strings, the next section briefly discusses Unicode and UTF-8, both of which are character encodings.

UNICODE AND UTF-8

A Unicode string consists of a sequence of numbers that are between 0 and 0x10ffff, where each number represents a group of bytes. An *encoding* is the manner in which a Unicode string is translated into a sequence of bytes. Among the various encodings, UTF-8 ("Unicode Transformation Format") is perhaps the most common, and it's also the default encoding for many systems. The digit 8 in UTF-8 indicates that the encoding uses 8-bit numbers, whereas UTF-16 uses 16-bit numbers (but this encoding is less common).

The ASCII character set is a subset of UTF-8, so a valid ASCII string can be read as a UTF-8 string without any re-encoding required. In addition, a Unicode string can be converted into a UTF-8 string.

WORKING WITH UNICODE

Python supports Unicode, which means that you can render characters in different languages. Unicode data can be stored and manipulated in the same way as strings. Create a Unicode string by prepending the letter "u," as shown here:

```
>>> u'Hello from Python!'
u'Hello from Python!'
```

Special characters can be included in a string by specifying their Unicode value. For example, the following Unicode string embeds a space (which has the Unicode value 0x0020) in a string:

```
>>> u'Hello\u0020from Python!'
u'Hello from Python!'
```

Listing 1.1 displays the content of `Unicode1.py` that illustrates how to display a string of characters in Japanese (Hiragana) and another string of characters in Chinese (Mandarin).

LISTING 1.1: Unicode1.py

```
chinese1 = u'\u5c07\u63a2\u8a0e HTML5 \u53ca\u5176\u4ed6'
hiragana = u'D3 \u306F \u304B\u3063\u3053\u3043\u3043 \u3067\u3059!'

print('Chinese:',chinese1)
print('Hiragana:',hiragana)
```

The output of Listing 1.2 is here:

```
Chinese: 將探討 HTML5 及其他
Hiragana: D3 は かっこいぃ です!
```

The next portion of this chapter shows you how to "slice and dice" text strings with built-in Python functions.

WORKING WITH STRINGS

A string in Python 3 is based on Unicode, whereas a string in Python 2 is a sequence of ASCII-encoded bytes. You can concatenate two strings using the + operator. The following example prints a string and then concatenates two single-letter strings:

```
>>> 'abc'
'abc'
>>> 'a' + 'b'
'ab'
```

You can use + or * to concatenate identical strings, as shown here:

```
>>> 'a' + 'a' + 'a'
'aaa'
>>> 'a' * 3
'aaa'
```

You can assign strings to variables and print them using the `print` command:

```
>>> print('abc')
abc
>>> x = 'abc'
>>> print(x)
abc
>>> y = 'def'
>>> print(x + y)
Abcdef
```

You can "unpack" the letters of a string and assign them to variables, as shown here:

```
>>> str = "World"
>>> x1,x2,x3,x4,x5 = str
>>> x1
'W'
>>> x2
'o'
>>> x3
'r'
>>> x4
'l'
>>> x5
'd'
```

The preceding code snippets shows you how easy it is to extract the letters in a text string. You can extract substrings of a string, as shown in the following examples:

```
>>> x = "abcdef"
>>> x[0]
'a'
>>> x[-1]
'f'
```

```
>>> x[1:3]
'bc'
>>> x[0:2] + x[5:]
'abf'
```

However, you will cause an error if you attempt to "subtract" two strings, as you probably expect:

```
>>> 'a' - 'b'
Traceback (most recent call last):
  File "<stdin>", line 1, in <module>
TypeError: unsupported operand type(s) for -: 'str' and 'str'
```

The `try/except` construct in Python (discussed later in this chapter) enables you to handle the preceding type of exception more gracefully.

Comparing Strings

You can use the methods `lower()` and `upper()` to convert a string to lowercase and uppercase, respectively, as shown here:

```
>>> 'Python'.lower()
'python'
>>> 'Python'.upper()
'PYTHON'
>>>
```

The methods `lower()` and `upper()` are useful for performing a case insensitive comparison of two ASCII strings. Listing 1.2 displays the content of `Compare.py` that uses the `lower()` function to compare two ASCII strings.

LISTING 1.2: Compare.py

```
x = 'Abc'
y = 'abc'

if(x == y):
  print('x and y: identical')
elif (x.lower() == y.lower()):
  print('x and y: case insensitive match')
else:
  print('x and y: different')
```

Since x contains mixed case letters and y contains lowercase letters, Listing 1.2 displays the following output:

```
x and y: different
```

Formatting Strings in Python

Python provides the functions `string.lstring()`, `string.rstring()`, and `string.center()` for positioning a text string so that it is left-justified, right-justified, and centered, respectively. As you saw in a previous section, Python also provides the `format()` method for advanced interpolation features. Now enter the following commands in the Python interpreter:

```
import string

str1 = 'this is a string'
print(string.ljust(str1, 10))
print(string.rjust(str1, 40))
print(string.center(str1,40))
```

The output is shown here:

```
this is a string
            this is a string
            this is a string
```

UNINITIALIZED VARIABLES AND THE VALUE NONE

Python distinguishes between an uninitialized variable and the value `None`. The former is a variable that has not been assigned a value, whereas the value `None` is a value that indicates "no value." Collections and methods often return the value `None`, and you can test for the value `None` in conditional logic.

The next portion of this chapter shows you how to "slice and dice" text strings with built-in Python functions.

SLICING AND SPLICING STRINGS

Python enables you to extract substrings of a string (called "slicing") using array notation. Slice notation is `start:stop:step`, where the `start`, `stop`, and `step` values are integers that specify the start value, end value, and the increment value. The interesting part about slicing in Python is that you can use the value –1, which operates from the right-side instead of the left-side of a string. Some examples of slicing a string are here:

```
text1 = "this is a string"
print('First 7 characters:',text1[0:7])
print('Characters 2-4:',text1[2:4])
print('Right-most character:',text1[-1])
print('Right-most 2 characters:',text1[-3:-1])
```

The output from the preceding code block is here:

```
First 7 characters: this is
Characters 2-4: is
Right-most character: g
Right-most 2 characters: in
```

Later in this chapter, you will see how to insert a string in the middle of another string.

Testing for Digits and Alphabetic Characters

Python enables you to examine each character in a string and then test whether that character is a digit or an alphabetic character. This section provides a simple introduction to regular expressions.

Listing 1.3 displays the content of `CharTypes.py` that illustrates how to determine if a string contains digits or characters. Although we have not discussed `if` statements in Python, the examples in Listing 1.3 are straightforward.

LISTING 1.3: CharTypes.py

```
str1 = "4"
str2 = "4234"
str3 = "b"
str4 = "abc"
str5 = "a1b2c3"

if(str1.isdigit()):
  print("this is a digit:",str1)

if(str2.isdigit()):
  print("this is a digit:",str2)

if(str3.isalpha()):
  print("this is alphabetic:",str3)
if(str4.isalpha()):
  print("this is alphabetic:",str4)

if(not str5.isalpha()):
  print("this is not pure alphabetic:",str5)

print("capitalized first letter:",str5.title())
```

Listing 1.3 initializes some variables, followed by two conditional tests that check whether `str1` and `str2` are digits using the `isdigit()` function. The next portion of Listing 1.3 checks if `str3`, `str4`, and `str5` are alphabetic strings using the `isalpha()` function. The output of Listing 1.3 is here:

```
this is a digit: 4
this is a digit: 4234
this is alphabetic: b
this is alphabetic: abc
this is not pure alphabetic: a1b2c3
capitalized first letter: A1B2C3
```

SEARCH AND REPLACE A STRING IN OTHER STRINGS

Python provides methods for searching and replacing a string in a second text string. Listing 1.4 displays the content of `FindPos1.py` that shows you how to use the `find()` function to search for the occurrence of one string in another string.

LISTING 1.4: FindPos1.py

```
item1 = 'abc'
item2 = 'Abc'
text = 'This is a text string with abc'

pos1 = text.find(item1)
pos2 = text.find(item2)

print('pos1=',pos1)
print('pos2=',pos2)
```

Listing 1.4 initializes the variables item1, item2, and text, and then searches for the index of the contents of item1 and item2 in the string text. The Python find() function returns the column number where the first successful match occurs; otherwise, the find() function returns a –1 if a match is unsuccessful.

The output from launching Listing 1.4 is here:

```
pos1 = 27
pos2 = -1
```

In addition to the find() method, you can use the in operator when you want to test for the presence of an element, as shown here:

```
>>> lst = [1,2,3]
>>> 1 in lst
True
```

Listing 1.5 displays the content of Replace1.py that shows you how to replace one string with another string.

LISTING 1.5: Replace1.py

```
text = 'This is a text string with abc'
print('text:',text)
text = text.replace('is a', 'was a')
print('text:',text)
```

Listing 1.5 starts by initializing the variable text and then printing its contents. The next portion of Listing 1.5 replaces the occurrence of "is a" with "was a" in the string text, and then prints the modified string. The output from launching Listing 1.5 is here:

```
text: This is a text string with abc
text: This was a text string with abc
```

REMOVE LEADING AND TRAILING CHARACTERS

Python provides the functions strip(), lstrip(), and rstrip() to remove characters in a text string. Listing 1.6 displays the content of Remove1.py that shows you how to search for a string.

LISTING 1.6: Remove1.py

```
text = '   leading and trailing white space   '
print('text1:','x',text,'y')

text = text.lstrip()
print('text2:','x',text,'y')

text = text.rstrip()
print('text3:','x',text,'y')
```

Listing 1.6 starts by concatenating the letter x and the contents of the variable text, and then printing the result. The second part of Listing 1.6 removes the leading white spaces in the string text and then appends the result to the letter x. The third part of Listing 1.6 removes the trailing white spaces in the string text (note that the leading white spaces have already been removed) and then appends the result to the letter x.

The output from launching Listing 1.6 is here:

```
text1: x   leading and trailing white space   y
text2: x leading and trailing white space   y
text3: x leading and trailing white space y
```

If you want to remove extra white spaces inside a text string, use the replace() function as discussed in the previous section. The following example illustrates how this can be accomplished, which also contains the re module for regular expressions:

```
import re
text = 'a     b'
a = text.replace(' ', '')
b = re.sub('\s+', ' ', text)

print(a)
print(b)
```

The result is here:

```
ab
a b
```

PRINTING TEXT WITHOUT NEWLINE CHARACTERS

If you need to suppress white space and a newline between objects output with multiple print statements, you can use concatenation or the write() function.

The first technique is to concatenate the string representations of each object using the str() function prior to printing the result. For example, execute the following statements in Python:

```
x = str(9)+str(0xff)+str(-3.1)
print('x: ',x)
```

The output is shown here:

```
x:    9255-3.1
```

The preceding line contains the concatenation of the numbers 9 and 255 (which is the decimal value of the hexadecimal number 0xff) and -3.1.

Incidentally, you can use the str() function with modules and user-defined classes. An example involving the Python built-in module sys is here:

```
>>> import sys
>>> print(str(sys))
<module 'sys' (built-in)>
```

The following code snippet illustrates how to use the write() function to display a string:

```
import sys
write = sys.stdout.write
write('123')
write('123456789')
```

The output is here:

```
1233
1234567899
```

TEXT ALIGNMENT

Python provides the methods ljust(), rjust(), and center() for aligning text. The ljust() and rjust() functions left justify and right justify a text string, respectively, whereas the center() function will center a string. An example is shown in the following code block:

```
text = 'Hello World'
text.ljust(20)
'Hello World '
>>> text.rjust(20)
' Hello World'
>>> text.center(20)
' Hello World '
```

You can use the Python format() function to align text. Use the <, >, or ^ characters, along with a desired width, to right justify, left justify, and center the text, respectively. The following examples illustrate how you can specify text justification:

```
>>> format(text, '>20')
'         Hello World'
>>>
>>> format(text, '<20')
'Hello World         '
>>>
>>> format(text, '^20')
'    Hello World     '
>>>
```

WORKING WITH DATES

Python provides a rich set of date-related functions that are documented online:

http://docs.python.org/2/library/datetime.html

Listing 1.7 displays the content of the Python script `Datetime2.py` that displays various date-related values, such as the current date and time; the day of the week, month, and year; and the time in seconds since the epoch.

LISTING 1.7: Datetime2.py

```
import time
import datetime

print("Time in seconds since the epoch: %s" %time.time())
print("Current date and time: " , datetime.datetime.now())
print("Or like this: " ,datetime.datetime.now().strftime("%y-%m-%d-%H-
%M"))

print("Current year: ", datetime.date.today().strftime("%Y"))
print("Month of year: ", datetime.date.today().strftime("%B"))
print("Week number of the year: ", datetime.date.today().strftime("%W"))
print("Weekday of the week: ", datetime.date.today().strftime("%w"))
print("Day of year: ", datetime.date.today().strftime("%j"))
print("Day of the month : ", datetime.date.today().strftime("%d"))
print("Day of week: ", datetime.date.today().strftime("%A"))
```

Listing 1.8 displays the output generated by executing the code in Listing 1.7.

LISTING 1.8: datetime2.out

```
Time in seconds since the epoch: 1375144195.66
Current date and time:  2013-07-29 17:29:55.664164
Or like this:  13-07-29-17-29
Current year:  2013
Month of year:  July
Week number of the year:  30
Weekday of the week:  1
Day of year:  210
Day of the month :  29
Day of week:  Monday
```

Python also enables you to perform arithmetic calculations with date-related values, as shown in the following code block:

```
>>> from datetime import timedelta
>>> a = timedelta(days=2, hours=6)
>>> b = timedelta(hours=4.5)
>>> c = a + b
>>> c.days
2
>>> c.seconds
```

```
37800
>>> c.seconds / 3600
10.5
>>> c.total_seconds() / 3600
58.5
```

Converting Strings to Dates

Listing 1.9 displays the content of `String2Date.py` that illustrates how to convert a string to a date and how to calculate the difference between two dates.

LISTING 1.9: String2Date.py

```
from datetime import datetime

text = '2014-08-13'
y = datetime.strptime(text, '%Y-%m-%d')
z = datetime.now()
diff = z - y
print('Date difference:',diff)
```

The output from Listing 1.9 is shown here:

```
Date difference: -210 days, 18:58:40.197130
```

EXCEPTION HANDLING

Unlike JavaScript, you cannot add a number and a string in Python. Fortunately, you can detect an illegal operation using the `try/except` construct in Python, which is similar to the `try/catch` construct in languages such as JavaScript and Java.

An example of a `try/except` block is here:

```
try:
  x = 4
  y = 'abc'
  z = x + y
except:
  print 'cannot add incompatible types:', x, y
```

When you run the preceding code in Python, the `print` statement in the `except` code block is executed because the variables x and y have incompatible types.

Earlier in the chapter, you also saw that subtracting two strings throws an exception:

```
>>> 'a' - 'b'
Traceback (most recent call last):
  File "<stdin>", line 1, in <module>
TypeError: unsupported operand type(s) for -: 'str' and 'str'
```

A simple way to handle this situation is to use a `try/except` block:

```
>>> try:
...   print('a' - 'b')
```

```
... except TypeError:
...   print('TypeError exception while trying to subtract two strings')
... except:
...   print('Exception while trying to subtract two strings')
...
```

The output from the preceding code block is here:

```
TypeError exception while trying to subtract two strings
```

As you can see, the preceding code block specifies the finer-grained exception called `TypeError`, followed by a "generic" `except` code block to handle all other exceptions that might occur during the execution of your Python code. This style resembles the exception handling in Java code.

Listing 1.10 displays the content of `Exception1.py` that illustrates how to handle various types of exceptions, which includes an exception due to a missing file.

LISTING 1.10: Exception1.py

```
import sys

try:
    f = open('myfile.txt')
    s = f.readline()
    i = int(s.strip())
except IOError as err:
    print("I/O error: {0}".format(err))
except ValueError:
    print("Could not convert data to an integer.")
except:
    print("Unexpected error:", sys.exc_info()[0])
    raise
```

Listing 1.10 contains a `try` block followed by three `except` statements. If an error occurs in the `try` block, the first `except` statement is compared with the type of exception that occurred. If there is a match, then the subsequent `print()` statement is executed, and the program terminates. If not, a similar test is performed with the second `except` statement. If neither `except` statement matches the exception, the third `except` statement handles the exception, which involves printing a message and then "raising" an exception.

Note that you can also specify multiple exception types in a single statement, as shown here:

```
except (NameError, RuntimeError, TypeError):
    print('One of three error types occurred')
```

The preceding code block is more compact, but you do not know which of the three error types occurred. Python allows you to define custom exceptions, but this topic is beyond the scope of this book.

HANDLING USER INPUT

Python enables you to read user input from the command line via the `input()` function (`raw_input()` for Python2.x). Typically, you assign user input to a variable, which will contain all characters that users enter from the keyboard. User input terminates when users press the <return> key (which is included with the input characters). Listing 1.11 displays the content of UserInput1.py that prompts users for their name and then uses interpolation to display a response.

LISTING 1.11: UserInput1.py

```
userInput = input("Enter your name: ")
print ("Hello %s, my name is Python" % userInput)
```

The output of Listing 1.11 is here (assume that the user entered the word Dave):

```
Hello Dave, my name is Python
```

The print() statement in Listing 1.11 uses string interpolation via %s, which substitutes the value of the variable after the % symbol. This functionality is obviously useful when you want to specify something that is determined at run-time. User input can cause exceptions (depending on the operations that your code performs), so it's important to include exception-handling code.

Listing 1.12 displays the content of UserInput2.py that prompts users for a string and attempts to convert the string to a number in a try/except block.

LISTING 1.12: UserInput2.py

```
userInput = input("Enter something: ")

try:
  x = 0 + eval(userInput)
  print('you entered the number:',userInput)
except:
  print(userInput,'is a string')
```

Listing 1.12 adds the number 0 to the result of converting a user's input to a number. If the conversion was successful, a message with the user's input is displayed. If the conversion failed, the except code block consists of a print() statement that displays a message.

This code sample uses the eval() function, which should be avoided so that your code does not evaluate arbitrary (and possibly destructive) commands.

Listing 1.13 displays the content of UserInput3.py that prompts users for two numbers and attempts to compute their sum in a pair of try/except blocks.

LISTING 1.13: UserInput3.py

```
sum = 0

msg = 'Enter a number:'
val1 = input(msg)

try:
  sum = sum + eval(val1)
```

```
except:
  print(val1,'is a string')

msg = 'Enter a number:'
val2 = input(msg)

try:
  sum = sum + eval(val2)
except:
  print(val2,'is a string')

print('The sum of',val1,'and',val2,'is',sum)
```

Listing 1.13 contains two `try` blocks, each of which is followed by an `except` statement. The first `try` block attempts to add the first user-supplied number to the variable `sum`, and the second `try` block attempts to add the second user-supplied number to the previously entered number. An error message occurs if either input string is not a valid number; if both are valid numbers, a message is displayed containing the input numbers and their sum. Be sure to read the caveat regarding the `eval()` function that is mentioned earlier in this chapter.

COMMAND-LINE ARGUMENTS

Python provides a `getopt` module to parse command-line options and arguments, and the `sys` module provides access to any command-line arguments via the `sys.argv`. This serves two purposes:

- `sys.argv` is the list of command-line arguments.
- `len(sys.argv)` is the number of command-line arguments.

Here, `sys.argv[0]` is the program name, so if the Python program is called `test.py`, it matches the value of `sys.argv[0]`.

Now you can provide input values for a Python program on the command line instead of providing input values by prompting users for their input. As an example, consider the script `test.py` shown here:

```
#!/usr/bin/python
import sys
print('Number of arguments:',len(sys.argv),'arguments')
print('Argument List:', str(sys.argv))
```

Run above script as follows:

```
python test.py arg1 arg2 arg3
```

This will produce following result:

```
Number of arguments: 4 arguments.
Argument List: ['test.py', 'arg1', 'arg2', 'arg3']
```

The ability to specify input values from the command line provides useful functionality. For example, suppose that you have a custom Python class that contains the methods `add` and `sub-tract` to add and subtract a pair of numbers.

You can use command-line arguments to specify which method to execute on a pair of numbers, as shown here:

```
python MyClass add 3 5
python MyClass subtract 3 5
```

This functionality is useful because you can programmatically execute different methods in a Python class, which means that you can write unit tests for your code as well.

Listing 1.14 displays the content of `Hello.py` that shows you how to use `sys.argv` to check the number of command line parameters.

LISTING 1.14: Hello.py

```python
import sys

def main():
  if len(sys.argv) >= 2:
    name = sys.argv[1]
  else:
    name = 'World'
  print('Hello', name)

# Standard boilerplate to invoke the main() function
if __name__ == '__main__':
  main()
```

Listing 1.14 defines the `main()` function that checks the number of command-line parameters: if this value is at least 2, then the variable `name` is assigned the value of the second parameter (the first parameter is `Hello.py`), otherwise `name` is assigned the value `Hello`. The `print()` statement then prints the value of the variable `name`. The final portion of Listing 1.14 uses conditional logic to determine whether to execute the `main()` function.

SUMMARY

This chapter showed you how to execute Python programs, as well as how to work with numbers and perform arithmetic operations on numbers in Python. Next, you learned how to work with strings and use string operations.

In addition, you learned about the difference between Unicode and ASCII in Python 3 and Python 2, respectively. Then you saw how to slice and splice strings, how to replace a string with another string, and also how to remove leading and trailing characters in a string.

Finally, you learned how to work with dates in Python, and then how to handle exceptions that can arise from user input.

## CHAPTER 2

WORKING WITH DATA

This chapter introduces you to various data types that you will encounter in datasets, how to scale data values, techniques for detecting outliers, and several ways for handling missing data values.

The first part of this chapter contains an overview of different types of data, and an explanation of how to normalize and standardize a set of numeric values by calculating the mean and standard deviation of a set of numbers. You will see how to map categorical data to a set of integers and how to perform a one-hot encoding.

The second part of this chapter discusses outliers, anomalies, and missing data, as well as various techniques for handling these scenarios. The third section discusses imbalanced data and several techniques, such as SMOTE, to deal with imbalanced classes in a dataset.

The fourth section contains details regarding the bias-variance tradeoff and various types of statistical bias; it also discusses ways to evaluate classifiers, such as LIME and ANOVA.

This chapter provides a high-level view of concepts that will help you work with datasets that require preprocessing before using them to train machine learning models. While the code samples reference APIs from Python libraries (such as NumPy and Pandas), the APIs are intuitive, such as `mean()` for calculating the mean of a set of numbers and `std()` for calculating the standard deviation of a set of numbers.

However, the code sample that involves Sklearn is marked "optional" because it uses the `EllipticEnvelope` class in `sklearn.covariance`, whose functionality is not intuitive (yet good to be aware of for future study).

DEALING WITH DATA: WHAT CAN GO WRONG?

In a perfect world, all datasets are in pristine condition, with no extreme values, no missing values, and no erroneous values. Every feature value is captured correctly, with no chance for any confusion. Moreover, no conversion is required between date formats, currency values, or languages because of the "One Universal Standard" that defines the correct formats and acceptable values for every possible set of data values.

Of course, all the scenarios mentioned in the previous paragraph can and do occur, which is the reason for the techniques that are discussed in this chapter. Even after you manage to create a wonderfully clean and robust dataset, other issues can arise, such as data drift, which is described in the next section.

In fact, the task of cleaning data is not necessarily complete even after a machine learning model is deployed to a production environment. For instance, an online system that gathers terabytes or petabytes of data on a daily basis can contain skewed values that adversely affect the performance of the model. Such adverse effects can be revealed through the changes in the metrics that are associated with the production model.

What is Data Drift?

The value of data is based on its accuracy, its relevance, and its age. *Data drift* refers to data that has become less relevant: in some cases, this happens over a period of time, and in other cases, it's because some data is no longer relevant because of feature-related changes in an application.

For example, online purchasing patterns in 2010 are probably not as relevant as data from 2020 because of various factors (such as the profile of different types of customers). Another example involves an inventory of cell phones: discontinued models have a diminished value in such a system. There might be multiple factors that can influence data drift in a specific dataset.

Two techniques for handling data drift are the *domain classifier* and *black-box shift detector*, both of which are discussed online:

https://blog.dataiku.com/towards-reliable-mlops-with-drift-detectors

Data drift is one of three types of drift, and all three types are listed here:

- Concept Drift
- Data Drift
- Upstream Data Changes

Perform an online search to find more information about these types of drift.

WHAT ARE DATASETS?

In simple terms, a *dataset* is a source of data (such as a text file) that contains rows and columns of data. Each row is typically called a *data point*, and each column is called a *feature*. A dataset can be in a variety of forms: CSV (comma separated values), TSV (tab separated values), Excel spreadsheet, a table in an RDMBS, a document in a NoSQL database, the output from a Web service, and so forth. As you will see, someone needs to analyze the dataset to determine which features are the most important and which features can be safely ignored in order to train a model with the given dataset.

A dataset can vary from very small (a couple of features and 100 rows) to very large (more than 1,000 features and more than one million rows). If you are unfamiliar with the problem domain, then you might struggle to determine the most important features in a large dataset. In this situation, you might need a domain expert who understands the importance of the features, their inter-dependencies (if any), and whether the data values for the features are valid.

In addition, there are algorithms (called *dimensionality reduction algorithms*) that can help you determine the most important features, such as PCA (Principal Component Analysis), which is outside the scope of this book.

Data Preprocessing

Data preprocessing is the initial step that involves validating the contents of a dataset, which involves making decisions about missing and incorrect data values:

- dealing with missing data values
- cleaning "noisy" text-based data
- removing HTML tags
- removing emoticons
- dealing with emojis/emoticons
- filtering data
- grouping data
- handling currency and date formats

Cleaning data is a subset of data wrangling that involves removing unwanted data and handling missing data. In the case of text-based data, you might need to remove HTML tags, punctuation, and so forth. In the case of numeric data, it's possible that alphabetic characters are mixed together with numeric data. However, a dataset with numeric features might have incorrect values or missing values (discussed later). In addition, calculating the minimum, maximum, mean, median, and standard deviation of the values of a feature obviously pertain only to numeric values.

After the preprocessing step is completed, *data wrangling* is performed, which refers to transforming data into a new format. For example, you might have to combine data from multiple sources into a single dataset. In this case, you might need to convert between different units of measurement (such as date formats and currency values) so that the data values can be represented in a consistent manner in a dataset.

Currency and date values are part of i18n (internationalization); L10n (localization) targets a specific nationality, language, or region. Hard-coded values (such as text strings) can be stored as resource strings in a file that's often called a *resource bundle*, where each string is referenced via a code. Each language has its own resource bundle.

DATA TYPES

If you have written computer programs, then you know that explicit data types exist in many programming languages, such as C, C++, Java, and TypeScript. Some programming languages, such as JavaScript and awk, do not require initializing variables with an explicit type: the type of a variable is inferred dynamically via an implicit type system (i.e., one that is not directly exposed to a developer).

In machine learning, datasets can contain features that have different types of data, such as a combination of one or more of the following:

- numeric data (integer/floating point and discrete/continuous)
- character/categorical data (different languages)
- date-related data (different formats)
- currency data (different formats)
- binary data (yes/no, 0/1, and so forth)
- nominal data (multiple unrelated values)
- ordinal data (multiple and related values)

Consider a dataset that contains real estate data, which can have as many as 30 columns (or even more), often with the following features:

- the number of bedrooms in a house: numeric value and a discrete value
- the number of square feet: a numeric value and (probably) a continuous value
- the name of the city: character data
- the construction date: a date value
- the selling price: a currency value and probably a continuous value
- the "for sale" status: binary data (either "yes" or "no")

An example of nominal data is the seasons in a year: although many countries have four distinct seasons, some countries only have two distinct seasons. However, seasons can be associated with different temperature ranges (summer versus winter). An example of ordinal data is an employee's pay grade: 1=entry level, 2=one year of experience, and so forth. Another example of nominal data is a set of colors, such as {Red, Green, Blue}.

An example of binary data is the pair {Male, Female}, and some datasets contain a feature with these two values. If such a feature is required for training a model, first convert {Male, Female} to a numeric counterpart, such as {0,1}. Similarly, if you need to include a feature whose values are the previous set of colors, you can replace {Red, Green, Blue} with the values {0,1,2}. Categorical data is discussed in more detail later in this chapter.

PREPARING DATASETS

If you have the good fortune to inherit a dataset that is in pristine condition, then data cleaning tasks (discussed later) are vastly simplified: in fact, it might not be necessary to perform *any* data cleaning for the dataset. However, if you need to create a dataset that combines data from multiple datasets that contain different formats for dates and currency, then you need to perform a conversion to a common format.

If you need to train a model that includes features that have categorical data, then you need to convert that categorical data to numeric data. For instance, the Titanic dataset contains a feature called "gender," which is either male or female. As you will see later in this chapter, Pandas makes it extremely simple to "map" male to 0 and female to 1.

Discrete Data vs. Continuous Data

Discrete data is a set of values that can be counted, whereas *continuous data* must be measured. Discrete data can reasonably fit in a drop-down list of values, but there is no exact value for making such a determination. One person might think that a list of 500 values is discrete, whereas another person might think it's continuous. For example, the list of provinces of Canada and the list of states of the USA are discrete data values, but is the same true for the number of countries in the world (roughly 200) or for the number of languages in the world (more than 7,000)?

Values for temperature, humidity, and barometric pressure are considered continuous. Currency is also treated as continuous, even though there is a measurable difference between two consecutive values. The smallest unit of currency for US currency is one penny, which is 1/100th of a dollar (accounting-based measurements use the "mil," which is 1/1,000th of a dollar).

Continuous data types can have subtle differences. For example, someone who is 200 centimeters tall is twice as tall as someone who is 100 centimeters tall (similarly for someone who is 100 kilograms versus a person who weighs 50 kilograms). However, temperature is different: 80 degrees Fahrenheit is not twice as hot as 40 degrees Fahrenheit.

Furthermore, the word "continuous" has a meaning in mathematics that is not necessarily the same as "continuous" in machine learning. In the former, a continuous variable (let's say in the 2D Euclidean plane) can have an uncountably infinite number of values. However, a feature in a dataset that can have more values that can be "reasonably" displayed in a drop-down list is treated *as though* it's a continuous variable.

For instance, values for stock prices are discrete: they must differ by at least a penny (or some other minimal unit of currency), which is to say, it's meaningless to say that the stock price changes by one-millionth of a penny. However, since there are so many possible stock values, it's treated as a continuous variable. The same comments apply to car mileage, ambient temperature, and barometric pressure.

"Binning" Continuous Data

The concept of *binning* refers to subdividing a set of values into multiple intervals, and then treating all the numbers in the same interval as though they had the same value.

As a simple example, suppose that a feature in a dataset contains the age of people in a dataset. The range of values is approximately between 0 and 120, and we could "bin" them into 12 equal intervals, where each consists of 10 values: 0 through 9, 10 through 19, 20 through 29, and so forth.

However, partitioning the values of people's age as described in the preceding paragraph can be problematic. Suppose that person A, person B, and person C are 29, 30, and 39, respectively. Then person A and person B are probably more similar to each other than person B and person C, but because of the way in which the ages are partitioned, B is classified as closer to C than to A. In fact, binning can increase Type I errors (false positive) and Type II errors (false negative), as discussed in the following blog post (along with some alternatives to binning):

https://medium.com/@peterflom/why-binning-continuous-data-is-almost-always-a-mistake-ad0b3a1d141f.

As another example, using quartiles is even more coarse-grained than the earlier age-related binning example. The issue with binning pertains to the consequences of classifying people in different bins, even though they are in close proximity to each other. For instance, some people struggle financially because they earn a meager wage, and they are disqualified from financial assistance because their salary is higher than the cut-off point for receiving any assistance.

Scaling Numeric Data via Normalization

A range of values can vary significantly and it's important to note that they often need to be scaled to a smaller range, such as values in the range [−1,1] or [0,1], which you can do via the tanh function or the sigmoid function, respectively.

For example, measuring a person's height in terms of meters involves a range of values between 0.50 meters and 2.5 meters (in the vast majority of cases), whereas measuring height in terms of centimeters ranges between 50 centimeters and 250 centimeters: these two units differ by a factor of 100. A person's weight in kilograms generally varies between 5 kilograms and 200 kilograms, whereas measuring weight in grams differs by a factor of 1,000. Distances between objects can be measured in meters or in kilometers, which also differ by a factor of 1,000.

In general, use units of measure so that the data values in multiple features are belong to a similar range of values. In fact, some machine learning algorithms require scaled data, often in the range of [0,1] or [−1,1]. In addition to the tanh and sigmoid functions, there are other techniques for scaling data, such as "standardizing" data (think Gaussian distribution) and "normalizing" data (linearly scaled so that the new range of values is in (0,1)).

The following examples involve a floating point variable X with different ranges of values that will be scaled so that the new values are in the interval [0,1].

- Example 1: If the values of X are in the range [0,2], then X/2 is in the range [0,1].
- Example 2: If the values of X are in the range [3,6], then X-3 is in the range [0,3], and (X-3)/3 is in the range [0,1].
- Example 3: If the values of X are in the range [−10,20], then X +10 is in the range [0,30], and (X +10)/30 is in the range of [0,1].

In general, suppose that X is a random variable whose values are in the range [a,b], where a < b. You can scale the data values by performing two steps:

```
Step 1: X-a is in the range [0,b-a]
Step 2: (X-1)/(b-a) is in the range [0,1]
```

If X is a random variable that has the values {x1, x2, x3, . . ., xn}, then the formula for normalization involves mapping each xi value to (xi - min)/(max - min), where min is the minimum value of X and max is the maximum value of X.

As a simple example, suppose that the random variable X has the values {−1, 0, 1}. Then min and max are 1 and −1, respectively, and the normalization of {−1, 0, 1} is the set of values {(-1-(-1))/2, (0-(-1))/2, (1-(-1))/2}, which equals {0, 1/2, 1}.

Scaling Numeric Data via Standardization

The standardization technique involves finding the mean mu and the standard deviation sigma, and then mapping each xi value to (xi - mu)/sigma. Recall the following formulas:

```
mu = [SUM (x)]/n
variance(x) = [SUM (x - xbar)*(x-xbar)]/n
sigma = sqrt(variance)
```

As a simple illustration of standardization, suppose that the random variable x has the values {-1, 0, 1}. Then `mu` and `sigma` are calculated as follows:

```
mu         = (SUM xi)/n = (-1 + 0 + 1)/3 = 0
variance = [SUM (xi- mu)^2]/n
           = [(-1-0)^2 + (0-0)^2 + (1-0)^2]/3
           = 2/3

sigma      = sqrt(2/3) = 0.816 (approximate value)
```

Hence, the standardization of `{-1, 0, 1}` is `{-1/0.816, 0/0.816, 1/0.816}`, which in turn equals the set of values `{-1.2254, 0, 1.2254}`.

As another example, suppose that the random variable x has the values `{-6, 0, 6}`. Then `mu` and `sigma` are calculated as follows:

```
mu         = (SUM xi)/n = (-6 + 0 + 6)/3 = 0

variance = [SUM (xi- mu)^2]/n
           = [(-6-0)^2 + (0-0)^2 + (6-0)^2]/3
           = 72/3
           = 24

sigma      = sqrt(24) = 4.899 (approximate value)
```

Hence, the standardization of `{-6, 0, 6}` is `{-6/4.899, 0/4.899, 6/4.899}`, which in turn equals the set of values `{-1.2247, 0, 1.2247}`.

In the preceding two examples, the mean equals 0 in both cases but the variance and standard deviation are significantly different. One other point: the normalization of a set of values *always* produces a set of numbers between 0 and 1.

However, the standardization of a set of values can generate numbers that are less than -1 and greater than 1: this will occur when `sigma` is less than the minimum value of every term `|mu - xi|`, where the latter is the absolute value of the difference between `mu` and each `xi` value. In the preceding example, the minimum difference equals 1, whereas `sigma` is 0.816, and therefore the largest standardized value is greater than 1.

Scaling Numeric Data via Robust Standardization

The *robust standardization* technique is a variant of standardization that computes the mean `mu` and the standard deviation `sigma` based on a subset of values. Specifically, use only the values that are between the 25th percentile and 75th percentile, which ignores the first and fourth quartiles that might contain outliers. Let's define the following variables:

```
X25 = 25th percentile
X75 = 75th percentile
XM = mean of {Xi} values
XR = robust standardization
```

Then XR is computed according to the following formula:

```
XR = (Xi - XM)/(X75 - X25)
```

The preceding technique is also called IQR, which is an acronym for *interquartile range*, and you can see a sample calculation here:

https://en.wikipedia.org/wiki/Interquartile_range

What to Look for in Categorical Data

This section contains various suggestions for handling inconsistent data values, and you can determine which ones to adopt based on any additional factors that are relevant to your particular task. For example, consider dropping columns that have very low cardinality (equal to or close to 1), as well as numeric columns with zero or very low variance.

Next, check the contents of categorical columns for inconsistent spellings or errors. A good example pertains to the gender category, which can consist of a combination of the following values:

```
male
Male
female
Female
m
f
M
F
```

The preceding categorical values for gender can be replaced with two categorical values (unless you have a valid reason to retain some of the other values). Moreover, if you are training a model whose analysis involves a single gender, then you need to determine which rows (if any) of a dataset must be excluded. Also check categorical data columns for redundant or missing whitespaces.

Check for data values that have multiple data types, such as a numerical column with numbers as numerals and some numbers as strings or objects. Also ensure there are consistent data formats (such as numbers as integers or floating numbers) and that dates have the same format (for example, do not mix mm/dd/yyyy date formats with another date format, such as dd/mm/yyyy).

Mapping Categorical Data to Numeric Values

Character data is often called *categorical data*, examples of which include people's names, home or work addresses, and email addresses. Many types of categorical data involve short lists of values. For example, the days of the week and the months in a year involve seven and twelve distinct values, respectively. Notice that the days of the week have a relationship: each day has a previous day and a next day, and this is similar for the months of a year.

However, the colors of an automobile are independent of each other: the color red is not better or worse than the color blue. However, cars of a certain color can have a statistically higher number of accidents, but we won't address this case here.

There are several well-known techniques for mapping categorical values to a set of numeric values. A simple example where you need to perform this conversion involves the gender feature in the Titanic dataset. This feature is one of the relevant features for training a machine learning model. The gender feature has {M,F} as its set of values. As you will see later in this chapter, Pandas makes it very easy to convert the set of values {M,F} to the set of values {0,1}.

Another mapping technique involves mapping a set of categorical values to a set of consecutive integer values. For example, the set {Red, Green, Blue} can be mapped to the set of integers {0,1,2}. The set {Male, Female} can be mapped to the set of integers {0,1}. The days of the week can be mapped to {0,1,2,3,4,5,6}. Note that the first day of the week depends on the country: in some cases, it's Sunday, and in other cases, it's Monday.

Another technique is called *one-hot encoding*, which converts each value to a *vector* (check Wikipedia if you need a refresher regarding vectors). Thus, {Male, Female} can be represented by the vectors `[1,0]` and `[0,1]`.

If you vertically "line up" the two vectors for gender, they form a 2x2 identity matrix, and doing the same for the colors {R,G,B} will form a 3x3 identity matrix, as shown here:

```
[1,0,0]
[0,1,0]
[0,0,1]
```

If you are familiar with matrices, you noticed that the preceding set of vectors looks like the 3x3 identity matrix. In fact, this technique generalizes in a straightforward manner. Specifically, if you have n distinct categorical values, you can map each of those values to one of the vectors in an nxn identity matrix.

As another example, the set of titles {`"Intern"`, `"Junior"`, `"Mid-Range"`, `"Senior"`, `"Project Leader"`, `"Dev Manager"`} have a hierarchical relationship in terms of their salaries (which can also overlap, but we'll skip that detail for now).

Another set of categorical data involves the seasons of the year: {`"Spring"`, `"Summer"`, `"Autumn"`, `"Winter"`} and while these values are generally independent of each other, there are cases in which the season is significant. For example, the values for the monthly rainfall, average temperature, crime rate, foreclosure rate can depend on the season, month, week, or even the day of the year.

If a feature has a large number of categorical values, then a one-hot encoding will produce many additional columns for each datapoint. Since the majority of the values in the new columns equal 0, this can increase the sparsity of the dataset, which in turn can result in more overfitting and hence adversely affect the accuracy of machine learning algorithms that you adopt during the training process.

Another solution is to use a sequence-based solution in which N categories are mapped to the integers 1, 2, . . ., N. Another solution involves examining the row frequency of each categorical value. For example, suppose that N equals 20, and there are 3 categorical values that occur in 95% of the values for a given feature. You can try the following:

1. Assign the values 1, 2, and 3 to those three categorical values.
2. Assign numeric values that reflect the relative frequency of those categorical values.
3. Assign the category "OTHER" to the remaining categorical values.
4. Delete the rows that whose categorical values belong to the 5%.

Working with Dates

The format for a calendar dates varies among different countries, and this belongs to something called *localization* of data (not to be confused with i18n, which is data internationalization). Some examples of date formats are shown below (and the first four are probably the most common):

```
MM/DD/YY
MM/DD/YYYY
DD/MM/YY
DD/MM/YYYY
YY/MM/DD
M/D/YY
D/M/YY
YY/M/D
MMDDYY
DDMMYY
YYMMDD
```

If you need to combine data from datasets that contain different date formats, then converting the disparate date formats to a single common date format will ensure consistency.

Working with Currency

The format for currency depends on the country, which includes different interpretations for a "," and "." in currency (and decimal values in general). For example, 1,124.78 equals "one thousand one hundred twenty-four point seven eight" in the US, whereas 1.124,78 has the same meaning in Europe (i.e., the "." symbol and the "," symbol are interchanged).

If you need to combine data from datasets that contain different currency formats, then you probably need to convert all the disparate currency formats to a single common currency format. There is another detail to consider: currency exchange rates can fluctuate on a daily basis, which in turn can affect the calculation of taxes, late fees, and so forth. Although you might be fortunate enough where you won't have to deal with these issues, it's still worth being aware of them.

WORKING WITH OUTLIERS AND ANOMALIES

In simplified terms, an *outlier* is an abnormal data value that is outside the range of "normal" values. For example, a person's height in centimeters is typically between 30 centimeters and 250 centimeters. Hence, a datapoint (e.g., a row of data in a spreadsheet) with a height of 5 centimeters or a height of 500 centimeters is an outlier. The consequences of these outlier values are unlikely to involve a significant financial or physical loss (though they could adversely affect the accuracy of a trained model).

Anomalies are also outside the "normal" range of values (just like outliers), and they are typically more problematic than outliers: anomalies can have more "severe" consequences than outliers. For example, consider the scenario in which someone who lives in California suddenly makes a credit card purchase in New York. If the person is on vacation (or a business trip), then the purchase is an outlier (it's "outside" the typical purchasing pattern), but it's not an issue. However, if that person was in California when the credit card purchase was made, then it's most likely to be credit card fraud, as well as an anomaly.

Unfortunately, there is no simple way to *decide* how to deal with anomalies and outliers in a dataset. Although you can drop rows that contain outliers, doing so might deprive the dataset (and therefore the trained model) of valuable information. You can try modifying the data values (described below), but again, this might lead to erroneous inferences in the trained model. Another possibility is to train a model with the dataset that contains anomalies and outliers, and then train a model with a dataset from which the anomalies and outliers have been removed. Compare the two results and see if you can infer anything meaningful regarding the anomalies and outliers.

Outlier Detection/Removal

Although the decision to keep or drop outliers is your decision to make, there are some techniques available that help you detect outliers in a dataset. Here is a short list of techniques, along with a very brief description and links for additional information:

- trimming
- winsorizing
- minimum covariance determinant
- local outlier factor
- Huber and Ridge regressions
- isolation forest (tree-based algorithm)
- one-class SVM

Perhaps *trimming* is the simplest technique (apart from dropping outliers), which involves removing rows whose feature value is in the upper 5% range or the lower 5% range. *Winsorizing* the data is an improvement over trimming: set the values in the top 5% range equal to the maximum value in the 95th percentile, and set the values in the bottom 5% range equal to the minimum in the 5th percentile.

The *Minimum Covariance Determinant* is a covariance-based technique, and a Python-based code sample that uses this technique is downloadable from the following site:

https://scikit-learn.org/stable/modules/outlier_detection.html

The *Local Outlier Factor* (LOF) technique is an unsupervised technique that calculates a local anomaly score via the kNN (k Nearest Neighbor) algorithm. Documentation and short code samples that use LOF are available online:

https://scikit-learn.org/stable/modules/generated/sklearn.neighbors.LocalOutlierFactor.html

Two other techniques involve the Huber and the Ridge classes, both of which are included as part of Sklearn. The Huber error is less sensitive to outliers because it's calculated via linear loss, similar to the MAE (Mean Absolute Error). A code sample that compares the Huber and Ridge regression algorithms is downloadable from the following site:

https://scikit-learn.org/stable/auto_examples/linear_model/plot_huber_vs_ridge.html

You can also explore the Theil-Sen estimator and RANSAC, which are "robust" against outliers:

https://scikit-learn.org/stable/auto_examples/linear_model/plot_theilsen.html

https://en.wikipedia.org/wiki/Random_sample_consensus

Four algorithms for outlier detection are discussed at the following site:

https://www.kdnuggets.com/2018/12/four-techniques-outlier-detection.html

One other scenario involves "local" outliers. For example, suppose that you use kMeans (or some other clustering algorithm) and determine that a value that is an outlier with respect to one of the clusters. While this value is not necessarily an "absolute" outlier, detecting such a value might be important for your use case.

FINDING OUTLIERS WITH NUMPY

Although we have not discussed the NumPy library, we will only use the NumPy array(), mean(), and std() methods in this section, all of which have intuitive functionality.

Listing 2.1 displays the content of numpy_outliers1.py that illustrates how to use NumPy methods to find outliers in an array of numbers.

LISTING 2.1: numpy_outliers1.py

```
import numpy as np

arr1 = np.array([2,5,7,9,9,40])
print("values:",arr1)

data_mean = np.mean(arr1)
data_std  = np.std(arr1)
print("data_mean:",data_mean)
print("data_std:" ,data_std)
print()

multiplier = 1.5
cut_off = data_std * multiplier
lower = data_mean - cut_off
upper = data_mean + cut_off
print("lower cutoff:",lower)
print("upper cutoff:",upper)
print()

outliers = [x for x in arr1 if x < lower or x > upper]
print('Identified outliers: %d' % len(outliers))
print("outliers:",outliers)
```

Listing 2.1 starts by defining a NumPy array of numbers and then calculates the mean and standard deviation of those numbers. The next block of code initializes two numbers that represent the upper and lower values that are based on the value of the cut_off variable. Any numbers in the array arr1 that lie to the left of the lower value or to the right of the upper value are treated as outliers.

The final section of code in Listing 2.1 initializes the variable `outliers` with the numbers that are determined to be outliers, and those values are printed. Launch the code in Listing 2.1 and you will see the following output:

```
values: [2   5   7   9   9   40]
data_mean: 12.0
data_std: 12.754084313139327

lower cutoff: -7.131126469708988
upper cutoff: 31.13112646970899

Identified outliers: 1
outliers: [40]
```

The preceding code sample specifies a hard-coded value in order to calculate the upper and lower range values.

Listing 2.2 is an improvement in that you can specify a set of values from which to calculate the upper and lower range values, and the new block of code is shown in bold.

LISTING 2.2: *numpy_outliers2.py*

```
import numpy as np

arr1 = np.array([2,5,7,9,9,40])
print("values:",arr1)

data_mean = np.mean(arr1)
data_std  = np.std(arr1)
print("data_mean:",data_mean)
print("data_std:" ,data_std)
print()

multipliers = np.array([0.5,1.0,1.5,2.0,2.5,3.0])
for multiplier in multipliers:
  cut_off = data_std * multiplier
  lower, upper = data_mean - cut_off, data_mean + cut_off
  print("=> multiplier:  ",multiplier)
  print("lower cutoff:",lower)
  print("upper cutoff:",upper)

  outliers = [x for x in df['data'] if x < lower or x > upper]
  print('Identified outliers: %d' % len(outliers))
  print("outliers:",outliers)
  print()
```

Listing 2.2 contains a block of new code that initializes the variable `multipliers` as an array of numeric values that are used for finding outliers. Although you will probably use a value of 2.0 or larger on a real dataset, this range of numbers can give you a better sense of detecting outliers. Launch the code in Listing 2.2 and you will see the following output:

```
values: [2   5   7   9   9   40]
data_mean: 12.0
```

```
data_std: 12.754084313139327

lower cutoff: -7.131126469708988
upper cutoff: 31.13112646970899

Identified outliers: 1
outliers: [40]
=> multiplier:    0.5
lower cutoff: 5.622957843430337
upper cutoff: 18.377042156569665
Identified outliers: 3
outliers: [2, 5, 40]

=> multiplier:    1.0
lower cutoff: -0.7540843131393267
upper cutoff: 24.754084313139327
Identified outliers: 1
outliers: [40]

=> multiplier:    1.5
lower cutoff: -7.131126469708988
upper cutoff: 31.13112646970899
Identified outliers: 1
outliers: [40]

=> multiplier:    2.0
lower cutoff: -13.508168626278653
upper cutoff: 37.50816862627865
Identified outliers: 1
outliers: [40]

=> multiplier:    2.5
lower cutoff: -19.88521078284832
upper cutoff: 43.88521078284832
Identified outliers: 0
outliers: []

=> multiplier:    3.0
lower cutoff: -26.262252939417976
upper cutoff: 50.26225293941798
Identified outliers: 0
outliers: []
```

FINDING OUTLIERS WITH PANDAS

Although we discuss Pandas in Chapter three, the code in this section only involves a very simple Pandas data frame, the mean() method, and the std() method.

Listing 2.3 displays the content of pandas_outliers1.py that illustrates how to use Pandas to find outliers in an array of numbers.

LISTING 2.3: pandas_outliers1.py

```python
import pandas as pd

df = pd.DataFrame([2,5,7,9,9,40])
df.columns = ["data"]

data_mean = df['data'].mean()
data_std  = df['data'].std()
print("data_mean:",data_mean)
print("data_std:" ,data_std)
print()

multiplier = 1.5
cut_off = data_std * multiplier
lower, upper = data_mean - cut_off, data_mean + cut_off
print("lower cutoff:",lower)
print("upper cutoff:",upper)
print()
outliers = [x for x in df['data'] if x < lower or x > upper]
print('Identified outliers: %d' % len(outliers))
print("outliers:",outliers)
```

Listing 2.3 starts by defining a Pandas data frame and then calculates the mean and standard deviation of those numbers. The next block of code initializes two numbers that represent the upper and lower values that are based on the value of the cut_off variable. Any numbers in the data frame that lie to the left of the lower value or to the right of the upper value are treated as outliers.

The final section of code in Listing 2.3 initializes the variable outliers with the numbers that are determined to be outliers, and those values are printed. Launch the code in Listing 2.3 and you will see the following output:

```
values: [2  5  7  9  9  40]
data_mean: 12.0
data_std: 12.754084313139327

lower cutoff: -7.131126469708988
upper cutoff: 31.13112646970899

Identified outliers: 1
outliers: [40]
```

The preceding code sample specifies a hard-coded value in order to calculate the upper and lower range values.

Listing 2.4 is an improvement in that you can specify a set of values from which to calculate the upper and lower range values, and the new block of code is shown in bold.

LISTING 2.4: pandas_outliers2.py

```python
import pandas as pd

#df = pd.DataFrame([2,5,7,9,9,40])
```

```
#df = pd.DataFrame([2,5,7,8,42,44])
df = pd.DataFrame([2,5,7,8,42,492])
df.columns = ["data"]
print("=> data values:")
print(df['data'])

data_mean = df['data'].mean()
data_std  = df['data'].std()
print("=> data_mean:",data_mean)
print("=> data_std:" ,data_std)
print()

multipliers = [0.5,1.0,1.5,2.0,2.5,3.0]
for multiplier in multipliers:
  cut_off = data_std * multiplier
  lower, upper = data_mean - cut_off, data_mean + cut_off
  print("=> multiplier:  ",multiplier)
  print("lower cutoff:",lower)
  print("upper cutoff:",upper)

  outliers = [x for x in df['data'] if x < lower or x > upper]
  print('Identified outliers: %d' % len(outliers))
  print("outliers:",outliers)
  print()
```

Listing 2.4 contains a block of new code that initializes the variable `multipliers` as an array of numeric values that are used for finding outliers. Although you will probably use a value of 2.0 or larger on a real dataset, this range of numbers can give you a better sense of detecting outliers. Launch the code in Listing 2.4 and you will see the following output:

```
=> data values:
0       2
1       5
2       7
3       8
4      42
5     492
Name: data, dtype: int64
=> data_mean: 92.66666666666667
=> data_std: 196.187325448579

=> multiplier:   0.5
lower cutoff: -5.42699605762283
upper cutoff: 190.76032939095617
Identified outliers: 1
outliers: [492]

=> multiplier:   1.0
lower cutoff: -103.52065878191233
upper cutoff: 288.85399211524566
Identified outliers: 1
outliers: [492]

=> multiplier:   1.5
lower cutoff: -201.6143215062018
```

```
upper cutoff: 386.9476548395352
Identified outliers: 1
outliers: [492]

=> multiplier:   2.0
lower cutoff: -299.7079842304913
upper cutoff: 485.0413175638247
Identified outliers: 1
outliers: [492]

=> multiplier:   2.5
lower cutoff: -397.80164695478084
upper cutoff: 583.1349802881142
Identified outliers: 0
outliers: []

=> multiplier:   3.0
lower cutoff: -495.8953096790703
upper cutoff: 681.2286430124036
Identified outliers: 0
outliers: []
```

Calculating Z-Scores to Find Outliers

The z-score of a set of numbers is calculated by standardizing those numbers, which involves subtracting their mean from each number and then dividing by their standard deviation. Although you can perform these steps manually, the Python SciPy library simplifies the steps involved. If need be, you can install this package with the following command:

```
pip3 install scipy
```

Listing 2.5 displays the content of `outliers_zscores.py` that illustrates how to find outliers in an array of numbers. As you will see, this code sample relies on convenience methods from NumPy, Pandas, and SciPy.

LISTING 2.5: outliers_zscores.py

```
import numpy as np
import pandas as pd
from scipy import stats

arr1 = np.array([2,5,7,9,9,40])
print("values:",arr1)

df = pd.DataFrame(arr1)

zscores = np.abs(stats.zscore(df))
print("z scores:")
print(zscores)
print()

upper = 2.0
lower = 0.5
print("=> upper outliers:")
print(zscores[np.where(zscores > upper)])
print()
```

```
print("=> lower outliers:")
print(zscores[np.where(zscores < lower)])
print()
```

Listing 2.5 starts with several `import` statements, followed by initializing the variable `arr1` as a NumPy array of numbers, and then displaying the values in `arr1`. The next code snippet initializes the variable `df` as a data frame that contains the values in the variable `arr1`.

Next, the variable `zscores` is initialized with the z-scores of the elements of the `df` data frame, as shown here:

```
zscores = np.abs(stats.zscore(df))
```

The next section of code initializes the variables `upper` and `lower`, and the z-scores whose values are less than the value of `lower` or greater than the value `upper` are treated as outliers, and those values are displayed. Launch the code in Listing 2.3 and you will see the following output:

```
values: [2  5  7  9  9  40]
z scores:
[[0.78406256]
 [0.54884379]
 [0.39203128]
 [0.23521877]
 [0.23521877]
 [2.19537517]]

=> upper outliers:
[2.19537517]

=> lower outliers:
[0.39203128 0.23521877 0.23521877]
```

FINDING OUTLIERS WITH SKLEARN (OPTIONAL)

This section is optional because the code involves the `EllipticEnvelope` class in `sklearn.covariance`, which we do not cover in this book. However, it's still worthwhile to peruse the code and compare this code with earlier code samples for finding outliers.

Listing 2.6 displays the content of `elliptic_envelope_outliers.py` that illustrates how to use Pandas to find outliers in an array of numbers.

LISTING 2.6: *elliptic_envelope_outliers.py*

```
# pip3 install scikit-learn as sklearn
from sklearn.covariance import EllipticEnvelope
import numpy as np
```

```
# Create a sample normal distribution:
Xdata = np.random.normal(loc=5, scale=2, size=10).reshape(-1, 1)
print("Xdata values:")
print(Xdata)
print()

# instantiate and fit the estimator:
envelope = EllipticEnvelope(random_state=0)
envelope.fit(Xdata)
# create a test set:
test = np.array([0, 2, 4, 6, 8, 10, 15, 20, 25, 30]).reshape(-1, 1)
print("test values:")
print(test)
print()

# predict() returns 1 for inliers and -1 for outliers:
print("envelope.predict(test):")
print(envelope.predict(test))
```

Listing 2.6 starts with several import statements and then initializes the variable Xdata as a column vector of random numbers from a Gaussian distribution. The next code snippet initializes the variable envelope as an instance of the EllipticEnvelope from sklearn (which will determine if there are any outliers in Xdata), and then trains on the data values in Xdata.

The next portion of Listing 2.6 initializes the variable test as a column vector, much like the initialization of Xdata. The final portion of Listing 2.6 makes a prediction on the values in the variable test and also displays the results: the value −1 indicates an outlet. Launch the code in Listing 2.6 and you will see the following output:

```
Xdata values:
[[5.21730452]
 [5.49182377]
 [2.87553776]
 [4.20297013]
 [8.29562026]
 [5.78097977]
 [4.86631006]
 [5.47184212]
 [4.77954946]
 [8.66184028]]

test values:
[[ 0]
 [ 2]
 [ 4]
 [ 6]
 [ 8]
 [10]
 [15]
 [20]
 [25]
 [30]]
envelope.predict(test):
[-1  1  1  1  1 -1 -1 -1 -1 -1]
```

See the following site for more information regarding data cleaning and preprocessing:

https://www.kdnuggets.com/2019/11/data-cleaning-preprocessing-beginners.html

WORKING WITH MISSING DATA

There are various reasons for missing values in a dataset, some of which are listed here:

- values are unavailable
- values were improperly collected
- inaccurate data entry

Although you might be tempted to *always* replace missing values with concrete values, there are situations in which you cannot determine a value. As a simple example, a survey that contains questions for people under 30 will have a missing value for respondents who are over 30, and in this case, specifying a value for the missing value would be incorrect. With these details in mind, there are various ways to fill missing values, some of which are listed here:

- Remove the lines with the data if the dataset is large enough *and* there is a high percentage of missing values (50% or larger).
- Fill null variables with 0 for numeric features.
- Use the `Imputerclass` from the scikit-learn library.
- Fill missing values with the value in an adjacent row.
- Replace missing data with the mean/median/mode value.
- Infer ("impute") the value for missing data.
- Delete rows with missing data.

Once again, the technique that you select for filling missing values is influenced by various factors, such as

- how you want to process the data
- the type of data involved
- the cause of missing values

Although the most common technique involves the mean value for numeric features, someone needs to determine which technique is appropriate for a given feature.

However, if you are not confident that you can impute a reasonable value, consider deleting the row with a missing value, and then train a model with the imputed value and also with the deleted row.

One problem that can arise after removing rows with missing values is that the resulting dataset is too small. In this case, consider using SMOTE (Synthetic Minority Oversampling Technique) to generate synthetic data.

Additional information for handling missing values through imputation can be found here:

https://www.kdnuggets.com/2020/09/missing-value-imputation-review.html

Imputing Values: When is Zero a Valid Value?

In general, replace a missing numeric value with zero is a risky choice: this value is obviously incorrect if the values of a feature are positive numbers between 1,000 and 5,000 (or some other range of positive numbers). For a feature that has numeric values, replacing a missing value with the mean of existing values can be better than the value zero (unless the average equals zero); also consider using the median value. For categorical data, consider using the mode to replace a missing value.

There are situations where you can use the mean of existing values to impute missing values but not the value zero, and vice versa. As a first example, suppose that an attribute contains the height in centimeters of a set of persons. In this case, the mean could be a reasonable imputation, whereas 0 suffers from the following issues:

1. It's an invalid value (nobody has height 0).
2. It will skew statistical quantities, such as the mean and variance.

You might be tempted to use the mean instead of 0 when the minimum allowable value is a positive number, but use caution when working with highly imbalanced datasets. As a second example, consider a small community of 50 residents with the following attributes:

1. 45 people have an average annual income of USD 50,000
2. 4 other residents have an annual income of 10,000,000
3. 1 resident has an unknown annual income

Although the preceding example might seem contrived, it's likely that the median income is preferable to the mean income, and certainly better than imputing a value of 0.

As a third example, suppose that a company generates weekly sales reports for multiple office branches, and a new office has been opened but has yet to make any sales. In this case, the use of the mean to impute missing values for this branch would produce fictitious results. Hence, it makes sense to use 0 for any missing sales-related quantities, which will accurately reflect the sales-related status of the new branch.

DEALING WITH IMBALANCED DATASETS

Imbalanced datasets contain at least once class that has many more values than another class in the dataset. For example, if class A has 99% of the data and class B has 1%, which classification algorithm would you use? Unfortunately, classification algorithms don't work well with this type of imbalanced dataset.

Imbalanced classification involves dealing with imbalanced datasets. The following list contains several well-known techniques for addressing an imbalance:

• Random resampling rebalances the class distribution.
• Random undersampling deletes examples from the majority class.
• Random oversampling duplicates data in the minority class.
• SMOTE (Synthetic Minority Oversampling Technique)

Random resampling rebalances the class distribution by resampling the data space. The *random undersampling* technique removes samples that belong to the majority class from the dataset, and involves the following:

- randomly removing samples from the majority class
- can be performed with or without replacement
- alleviating an imbalance in the dataset
- may increase the variance of the classifier
- may discard useful or important samples

However, random undersampling does not work well with extremely unbalanced datasets, such as a 99% and 1% split into two classes. Moreover, undersampling can result in losing information that is useful for a model.

Random oversampling generates new samples from a minority class: this technique duplicates examples from the minority class.

Another option to consider is the Python package `imbalanced-learn` in the `scikit-learn-contrib` project. This project provides various re-sampling techniques for datasets that exhibit class imbalance. More details are available online:

https://github.com/scikit-learn-contrib/imbalanced-learn

Another well-known technique is called SMOTE, which involves data augmentation (i.e., synthesizing new data samples). SMOTE was initially developed by means of the kNN algorithm (other options are available), and it can be an effective technique for handling imbalanced classes. SMOTE is discussed in more detail in the next section.

WHAT IS SMOTE?

SMOTE (Synthetic Minority Oversampling Technique) is a technique for synthesizing new samples for a dataset. This technique is based on linear interpolation:

- Step 1: Select samples that are close in the feature space.
- Step 2: Draw a line between the samples in the feature space.
- Step 3: Draw a new sample at a point along that line.

A more detailed explanation of the SMOTE algorithm is as follows:

- Select a random sample "a" from the minority class.
- Find k nearest neighbors for that example.
- Select a random neighbor "b" from the nearest neighbors.
- Create a line L that connects "a" and "b."
- Randomly select one or more points "c" on line L.

If need be, you can repeat this process for the other (k–1) nearest neighbors to distribute the synthetic values more evenly among the nearest neighbors.

SMOTE Extensions

The initial SMOTE algorithm is based on the kNN classification algorithm, which has been extended in various ways, such as replacing kNN with SVM. A list of SMOTE extensions is as follows:

- selective synthetic sample generation
- Borderline-SMOTE (kNN)
- Borderline-SMOTE (SVM)
- Adaptive Synthetic Sampling (ADASYN)

Perform an Internet search for more details about these algorithms, and also navigate to the following URL:

https://en.wikipedia.org/wiki/Oversampling_and_undersampling_in_data_analysis

THE BIAS-VARIANCE TRADEOFF

This section is presented from the viewpoint of machine learning, but the concepts of bias and variance are highly relevant outside of machine learning, so it's probably still worthwhile to read this section as well as the previous section.

Bias in machine learning can be due to an error from wrong assumptions in a learning algorithm. High bias might cause an algorithm to miss relevant relations between features and target outputs (underfitting). Prediction bias can occur because of "noisy" data, an incomplete feature set, or a biased training sample.

Error due to bias is the difference between the expected (or average) prediction of your model and the correct value that you want to predict. Repeat the model building process multiple times, gather new data each time, and perform an analysis to produce a new model. The resulting models have a range of predictions because the underlying data sets have a degree of randomness. Bias measures the extent to the predictions for these models are from the correct value.

Variance in machine learning is the expected value of the squared deviation from the mean. High variance can cause an algorithm to model the random noise in the training data, rather than the intended outputs (*overfitting*). Moreover, adding parameters to a model increases its complexity, increases the variance, and decreases the bias.

The point to remember: dealing with bias and variance involves dealing with underfitting and overfitting.

Error due to variance is the variability of a model prediction for a given data point. As before, repeat the entire model building process, and the variance is the extent to which predictions for a given point vary among different instances of the model.

If you have worked with datasets and performed data analysis, you already know that finding well-balanced samples can be difficult or highly impractical. Moreover, performing an analysis of the data in a dataset is vitally important, yet there is no guarantee that you can produce a dataset that is 100% "clean."

A *biased statistic* is a statistic that is systematically different from the entity in the population that is being estimated. In more casual terminology, if a data sample "favors" or "leans" toward one aspect of the population, then the sample has bias. For example, if you prefer movies that are comedies more so than any other type of movie, then clearly you are more likely to select a comedy instead of a dramatic movie or a science fiction movie. Thus, a frequency graph of the movie types in a sample of your movie selections will be more closely clustered around comedies.

However, if you have a wide-ranging set of preferences for movies, then the corresponding frequency graph will be more varied, and therefore have a larger spread of values.

As a simple example, suppose you are given an assignment that involves writing a term paper on a controversial subject that has many opposing viewpoints. Since you want a bibliography that supports your well-balanced term paper that takes into account multiple viewpoints, your bibliography will contain a wide variety of sources.

In other words, your bibliography will have a larger variance and a smaller bias. If most (or all) the references in your bibliography espouse the same point of view, then you will have a smaller variance and a larger bias (it's just an analogy, so it's not a perfect counterpart to bias-versus-variance).

The bias-variance trade-off can be stated in simple terms: in general, reducing the bias in samples can increase the variance, whereas reducing the variance tends to increase the bias.

Types of Bias in Data

In addition to the bias-variance trade-off that is discussed in the previous section, there are several types of bias:

- availability bias
- confirmation bias
- false causality
- sunk cost fallacy
- survivorship bias

Availability bias is akin to making a "rule" based on an exception. For example, there is a known link between smoking cigarettes and cancer, but there are exceptions. If you find someone who has smoked three packs of cigarettes on a daily basis for four decades and is still healthy, can you assert that smoking does not lead to cancer?

Confirmation bias refers to the tendency to focus on data that confirms their beliefs and simultaneously ignore data that contradicts a belief.

False causality occurs when you incorrectly assert that the occurrence of a particular event causes another event to occur as well. One of the most well-known examples involves ice cream consumption and violent crime in New York during the summer. Since more people eat ice cream in the summer, that "causes" more violent crime, which is a false causality. Other factors, such as the increase in temperature, may be linked to the increase in crime. However, it's important to distinguish between correlation and causality: the latter is a much stronger link than the former, and it's also more difficult to establish causality instead of correlation.

Sunk cost refers to something (often money) that has been spent or incurred that cannot be recouped. A common example pertains to gambling at a casino: people fall into the pattern of spending more money to recoup a substantial amount of money that has already been lost. While there are cases in which people do recover their money, in many (most?) cases, people simply incur an even greater loss because they continue to spend their money. (Hence, we have the expression, "it's time to cut your losses and walk away.")

Survivorship bias refers to analyzing a particular subset of "positive" data while ignoring the "negative" data. This bias occurs in various situations, such as being influenced by individuals who recount their rags-to-riches success story ("positive" data) while ignoring the fate of the people (which is often a very high percentage) who did not succeed (the "negative" data) in a similar quest. So, while it's certainly possible for an individual to overcome many difficult obstacles to succeed, is the success rate one in one thousand (or even lower)?

ANALYZING CLASSIFIERS (OPTIONAL)

This section is marked "optional" because its contents pertain to machine learning classifiers, which is not the focus of this book. However, it's still worthwhile to glance through the material, or perhaps return to this section after you have a basic understanding of machine learning classifiers.

Several well-known techniques are available for analyzing the quality of machine learning classifiers. Two techniques are LIME and ANOVA, both of which are discussed in the following subsections.

What is LIME?

LIME is an acronym for Local Interpretable Model-Agnostic Explanations. LIME is a model-agnostic technique that can be used with machine learning models. The intuition for this technique is straightforward: make small random changes to data samples and then observe the manner in which predictions change (or not). The intuition involves changing the output (slightly) and then observe what happens to the output.

By way of analogy, consider food inspectors who test for bacteria in truckloads of perishable food. Clearly, it's infeasible to test every food item in a truck (or a train car), so inspectors perform "spot checks" that involve testing randomly selected items. In an analogous fashion, LIME makes small changes to input data in random locations and then analyzes the changes in the associated output values.

However, there are two caveats to keep in mind when you use LIME with input data for a given model:

1. The actual changes to input values are model-specific.
2. This technique works on input that is interpretable.

Examples of interpretable input include machine learning classifiers (such as trees and random forests) and NLP techniques such as BoW. Non-interpretable input involves "dense" data, such as a word embedding (which is a vector of floating point numbers).

You could also substitute your model with another model that involves interpretable data, but then you need to evaluate how accurate the approximation is to the original model.

What is ANOVA?

ANOVA is an acronym for *analysis of variance*, which attempts to analyze the differences among the mean values of a sample that's taken from a population. ANOVA enables you to test if multiple mean values are equal. More importantly, ANOVA can assist in reducing Type I (false positive) errors and Type II errors (false negative) errors. For example, suppose that person A is diagnosed with cancer and person B is diagnosed as healthy, and that both diagnoses are incorrect. Then the result for person A is a false positive whereas the result for person B is a false negative. In general, a test result of false positive is *much* preferable to a test result of false negative.

ANOVA pertains to the design of experiments and hypothesis testing, which can produce meaningful results in various situations. For example, suppose that a dataset contains a feature that can be partitioned into several reasonably homogenous groups. Next, analyze the variance in each group and perform comparisons with the goal of determining different sources of variance for the values of a given feature. For more information about ANOVA, navigate to the following link:

https://en.wikipedia.org/wiki/Analysis_of_variance

SUMMARY

This chapter started with an explanation of datasets, a description of data wrangling, and details regarding various types of data. Then you learned about techniques for scaling numeric data, such as normalization and standardization. You saw how to convert categorical data to numeric values, and how to handle dates and currency.

Then you learned how to work with outliers, anomalies, and missing data, along with various techniques for handling these scenarios. You also learned about imbalanced data and evaluating the use of SMOTE to deal with imbalanced classes in a dataset. In addition, you learned about the bias-variance tradeoff and various types of statistical bias. Finally, you learned about classifiers using two techniques, LIME and ANOVA.

## CHAPTER 3

INTRODUCTION TO PANDAS

This chapter introduces the Pandas library and contains various code samples that illustrate some useful Pandas features. The title of each section clearly indicates its contents, so you can easily scan this chapter for those sections that contain material that is new to you. This approach will help you make efficient use of your time when you read the contents of this chapter.

The first part of this chapter contains a brief introduction to Pandas, followed by code samples that illustrate how to define Pandas data frames and also display their attributes. Please keep in mind that this chapter is devoted to Pandas data frames. There is one code block that illustrates how to define a Pandas `Series`, and if you want to learn more about this Pandas `Series`, you can search online for more information.

The second part of this chapter discusses various types of data frames that you can create, such as numeric and Boolean data frames. In addition, you will see examples of creating data frames with NumPy functions and random numbers. You will also see examples of converting between Python dictionaries and JSON-based data, and how to create a Pandas data frame from JSON-based data.

WHAT IS PANDAS?

Pandas is a Python library that is compatible with other Python libraries, such as NumPy and Matplotlib. Install Pandas by opening a command shell and invoking the following command for Python 3.x:

```
pip3 install pandas
```

In many ways, the Pandas library has the semantics of a spreadsheet, and it also works with various file types, such as XSL, XML, HTML, and CSV. Pandas provides a data type called a data frame (similar to a Python dictionary) with extremely powerful functionality (similar to the functionality of a spreadsheet).

Pandas Data Frames

In simplified terms, a Pandas data frame is a two-dimensional data structure, and it's convenient to think of the data structure in terms of rows and columns. Data frames can be labeled (rows as well as columns), and the columns can contain different data types. The source of the dataset can be a data file, database tables, or Web service. Pandas data frame features include the following:

- Data Frame Methods
- Data Frame Statistics
- Grouping, Pivoting, and Reshaping
- Handle Missing Data
- Join Data Frames

Data Frames and Data Cleaning Tasks

The specific tasks that you need to perform depend on the structure and contents of a dataset. In general, you will perform a workflow with the following steps (not necessarily always in this order), all of which can be performed with a Pandas data frame:

- Read data into a data frame
- Display top of data frame
- Display column data types
- Display `non_missing` values
- Replace NA with a value
- Iterate through the columns
- Statistics for each column
- Find missing values
- Total missing values
- Percentage of missing values
- Sort table values
- Print summary information
- Find columns with > 50% missing values
- Rename columns

A PANDAS DATA FRAME EXAMPLE

Listing 3.1 displays the content of `pandas_df.py` that illustrates how to define several Pandas data frames and display their contents.

LISTING 3.1: pandas_df.py

```
import pandas as pd
import numpy as np
myvector1 = np.array([1,2,3,4,5])
print("myvector1:")
```

```
print(myvector1)
print()

mydf1 = pd.DataFrame(myvector1)
print("mydf1:")
print(mydf1)
print()

myvector2 = np.array([i for i in range(1,6)])
print("myvector2:")
print(myvector2)
print()

mydf2 = pd.DataFrame(myvector2)
print("mydf2:")
print(mydf2)
print()

myarray = np.array([[10,30,20], [50,40,60],[1000,2000,3000]])
print("myarray:")
print(myarray)
print()

mydf3 = pd.Data frame(myarray)
print("mydf3:")
print(mydf3)
print()
```

Listing 3.1 starts with a standard `import` statement for Pandas and NumPy, followed by the definition of two one-dimensional NumPy arrays and a two-dimensional NumPy array. The NumPy syntax should be familiar to you (many basic tutorials are available online). Each NumPy variable is followed by a corresponding Pandas data frame `mydf1`, `mydf2`, and `mydf3`. Launch the code in Listing 3.1. You will see the following output, and you can compare the NumPy arrays with the Pandas data frames:

```
myvector1:
[1 2 3 4 5]

mydf1:
   0
0  1
1  2
2  3
3  4
4  5

myvector2:
[1 2 3 4 5]
mydf2:
   0
0  1
1  2
```

```
2    3
3    4
4    5

myarray:
[[   10    30    20]
 [   50    40    60]
 [1000 2000 3000]]

mydf3:
        0     1     2
0      10    30    20
1      50    40    60
2    1000  2000  3000
```

By contrast, the following code block illustrates how to define a Pandas `Series`:

```
names = pd.Series(['SF', 'San Jose', 'Sacramento'])
sizes = pd.Series([852469, 1015785, 485199])
df = pd.DataFrame({ 'Cities': names, 'Size': sizes })
print(df)
```

Create a Python file with the preceding code (along with the required `import` statement). When you launch that code, you will see the following output:

```
     City name      sizes
0           SF     852469
1     San Jose    1015785
2    Sacramento    485199
```

DESCRIBING A PANDAS DATA FRAME

Listing 3.2 displays the content of `pandas_df_describe.py` that illustrates how to define a Pandas data frame that contains a 3×3 `NumPy` array of integer values, where the rows and columns of the data frame are labeled. Various other aspects of the data frame are also displayed.

LISTING 3.2: pandas_df_describe.py

```
import numpy as np
import pandas as pd

myarray = np.array([[10,30,20], [50,40,60],[1000,2000,3000]])

rownames = ['apples', 'oranges', 'beer']
colnames = ['January', 'February', 'March']
mydf = pd.Data frame(myarray, index=rownames, columns=colnames)
print("contents of df:")
print(mydf)
print()
```

```
print("contents of January:")
print(mydf['January'])
print()

print("Number of Rows:")
print(mydf.shape[0])
print()

print("Number of Columns:")
print(mydf.shape[1])
print()

print("Number of Rows and Columns:")
print(mydf.shape)
print()

print("Column Names:")
print(mydf.columns)
print()

print("Column types:")
print(mydf.dtypes)
print()

print("Description:")
print(mydf.describe())
print()
```

Listing 3.2 starts with two standard import statements followed by the variable myarray, which is a 3x3 NumPy array of numbers. The variables rownames and colnames provide names for the rows and columns, respectively, of the Pandas data frame mydf, which is initialized as a Pandas data frame with the specified data source (i.e., myarray).

The first portion of the output below requires a single print() statement (which simply displays the contents of mydf). The second portion of the output is generated by invoking the describe() method that is available for any NumPy data frame. The describe() method is useful: you will see various statistical quantities, such as the mean, standard deviation minimum, and maximum performed column_wise (not row_wise), along with values for the 25th, 50th, and 75th percentiles. The output of Listing 3.2 is here:

```
contents of df:
        January  February  March
apples       10        30     20
oranges      50        40     60
beer       1000      2000   3000

contents of January:
apples       10
oranges      50
beer       1000
Name: January, dtype: int64
```

```
Number of Rows:
3

Number of Columns:
3

Number of Rows and Columns:
(3, 3)

Column Names:
Index(['January', 'February', 'March'], dtype='object')

Column types:
January      int64
February     int64
March        int64
dtype: object

Description:
            January     February      March
count      3.000000     3.000000    3.000000
mean     353.333333   690.000000 1026.666667
std      560.386771  1134.504297 1709.073823
min       10.000000    30.000000   20.000000
25%       30.000000    35.000000   40.000000
50%       50.000000    40.000000   60.000000
75%      525.000000  1020.000000 1530.000000
max     1000.000000  2000.000000 3000.000000
```

PANDAS BOOLEAN DATA FRAMES

Pandas supports Boolean operations on data frames, such as the logical or, the logical and, and the logical negation of a pair of data frames. Listing 3.3 displays the content of pandas_boolean_df.py that illustrates how to define a Pandas data frame whose rows and columns are Boolean values.

LISTING 3.3: pandas_boolean_df.py

```
import pandas as pd

df1 = pd.Data frame({'a': [1, 0, 1], 'b': [0, 1, 1] }, dtype=bool)
df2 = pd.Data frame({'a': [0, 1, 1], 'b': [1, 1, 0] }, dtype=bool)

print("df1 & df2:")
print(df1 & df2)

print("df1 | df2:")
print(df1 | df2)

print("df1 ^ df2:")
print(df1 ^ df2)
```

Listing 3.3 initializes the `data frames df1` and `df2`, and then computes `df1 & df2`, `df1 | df2`, `df1 ^ df2`, which represent the logical AND, the logical OR, and the logical negation, respectively, of `df1` and `df2`. The output from launching the code in Listing 3.3 is here:

```
df1 & df2:
       a        b
0  False    False
1  False     True
2   True    False
df1 | df2:
       a        b
0   True     True
1   True     True
2   True     True
df1 ^ df2:
       a        b
0   True     True
1   True    False
2  False     True
```

Transposing a Pandas Data Frame

The `T` attribute (as well as the transpose function) enables you to generate the transpose of a Pandas data frame, similar to a NumPy `ndarray`.

For example, the following code snippet defines a Pandas data frame `df1` and then displays the transpose of `df1`:

```
df1 = pd.DataFrame({'a': [1, 0, 1], 'b': [0, 1, 1] }, dtype=int)

print("df1.T:")
print(df1.T)
```

The output is here:

```
df1.T:
   0  1  2
a  1  0  1
b  0  1  1
```

The following code snippet defines Pandas data frames `df1` and `df2` and then displays their sum:

```
df1 = pd.DataFrame({'a' : [1, 0, 1], 'b' : [0, 1, 1] }, dtype=int)
df2 = pd.DataFrame({'a' : [3, 3, 3], 'b' : [5, 5, 5] }, dtype=int)

print("df1 + df2:")
print(df1 + df2)
```

The output is here:

```
df1 + df2:
   a  b
0  4  5
1  3  6
2  4  6
```

PANDAS DATA FRAMES AND RANDOM NUMBERS

Listing 3.4 displays the content of `pandas_random_df.py` that illustrates how to create a Pandas data frame with random numbers.

LISTING 3.4: pandas_random_df.py

```
import pandas as pd
import numpy as np

df = pd.DataFrame(np.random.randint(1, 5, size=(5, 2)),
columns=['a','b'])
df = df.append(df.agg(['sum', 'mean']))

print("Contents of data frame:")
print(df)
```

Listing 3.4 defines the Pandas data frame `df` that consists of 5 rows and 2 columns that contain random integers between 1 and 5. Notice that the columns of `df` are labeled "a" and "b." In addition, the next code snippet appends two rows consisting of the sum and the mean of the numbers in both columns. The output of Listing 3.4 is here:

```
a     b
0      1.0  2.0
1      1.0  1.0
2      4.0  3.0
3      3.0  1.0
4      1.0  2.0
sum   10.0  9.0
mean   2.0  1.8
```

Listing 3.5 displays the content of `pandas_combine_df.py` that illustrates how to define a Pandas data frame that is based on two NumPy arrays of numbers.

LISTING 3.5: pandas_combine_df.py

```
import pandas as pd
import numpy as np

df = pd.DataFrame({'foo1' : np.random.randn(5),
                   'foo2' : np.random.randn(5)})

print("contents of df:")
print(df)
```

```
print("contents of foo1:")
print(df.foo1)

print("contents of foo2:")
print(df.foo2)
```

Listing 3.5 defines the Pandas data frame df that consists of 5 rows and 2 columns (labeled foo1 and foo2) of random real numbers between 0 and 5. The next portion of Listing 3.5 displays the contents of df and foo1. The output of Listing 3.5 is here:

```
contents of df:
        foo1        foo2
0   0.274680  _0.848669
1  _0.399771  _0.814679
2   0.454443  _0.363392
3   0.473753   0.550849
4  _0.211783  _0.015014
contents of foo1:
0      0.256773
1      1.204322
2      1.040515
3     _0.518414
4      0.634141
Name: foo1, dtype: float64
contents of foo2:
0     _2.506550
1     _0.896516
2     _0.222923
3      0.934574
4      0.527033
Name: foo2, dtype: float64
```

CONVERTING CATEGORICAL DATA TO NUMERIC DATA

One common task in machine learning involves converting a feature containing character data into a feature that contains numeric data.

Listing 3.6 displays the content of sometext.tsv that contains labeled data (spam or ham), which is used in the code sample displayed in Listing 3.7.

LISTING 3.6: sometext.tsv

```
type      text
ham       I'm telling the truth
spam      What a deal such a deal!
spam      Free vacation for your family
ham       Thank you for your help
spam      Spring break next week!
ham       I received the documents
spam      One million dollars for you
ham       My wife got covid19
spam      You might have won the prize
ham       Everyone is in good health
```

Listing 3.7 displays the content of `cat2numeric.py` that illustrates how to replace a text field with a corresponding numeric field.

LISTING 3.7: cat2numeric.py

```
import pandas as pd
import numpy as np

df = pd.read_csv('sometext.tsv', delimiter='\t')

print("=> First five rows (before):")
print(df.head(5))
print("------------------------")

# map ham/spam to 0/1 values:
df['type'] = df['type'].map( {'ham':0 , 'spam':1} )

print("=> First five rows (after):")
print(df.head(5))
print("------------------------")
```

Listing 3.7 initializes the data frame `df` with the contents of the CSV file `sometext.tsv`, and then displays the contents of the first five rows by invoking `df.head(5)`, which is also the default number of rows to display. The next code snippet in Listing 3.7 invokes the `map()` method to replace occurrences of `ham` with 0 and replace occurrences of `spam` with 1 in the column labeled type, as shown here:

```
df['type'] = df['type'].map( {'ham':0 , 'spam':1} )
```

The last portion of Listing 3.7 invokes the `head()` method again to display the first five rows of the dataset after having renamed the contents of the column type. Launch the code in Listing 3.7 and you will see the following output:

```
=> First five rows (before):
    type                          text
0   ham            I'm telling the truth
1   spam          What a deal such a deal!
2   spam    Free vacation for your family
3   ham              Thank you for your help
4   spam            Spring break next week!
------------------------
=> First five rows (after):
    type                          text
0     0              I'm telling the truth
1     1            What a deal such a deal!
2     1    Free vacation for your family
3     0              Thank you for your help
4     1              Spring break next week!
------------------------
```

As another example, Listing 3.8 displays the content of `shirts.csv` and Listing 3.9 displays the content of `shirts.py` that illustrates four techniques for converting categorical data to numeric data.

LISTING 3.8: shirts.csv

```
type,ssize
shirt,xxlarge
shirt,xxlarge
shirt,xlarge
shirt,xlarge
shirt,xlarge
shirt,large
shirt,medium
shirt,small
shirt,small
shirt,xsmall
shirt,xsmall
shirt,xsmall
```

LISTING 3.9: shirts.py

```python
import pandas as pd

shirts = pd.read_csv("shirts.csv")
print("shirts before:")
print(shirts)
print()

# TECHNIQUE #1:
#shirts.loc[shirts['ssize']=='xxlarge','size'] = 4
#shirts.loc[shirts['ssize']=='xlarge', 'size'] = 4
#shirts.loc[shirts['ssize']=='large',  'size'] = 3
#shirts.loc[shirts['ssize']=='medium', 'size'] = 2
#shirts.loc[shirts['ssize']=='small',  'size'] = 1
#shirts.loc[shirts['ssize']=='xsmall', 'size'] = 1

# TECHNIQUE #2:
#shirts['ssize'].replace('xxlarge', 4, inplace=True)
#shirts['ssize'].replace('xlarge',  4, inplace=True)
#shirts['ssize'].replace('large',   3, inplace=True)
#shirts['ssize'].replace('medium',  2, inplace=True)
#shirts['ssize'].replace('small',   1, inplace=True)
#shirts['ssize'].replace('xsmall',  1, inplace=True)

# TECHNIQUE #3:
#shirts['ssize'] = shirts['ssize'].apply({'xxlarge':4, 'xlarge':4, 'large':3,
'medium':2, 'small':1, 'xsmall':1}.get)

# TECHNIQUE #4:
shirts['ssize'] = shirts['ssize'].replace(regex='xlarge', value=4)
shirts['ssize'] = shirts['ssize'].replace(regex='large',  value=3)
shirts['ssize'] = shirts['ssize'].replace(regex='medium', value=2)
shirts['ssize'] = shirts['ssize'].replace(regex='small',  value=1)

print("shirts after:")
print(shirts)
```

Listing 3.9 starts with a code block of six statements that uses direct comparison with strings to make numeric replacements. For example, the following code snippet replaces all occurrences of the string xxlarge with the value 4:

```
shirts.loc[shirts['ssize']=='xxlarge','size'] = 4
```

The second code block consists of six statements that use the replace() method to perform the same updates, an example of which is shown here:

```
shirts['ssize'].replace('xxlarge', 4, inplace=True)
```

The third code block consists of a single statement that uses the apply() method to perform the same updates, as shown here:

```
shirts['ssize'] = shirts['ssize'].apply({'xxlarge':4, 'xlarge':4,
'large':3, 'medium':2, 'small':1, 'xsmall':1}.get)
```

The fourth code block consists of four statements that use regular expressions to perform the same updates, an example of which is shown here:

```
shirts['ssize'] = shirts['ssize'].replace(regex='xlarge', value=4)
```

Since the preceding code snippet matches xxlarge as well as xlarge, we only need *four* statements instead of six statements. If you are unfamiliar with regular expressions, you can read online tutorials regarding this topic. Launch the code in Listing 3.9 and you will see the following output:

```
shirts before
        type      size
0      shirt    xxlarge
1      shirt    xxlarge
2      shirt     xlarge
3      shirt     xlarge
4      shirt     xlarge
5      shirt      large
6      shirt     medium
7      shirt      small
8      shirt      small
9      shirt     xsmall
10     shirt     xsmall
11     shirt     xsmall

shirts after:
        type    size
0      shirt      4
1      shirt      4
2      shirt      4
3      shirt      4
4      shirt      4
5      shirt      3
6      shirt      2
7      shirt      1
8      shirt      1
```

```
9    shirt    1
10   shirt    1
11   shirt    1
```

MERGING AND SPLITTING COLUMNS IN PANDAS

Listing 3.10 displays the content of `employees.csv` and Listing 3.11 displays the content of `emp_merge_split.py` that illustrates how to merge columns and split columns of a CSV file.

LISTING 3.10: employees.csv

```
name,year,month
Jane-Smith,2015,Aug
Dave-Smith,2020,Jan
Jane-Jones,2018,Dec
Jane-Stone,2017,Feb
Dave-Stone,2014,Apr
Mark-Aster,,Oct
Jane-Jones,NaN,Jun
```

LISTING 3.11: emp_merge_split.py

```python
import pandas as pd

emps = pd.read_csv("employees.csv")
print("emps:")
print(emps)
print()

emps['year']  = emps['year'].astype(str)
emps['month'] = emps['month'].astype(str)
# separate column for first name and for last name:
emps['fname'],emps['lname'] = emps['name'].str.split("-",1).str

# concatenate year and month with a "#" symbol:
emps['hdate1'] = emps['year'].astype(str)+"#"+emps['month'].astype(str)

# concatenate year and month with a "-" symbol:
emps['hdate2'] = emps[['year','month']].agg('-'.join, axis=1)

print(emps)
print()
```

Listing 3.11 initializes the data frame `df` with the contents of the CSV file `employees.csv`, and then displays the contents of the data frame. The next pair of code snippets invoke the `astype()` method to convert the contents of the `year` and `month` columns to strings.

The next code snippet in Listing 3.11 uses the `split()` method to split the name column into the columns `fname` and `lname`, which contain the first name and last name, respectively, of each employee's name:

```python
emps['fname'],emps['lname'] = emps['name'].str.split("-",1).str
```

The next code snippet concatenates the contents of the year and month string with a "#" character to create a new column called hdate1, as shown here:

```
emps['hdate1'] = emps['year'].astype(str)+"#"+emps['month'].astype(str)
```

The final code snippet concatenates the contents of the year and month string with a "-" to create a new column called hdate2, as shown here:

```
emps['hdate2'] = emps[['year','month']].agg('-'.join, axis=1)
```

Launch the code in Listing 3.11 and you will see the following output:

```
emps:
        name     year   month
0  Jane-Smith   2015.0   Aug
1  Dave-Smith   2020.0   Jan
2  Jane-Jones   2018.0   Dec
3  Jane-Stone   2017.0   Feb
4  Dave-Stone   2014.0   Apr
5  Mark-Aster      NaN   Oct
6  Jane-Jones      NaN   Jun

        name     year month fname   lname      hdate1        hdate2
0  Jane-Smith   2015.0   Aug  Jane   Smith  2015.0#Aug    2015.0-Aug
1  Dave-Smith   2020.0   Jan  Dave   Smith  2020.0#Jan    2020.0-Jan
2  Jane-Jones   2018.0   Dec  Jane   Jones  2018.0#Dec    2018.0-Dec
3  Jane-Stone   2017.0   Feb  Jane   Stone  2017.0#Feb    2017.0-Feb
4  Dave-Stone   2014.0   Apr  Dave   Stone  2014.0#Apr    2014.0-Apr
5  Mark-Aster      nan   Oct  Mark   Aster     nan#Oct       nan-Oct
6  Jane-Jones      nan   Jun  Jane   Jones     nan#Jun       nan-Jun
```

There is one other detail regarding the following code snippet:

```
#emps['fname'],emps['lname'] = emps['name'].str.split("-",1).str
```

The following deprecation message is displayed:

```
#FutureWarning: Columnar iteration over characters
#will be deprecated in future releases.
```

COMBINING PANDAS DATA FRAMES

Pandas supports the concat() method to concatenate data frames. Listing 3.12 displays the content of concat_frames.py that illustrates how to combine two Pandas data frames.

LISTING 3.12: concat_frames.py

```
import pandas as pd

can_weather = pd.Data frame({
    "city": ["Vancouver","Toronto","Montreal"],
```

```
        "temperature": [72,65,50],
        "humidity": [40, 20, 25]
})

us_weather = pd.Data frame({
    "city": ["SF","Chicago","LA"],
    "temperature": [60,40,85],
    "humidity": [30, 15, 55]
})

df = pd.concat([can_weather, us_weather])
print(df)
```

The first line in Listing 3.12 is an `import` statement, followed by the definition of the Pandas data frames `can_weather` and `us_weather` that contain weather-related information for cities in Canada and the USA, respectively. The Pandas data frame `df` is the concatenation of `can_weather` and `us_weather`. The output from Listing 3.12 is here:

```
0   Vancouver        40        72
1     Toronto        20        65
2    Montreal        25        50
0          SF        30        60
1     Chicago        15        40
2          LA        55        85
```

DATA MANIPULATION WITH PANDAS DATA FRAMES

As a simple example, suppose that we have a two-person company that keeps track of income and expenses on a quarterly basis. We want to calculate the profit/loss for each quarter, as well as the overall profit/loss.

Listing 3.13 displays the content of `pandas_quarterly_df1.py` that illustrates how to define a Pandas data frame consisting of income-related values.

LISTING 3.13: pandas_quarterly_df1.py

```
import pandas as pd

summary = {
    'Quarter': ['Q1', 'Q2', 'Q3', 'Q4'],
    'Cost':    [23500, 34000, 57000, 32000],
    'Revenue': [40000, 40000, 40000, 40000]
}

df = pd.DataFrame(summary)

print("Entire Dataset:\n",df)
print("Quarter:\n",df.Quarter)
print("Cost:\n",df.Cost)
print("Revenue:\n",df.Revenue)
```

Listing 3.13 defines the variable `summary` that contains hard-coded quarterly information about cost and revenue for our two-person company. In general, these hard-coded values would be replaced by data from another source (such as a CSV file), so think of this code sample as a simple way to illustrate some of the functionality that is available in Pandas data frames.

The variable `df` is a Pandas data frame based on the data in the `summary` variable. The three `print()` statements display the quarters, the cost per quarter, and the revenue per quarter. The output from Listing 3.13 is here:

```
Entire Dataset:
      Cost Quarter   Revenue
0   23500      Q1     40000
1   34000      Q2     60000
2   57000      Q3     50000
3   32000      Q4     30000
Quarter:
  0     Q1
1     Q2
2     Q3
3     Q4
Name: Quarter, dtype: object
Cost:
  0     23500
1     34000
2     57000
3     32000
Name: Cost, dtype: int64
Revenue:
  0     40000
1     60000
2     50000
3     30000
Name: Revenue, dtype: int64
```

PANDAS DATA FRAMES AND CSV FILES

The code samples in several earlier sections contain hard-coded data inside the Python scripts. However, it's also very common to read data from a CSV file. You can use the Python `csv.reader()` function, the NumPy `loadtxt()` function, or the Pandas function `read_csv()` function (shown in this section) to read the contents of CSV files.

Listing 3.14 displays the content of the CSV file `weather_data.csv` and Listing 3.15 displays the content of `weather_data.py` that illustrates how to read the file `weather_data.csv`.

LISTING 3.14: *weather_data.py*

```
day,temperature,windspeed,event
7/1/2018,42,16,Rain
7/2/2018,45,3,Sunny
7/3/2018,78,12,Snow
7/4/2018,74,9,Snow
7/5/2018,42,24,Rain
7/6/2018,51,32,Sunny
```

LISTING 3.15: weather_data.py

```python
import pandas as pd

df = pd.read_csv("weather_data.csv")

print(df)
print(df.shape)   # rows, columns
print(df.head())  # df.head(3)
print(df.tail())
print(df[1:3])
print(df.columns)
print(type(df['day']))
print(df[['day','temperature']])
print(df['temperature'].max())
```

Listing 3.15 invokes the Pandas `read_csv()` function to read the contents of the CSV file `weather_data.csv`, followed by a set of Python `print()` statements that display various portions of the CSV file. The output from Listing 3.15 is here:

```
        day  temperature  windspeed      event
0  7/1/2018           42         16   Rain
1  7/2/2018           45          3  Sunny
2  7/3/2018           78         12   Snow
3  7/4/2018           74          9  Snow
4  7/5/2018           42         24   Rain
5  7/6/2018           51         32  Sunny
(6, 4)
        day  temperature  windspeed      event
0  7/1/2018           42         16   Rain
1  7/2/2018           45          3  Sunny
2  7/3/2018           78         12   Snow
3  7/4/2018           74          9  Snow
4  7/5/2018           42         24   Rain
        day  temperature  windspeed      event
1  7/2/2018           45          3  Sunny
2  7/3/2018           78         12   Snow
3  7/4/2018           74          9  Snow
4  7/5/2018           42         24   Rain
5  7/6/2018           51         32  Sunny
        day  temperature  windspeed      event
1  7/2/2018           45          3  Sunny
2  7/3/2018           78         12   Snow
Index(['day', 'temperature', 'windspeed', 'event'], dtype='object')
<class 'pandas.core.series.Series'>
        day  temperature
0  7/1/2018           42
1  7/2/2018           45
2  7/3/2018           78
3  7/4/2018           74
4  7/5/2018           42
5  7/6/2018           51
78
```

In some situations, you might need to apply Boolean conditional logic to "filter out" some rows of data, based on a conditional condition that's applied to a column value.

Listing 3.16 displays the content of the CSV file `people.csv` and Listing 3.17 displays the content of `people_pandas.py` that illustrates how to define a Pandas data frame that reads the CSV file and manipulates the data.

LISTING 3.16: people.csv

```
fname,lname,age,gender,country
john,smith,30,m,usa
jane,smith,31,f,france
jack,jones,32,m,france
dave,stone,33,m,italy
sara,stein,34,f,germany
eddy,bower,35,m,spain
```

LISTING 3.17: people_pandas.py

```
import pandas as pd

df = pd.read_csv('people.csv')
df.info()
print('fname:')
print(df['fname'])
print('_____')
print('age over 33:')
print(df['age'] > 33)
print('_____')
print('age over 33:')
myfilter = df['age'] >  33
print(df[myfilter])
```

Listing 3.17 populates the Pandas data frame `df` with the contents of the CSV file `people.csv`. The next portion of Listing 3.17 displays the structure of `df`, followed by the first names of all the people. The next portion of Listing 3.17 displays a tabular list of six rows containing either True or False depending on whether a person is over 33 or at most 33, respectively. The final portion of Listing 3.17 displays a tabular list of two rows containing all the details of the people who are over 33. The output from Listing 3.17 is here:

```
myfilter = df['age'] >  33
<class 'pandas.core.frame.Data frame'>
RangeIndex: 6 entries, 0 to 5
Data columns (total 5 columns):
fname       6 non_null object
lname       6 non_null object
age         6 non_null int64
gender      6 non_null object
country     6 non_null object
dtypes: int64(1), object(4)
memory usage: 320.0+ bytes
fname:
```

```
0    john
1    jane
2    jack
3    dave
4    sara
5    eddy
Name: fname, dtype: object
```

```
age over 33:
0    False
1    False
2    False
3    False
4     True
5     True
Name: age, dtype: bool
```

```
age over 33:
   fname  lname  age gender country
4   sara  stein   34      f  france
5   eddy  bower   35      m  france
```

Useful Options for the Pandas read_csv() Function

Skip the initial header information contained in the first row with this code snippet:

```
df = pd.read_csv("data.csv", header=None)
```

The following code snippet shows you how to save a Pandas data frame to a CSV file *without* including the indices:

```
df.to_csv("data.csv", sep=",", index=False)
```

If need be, you can remove the first line immediately following the header row with this code snippet:

```
my_dataset = pd.read_csv("dataset.csv", skiprows=1, low_memory=False)
```

Skip the first three rows of a CSV file:

```
df = pd.read_csv("data.csv", skiprows=3, header=None)
```

Skip a range of rows that are specified by index:

```
df = pd.read_csv("data.csv", skiprows=[0,2])
```

Reading Selected Rows from CSV Files

You have seen Pandas-based examples of reading the entire contents of CSV files into a Pandas data frame and then selecting subsets of those rows for additional processing. In this section, you will see how to read portions of CSV files, which eliminates the need to drop redundant rows from Pandas data frames.

This technique involves reading portions of CSV files by specifying the `chunksize` parameter, that is useful for large datasets: Pandas will process the dataset in sequential chunks without reading the entire file into memory. Although the CSV dataset in this example is very small, you now know how to specify this parameter.

Listing 3.18 displays the content of `fruits.csv` that is referenced in Listing 3.19 that retrieves a subset of rows from `fruits.csv`.

LISTING 3.18: fruits.csv

```
name,month,day
avocado,Aug,13
persimmon,Jul,28
apples,Sept,25
oranges,Aug,30
bananas,Dec,20
cantelope,Nov,18
```

Listing 3.19 displays the content of `pandas_csv1.py` that illustrates how to read a subset of rows from a CSV file based on some conditional logic.

LISTING 3.19: pandas_csv1.py

```
import pandas as pd

csv_file="fruits.csv"

df1 = pd.read_csv(csv_file)
print("df1 set of rows:")
print(df1)
print()

df1 = pd.read_csv(csv_file, chunksize=10000000)
df2 = pd.concat((item.query("name == 'oranges'") for item in df1),
ignore_index=True)
print("df2:")
print(df2)
print()
```

Listing 3.19 initialized the string variable `csv_file` with the value of `fruits.csv`, populates the Pandas data frame `df1` with the contents of `fruits.csv`, and then displays the contents of `df1`.

The next portion of Listing 3.19 initializes the Pandas data frame `df2` with the subset of rows in `df1` whose `name` attribute equals `oranges`. Launch the code in Listing 3.19 and you will see the following output:

```
df1 set of rows:
        name month  day
0    avocado   Aug   13
1  persimmon   Jul   28
2     apples  Sept   25
3    oranges   Aug   30
```

```
4     bananas    Dec    20
5   cantelope    Nov    18
df2 rows with oranges:
     name month   day
0   oranges     Aug    30
```

Listing 3.20 displays the content of `pandas_schema1.py` that illustrates how to read a subset of rows from a CSV file based on some conditional logic.

LISTING 3.20: pandas_schema1.py

```
import pandas as pd

csv_file="emp_ages.csv"

schema = { "age": int }

df1 = pd.read_csv(csv_file, dtype=schema, chunksize=10000000)
df2 = pd.concat((item.query("'age' >= 45") for item in df1), ignore_
index=True)

print("df2 ages at least 45:")
print(df2)
```

Listing 3.20 initializes the string variable `csv_file` with the value `emp_ages.csv` and then initializes the string variable schema with a JSON-based string. The next code snippet initializes the Pandas data frame `df1` with the contents of the CSV file `emp_ages.csv`.

Next, the Pandas data frame `df2` is initialized with the subset of rows in `df1` whose age attribute is at least 45. The backquotes in this code snippet are required when you specify an attribute that has an embedded whitespace. Launch the code in Listing 3.20 and you will see the following output:

```
df2 ages at least 45:
   fname   lname   age
0   Jane   Jones    65
1   Jane   Jones    65
2   Dave   Stone    45
3   Mark   Aster    53
4   Jane   Jones    58
```

Listing 3.21 displays the content of `pandas_schema2.py` that illustrates how to read a subset of rows from a CSV file based on some conditional logic.

LISTING 3.21: pandas_schema2.py

```
import pandas as pd

csv_file="emp_ages.csv"

schema = { "age": int, "fname":str}
```

```
df1 = pd.read_csv(csv_file, dtype=schema, chunksize=10000000)
df2 = pd.concat((item.query("age >= 45 | age < 20") for item in df1),
ignore_index=True)

print("df2 ages at least 45 or less than 20:")
print(df2)
```

Listing 3.21 extends the code in Listing 3.20 by specifying a compound condition for the rows in the Pandas data frame df2, which involves the rows in df1 whose age attribute is at least 45 *or* the rows in df1 whose age attribute is *less than* 20. Launch the code in Listing 3.21 and you will see the following output:

```
df2 ages at least 45 or less than 20:
   fname  lname  age
0  Dave   Smith  10
1  Jane   Jones  65
2  Jane   Jones  65
3  Dave   Stone  45
4  Mark   Aster  53
5  Jane   Jones  58
```

PANDAS DATA FRAMES AND EXCEL SPREADSHEETS

Listing 3.22 displays the content of write_people_xlsx.py that illustrates how to read data from a CSV file and then create an Excel spreadsheet with that data.

LISTING 3.22: write_people_xlsx.py

```
import pandas as pd

df1 = pd.read_csv("people.csv")
df1.to_excel("people.xlsx")

#optionally specify the sheet name:
#df1.to_excel("people.xlsx", sheet_name='Sheet_name_1')
```

Listing 3.22 initializes the Pandas data frame df1 with the contents of the CSV file people.csv and then invokes the to_excel() method to save the contents of the data frame to the Excel spreadsheet people.xlsx.

Listing 3.23 displays the content of read_people_xlsx.py that illustrates how to read data from the Excel spreadsheet people.xlsx and create a Pandas data frame with that data.

LISTING 3.23: read_people_xlsx.py

```
import pandas as pd

df = pd.read_excel("people.xlsx")
print("Contents of Excel spreadsheet:")
print(df)
```

Listing 3.23 is straightforward: the Pandas data frame `df` is initialized with the contents of the spreadsheet `people.xlsx` (whose contents are the same as `people.csv`) via the Pandas function `read_excel()`. The output from Listing 3.23 is here:

```
df1:
     Unnamed: 0  fname   lname   age  gender   country
0             0  john    smith   30       m       usa
1             1  jane    smith   31       f    france
2             2  jack    jones   32       m    france
3             3  dave    stone   33       m     italy
4             4  sara    stein   34       f   germany
5             5  eddy    bower   35       m     spain
```

Useful Options for Reading Excel Spreadsheets

Sometimes you need extra control over the values that you read from an Excel spreadsheet into a Pandas data frame, just as you do with CSV files.

Skip the header and the footer in an Excel spreadsheet with this code snippet:

```
df = pd.read_excel("myfile.xls",header=15,skipfooter=_Y_)
```

SELECT, ADD, AND DELETE COLUMNS IN DATA FRAMES

This section contains short code blocks that illustrate how to perform operations on a data frame that resemble the operations on a Python dictionary. For example, getting, setting, and deleting columns works with the same syntax as the analogous Python `dict` operations, as shown here:

```
df = pd.DataFrame.from_dict(dict([('A',[1,2,3]),('B',[4,5,6])]),
                orient='index', columns=['one', 'two', 'three'])

print(df)
```

The output from the preceding code snippet is here:

```
   one  two  three
A    1    2      3
B    4    5      6
```

Look at the following operation that appends a new column to the contents of the data frame `df`:

```
df['four'] = df['one'] * df['two']
print(df)
```

The output from the preceding code block is here:

```
   one  two  three  four
A    1    2      3     2
B    4    5      6    20
```

The following operation squares the contents of a column in the data frame `df`:

```
df['three'] = df['two'] * df['two']
print(df)
```

The output from the preceding code block is here:

```
   one  two  three  four
A    1    2      4     2
B    4    5     25    20
```

The following operation inserts a column of random numbers in index position 1 (which is the second column) in the data frame `df`:

```
import numpy as np
rand = np.random.randn(2)
df.insert(1, 'random', rand)
print(df)
```

The output from the preceding code block is here:

```
   one    random  two  three  four
A    1 -1.703111    2      4     2
B    4  1.139189    5     25    20
```

The following operation appends a new column called `flag` that contains `True` or `False`, based on whether the numeric value in the "one" column is greater than 2:

```
import numpy as np
rand = np.random.randn(2)
df.insert(1, 'random', rand)
print(df)
```

The output from the preceding code block is here:

```
   one    random  two  three  four   flag
A    1 -1.703111    2      4     2  False
B    4  1.139189    5     25    20   True
```

Columns can be deleted, as shown in following code snippet that deletes the "two" column:

```
del df['two']
print(df)
```

The output from the preceding code block is here:

```
   one    random  three  four   flag
A    1 -0.460401      4     2  False
B    4  1.211468     25    20   True
```

Columns can be deleted via the `pop()` method, as shown in following code snippet that deletes the "three" column:

```
three = df.pop('three')
print(df)
```

```
      one     random   four    flag
A      1   -0.544829       2   False
B      4    0.581476      20    True
```

When inserting a scalar value, it will naturally be propagated to fill the column:

```
df['foo'] = 'bar'
print(df)
```

The output from the preceding code snippet is here:

```
      one     random   four    flag   foo
A      1   -0.187331       2   False   bar
B      4   -0.169672      20    True   bar
```

HANDLING OUTLIERS IN PANDAS

If you are unfamiliar with outliers and anomalies, please read the sections in the appendix that discuss these two concepts because this section uses Pandas to find outliers in a dataset. The key idea involves finding the "z-score" of the values in the dataset, which involves calculating the mean sigma and standard deviation std, and then mapping each value x in the dataset to the value (x-sigma)/std.

Next, you specify a value of z (such as 3) and find the rows whose z-score is greater than 3. These are the rows that contain values that are considered outliers. *Note that a suitable value for the z-score is your decision (not some other external factor).*

Listing 3.24 displays the content of outliers_zscores.py that illustrates how to find rows of a dataset whose z-score greater than (or less than) a specified value.

LISTING 3.24: outliers_zscores.py

```
import numpy as np
import pandas as pd
from scipy import stats
from scikit-learn import datasets

df = datasets.load_iris()
columns = df.feature_names
iris_df = pd.DataFrame(df.data)
iris_df.columns = columns

print("=> iris_df.shape:",iris_df.shape)
print(iris_df.head())
print()

z = np.abs(stats.zscore(iris_df))
print("z scores for iris:")
print("z.shape:",z.shape)

upper = 2.5
lower = 0.01
print("=> upper outliers:")
```

```
print(z[np.where(z > upper)])
print()

outliers = iris_df[z < lower]
print("=> lower outliers:")
print(outliers)
print()
```

Listing 3.24 initializes the variable df with the contents of the built-in Iris dataset. Next, the variable columns is initialized with the column names, and the data frame iris_df is initialized from the content of df.data that contains the actual data for the Iris dataset. In addition, iris_df.columns is initialized with the contents of the variable columns.

The next portion of Listing 3.24 displays the shape of the data frame iris_df, followed by the zscore of the iris_df data frame, which is computed by subtracting the mean and then dividing by the standard deviation (performed for each row).

The last two portions of Listing 3.24 display the outliers (if any) whose zscore is outside the interval [0.01, 2.5]. Launch the code in Listing 3.24 and you will see the following output:

```
=> iris_df.shape: (150, 4)
   sepal length (cm)  sepal width (cm)  petal length (cm)  petal width (cm)
0         5.1               3.5               1.4               0.2
1         4.9               3.0               1.4               0.2
2         4.7               3.2               1.3               0.2
3         4.6               3.1               1.5               0.2
4         5.0               3.6               1.4               0.2
z scores for iris:
z.shape: (150, 4)

=> upper outliers:
[3.09077525 2.63038172]
=> lower outliers:
   sepal length (cm)  sepal width (cm)  petal length (cm)  petal width (cm)
73        6.1               2.8               4.7               1.2
82        5.8               2.7               3.9               1.2
90        5.5               2.6               4.4               1.2
92        5.8               2.6               4.0               1.2
95        5.7               3.0               4.2               1.2
```

PANDAS DATA FRAMES AND SIMPLE STATISTICS

Listing 3.25 displays the content of housing_stats.py that illustrates how to gather basic statistics from data in a Pandas data frame.

LISTING 3.25: housing_stats.py

```
import pandas as pd

df = pd.read_csv("Housing.csv")

minimum_bdrms = df["bedrooms"].min()
median_bdrms  = df["bedrooms"].median()
maximum_bdrms = df["bedrooms"].max()
```

```
print("minimum # of bedrooms:",minimum_bdrms)
print("median  # of bedrooms:",median_bdrms)
print("maximum # of bedrooms:",maximum_bdrms)
print("")

print("median values:",df.median().values)
print("")

prices = df["price"]
print("first 5 prices:")
print(prices.head())
print("")

median_price = df["price"].median()
print("median price:",median_price)
print("")

corr_matrix = df.corr()
print("correlation matrix:")
print(corr_matrix["price"].sort_values(ascending=False))
```

Listing 3.25 initializes the Pandas data frame `df` with the contents of the CSV file `housing.csv`. The next three variables are initialized with the minimum, median, and maximum number of bedrooms, respectively, and then these values are displayed.

The next portion of Listing 3.25 initializes the variable `prices` with the contents of the prices column of the Pandas data frame `df`. Next, the first five rows are printed via the `prices.head()` statement, followed by the median value of the prices.

The final portion of Listing 3.25 initializes the variable `corr_matrix` with the contents of the correlation matrix for the Pandas data frame `df`, and then displays its contents. The output from Listing 3.25 is here:

```
Apples
10
```

FINDING DUPLICATE ROWS IN PANDAS

Listing 3.26 displays the content of `duplicates.csv` and Listing 3.27 displays the content of `duplicates.py` that illustrates how to find duplicate rows in a Pandas data frame.

LISTING 3.26: duplicates.csv

```
fname,lname,level,dept,state
Jane,Smith,Senior,Sales,California
Dave,Smith,Senior,Devel,California
Jane,Jones,Year1,Mrktg,Illinois
Jane,Jones,Year1,Mrktg,Illinois
Jane,Stone,Senior,Mrktg,Arizona
Dave,Stone,Year2,Devel,Arizona
Mark,Aster,Year3,BizDev,Florida
Jane,Jones,Year1,Mrktg,Illinois
```

LISTING 3.27: duplicates.py

```
import pandas as pd

df = pd.read_csv("duplicates.csv")
print("Contents of data frame:")
print(df)
print()

print("Duplicate rows:")
#df2 = df.duplicated(subset=None)
df2 = df.duplicated(subset=None, keep='first')
print(df2)
print()

print("Duplicate first names:")
df3 = df[df.duplicated(['fname'])]
print(df3)
print()

print("Duplicate first name and level:")
df3 = df[df.duplicated(['fname','level'])]
print(df3)
print()
```

Listing 3.27 initializes the data frame df with the contents of the CSV file duplicates.csv, and then displays the contents of the data frame. The next portion of Listing 3.27 displays the duplicate rows by invoking the duplicated() method, whereas the next portion of Listing 3.27 displays only the first name fname of the duplicate rows. The final portion of Listing 3.27 displays the first name fname as well as the level of the duplicate rows. Launch the code in Listing 3.27 and you will see the following output:

```
Contents of data frame:
    fname  lname   level    dept       state
0   Jane   Smith   Senior   Sales   California
1   Dave   Smith   Senior   Devel   California
2   Jane   Jones   Year1    Mrktg     Illinois
3   Jane   Jones   Year1    Mrktg     Illinois
4   Jane   Stone   Senior   Mrktg      Arizona
5   Dave   Stone   Year2    Devel      Arizona
6   Mark   Aster   Year3    BizDev     Florida
7   Jane   Jones   Year1    Mrktg     Illinois

Duplicate rows:
0      False
1      False
2      False
3       True
4      False
5      False
6      False
7       True
dtype: bool
```

```
Duplicate first names:
   fname  lname   level    dept      state
2   Jane  Jones   Year1   Mrktg   Illinois
3   Jane  Jones   Year1   Mrktg   Illinois
4   Jane  Stone   Senior  Mrktg    Arizona
5   Dave  Stone   Year2   Devel    Arizona
7   Jane  Jones   Year1   Mrktg   Illinois

Duplicate first name and level:
   fname  lname   level    dept      state
3   Jane  Jones   Year1   Mrktg   Illinois
4   Jane  Stone   Senior  Mrktg    Arizona
7   Jane  Jones   Year1   Mrktg   Illinois
```

Listing 3.28 displays the content of `drop_duplicates.py` that illustrates how to drop duplicate rows in a Pandas data frame.

LISTING 3.28: drop_duplicates.py

```
import pandas as pd

df = pd.read_csv("duplicates.csv")
print("Contents of data frame:")
print(df)
print()

fname_filtered = df.drop_duplicates(['fname'])
print("Drop duplicate first names:")
print(fname_filtered)
print()

fname_lname_filtered = df.drop_duplicates(['fname','lname'])
print("Drop duplicate first and last names:")
print(fname_lname_filtered)
print()
```

Listing 3.28 initializes the data frame `df` with the contents of the CSV file `duplicates.csv`, and then displays the contents of the data frame. The next portion of Listing 3.28 deletes the rows that have duplicate `fname` values, followed by a code block that drops rows with duplicate `fname` and `lname` values. Launch the code in Listing 3.28 and you will see the following output:

```
Contents of data frame:
   fname  lname   level    dept       state
0   Jane  Smith   Senior   Sales  California
1   Dave  Smith   Senior   Devel  California
2   Jane  Jones   Year1    Mrktg    Illinois
3   Jane  Jones   Year1    Mrktg    Illinois
4   Jane  Stone   Senior   Mrktg     Arizona
5   Dave  Stone   Year2    Devel     Arizona
6   Mark  Aster   Year3   BizDev     Florida
7   Jane  Jones   Year1    Mrktg    Illinois
```

```
Drop duplicate first names:
   fname  lname   level   dept     state
0  Jane   Smith   Senior  Sales    California
1  Dave   Smith   Senior  Devel    California
6  Mark   Aster   Year3   BizDev   Florida

Drop duplicate first and last names:
   fname  lname   level   dept     state
0  Jane   Smith   Senior  Sales    California
1  Dave   Smith   Senior  Devel    California
2  Jane   Jones   Year1   Mrktg    Illinois
4  Jane   Stone   Senior  Mrktg    Arizona
5  Dave   Stone   Year2   Devel    Arizona
6  Mark   Aster   Year3   BizDev   Florida
```

FINDING MISSING VALUES IN PANDAS

Listing 3.29 displays the content of `employees2.csv` and Listing 3.30 displays the content of `missing_values.py` that illustrates how to display rows of a data frame that have missing values in a Pandas data frame.

LISTING 3.29: employees2.csv

```
name,year,month
Jane-Smith,2015,Aug
Jane-Smith,2015,Aug
Dave-Smith,2020,
Dave-Stone,,Apr
Jane-Jones,2018,Dec
Jane-Stone,2017,Feb
Jane-Stone,2017,Feb
Mark-Aster,,Oct
Jane-Jones,NaN,Jun
```

LISTING 3.30: missing_values.py

```
import pandas as pd
import matplotlib.pyplot as plt
import numpy as np

df = pd.read_csv("employees2.csv")

print("=> contents of CSV file:")
print(df)
print()

#NA:  Not Available (Pandas)
#NaN: Not a Number (Pandas)
#NB:  NumPy uses np.nan() to check for NaN values

df = pd.read_csv("employees2.csv")
```

```
print("=> contents of CSV file:")
print(df)
print()

print("=> any NULL values per column?")
print(df.isnull().any())
print()

print("=> count of NAN/MISSING values in each column:")
print(df.isnull().sum())
print()

print("=> count of NAN/MISSING values in each column:")
print(pd.isna(df).sum())
print()

print("=> count of NAN/MISSING values in each column (sorted):")
print(df.isnull().sum().sort_values(ascending=False))
print()

nan_null = df.isnull().sum().sum()
miss_values = df.isnull().any().sum()

print("=> count of NaN/MISSING values:",nan_null)
print("=> count of MISSING values:",miss_values)
print("=> count of NaN values:",nan_null-miss_values)
```

Listing 3.30 initializes the data frame df with the contents of the CSV file employees2.csv, and then displays the contents of the data frame. The next portion of Listing 3.30 displays the number of null values that appear in any row or column. The next portion of Listing 3.30 displays the fields and the names of the fields that have null values.

The next portion of Listing 3.30 displays the number of duplicate rows, followed by the row numbers that are duplicates. Launch the code in Listing 3.30 and you will see the following output:

```
=> contents of CSV file:
          name    year month
0  Jane-Smith  2015.0   Aug
1  Jane-Smith  2015.0   Aug
2  Dave-Smith  2020.0   NaN
3  Dave-Stone     NaN   Apr
4  Jane-Jones  2018.0   Dec
5  Jane-Stone  2017.0   Feb
6  Jane-Stone  2017.0   Feb
7  Mark-Aster     NaN   Oct
8  Jane-Jones     NaN   Jun

=> any NULL values per column?
name      False
year       True
month      True
dtype: bool
```

```
=> count of NAN/MISSING values in each column:
name     0
year     3
month    1
dtype: int64

=> count of NAN/MISSING values in each column:
name     0
year     3
month    1
dtype: int64

=> count of NAN/MISSING values in each column (sorted):
year     3
month    1
name     0
dtype: int64
=> count of NaN/MISSING values: 4
=> count of MISSING values: 2
=> count of NaN values: 2
```

MISSING VALUES IN AN IRIS-BASED DATASET

This section shows you how to replace missing values in the dataset nan_iris.csv that was created as follows:

- copy the header and the first 50 data rows of the Iris dataset
- substitute NaN in randomly selected rows and columns

For your convenience, the iris.csv dataset and the nan_iris.csv dataset are included in the companion files for this book (see the Preface for details).

Listing 3.32 displays an initial portion of the contents of nan_iris.csv, whereas Listing 3.33 displays the content of missingdatairis.py that illustrates how to replace the NaN values with meaningful values.

LISTING 3.32: nan_iris.csv

```
SepalLength,SepalWidth,PetalLength,PetalWidth,Name
5.1,3.5,1.4,0.2,Iris-setosa
4.9,3,1.4,0.2,Iris-setosa
NaN,3.2,NaN,0.2,Iris-setosa
4.6,3.1,1.5,0.2,Iris-setosa
5,3.6,1.4,0.2,Iris-setosa
NaN,3.9,1.7,0.4,Iris-setosa
4.6,3.4,1.4,0.3,Iris-setosa
NaN,3.4,1.5,0.2,Iris-setosa
4.4,2.9,1.4,0.2,Iris-setosa
4.9,3.1,NaN,0.1,NaN
// details omitted for brevity
4.5,2.3,1.3,0.3,Iris-setosa
```

```
4.4,NaN,NaN,NaN,NaN
5,3.5,NaN,NaN,Iris-setosa
5.1,3.8,1.9,0.4,Iris-setosa
4.8,3,1.4,0.3,Iris-setosa
5.1,3.8,1.6,0.2,Iris-setosa
4.6,3.2,1.4,0.2,Iris-setosa
5.3,3.7,1.5,0.2,Iris-setosa
5,3.3,1.4,0.2,Iris-setosa
```

LISTING 3.33: *missingdatairis.py*

```python
import numpy as np
import pandas as pd

# Step 1:
data = pd.read_csv('nan_iris.csv')
# Step 2:
print("=> Details of dataset columns:")
print(data.info())
print()

# Step 3:
print("=> Missing values per column:")
print(data.isnull().sum())
print()

# Step 4:
print("=> First range from 40 to 45:")
print(data[40:45])
print()

# Step 5:
print("=> List of Mean Values:")
print(data.mean())
print()

# list of column labels:
# SepalLength SepalWidth PetalLength PetalWidth Name

# Step 6:
# fill numeric columns with the mean (per column):
data.fillna(data.mean(), inplace=True)

# Step 7:
print("=> Second range from 40 to 45:")
print(data[40:45])
print()

# Step 8:
# create a new category for categorical data:
data['Name'] = data['Name'].fillna('UNKNOWN')

# Step 9:
print("=> Third range from 40 to 45:")
print(data[40:45])
```

Listing 3.33 contains various blocks of code with self-explanatory comments that explain the purpose of the code, starting with the first step that reads the contents of nan_iris.csv into the data frame data, followed by the block of code that displays the details of the dataset.

Next, the third block of code displays the number of missing values in each column of the dataset, followed by a block of code that display the contents of rows 40 through 45.

The fifth block of code displays the mean values for each column in the dataset, followed by a block of code that replaces the missing numeric values with the mean value, on a column-by-column basis, via the following code snippet:

```
data.fillna(data.mean(), inplace=True)
```

The seventh block of code displays the updated contents of the dataset, followed by a block of code that replaces the NaN values with UNKNOWN in the Name column.

The final block of code displays the data in rows 40 through 45, and at this point, all the NaN values in the data frame have been replaced with a numeric value or the string UNKNOWN. Launch the code in Listing 3.33 and you will see the following output:

```
=> Details of dataset columns:
<class 'pandas.core.frame.DataFrame'>
RangeIndex: 50 entries, 0 to 49
Data columns (total 5 columns):
 #   Column       Non-Null Count  Dtype
---  ------       --------------  -----
 0   SepalLength  39 non-null     float64
 1   SepalWidth   49 non-null     float64
 2   PetalLength  46 non-null     float64
 3   PetalWidth   48 non-null     float64
 4   Name         46 non-null     object
dtypes: float64(4), object(1)
memory usage: 2.1+ KB
None

=> Missing values per column:
SepalLength    11
SepalWidth      1
PetalLength     4
PetalWidth      2
Name            4
dtype: int64

=> First range from 40 to 45:
     SepalLength  SepalWidth  PetalLength  PetalWidth         Name
40           NaN         3.5          1.3         0.3  Iris-setosa
41           4.5         2.3          1.3         0.3  Iris-setosa
42           4.4         NaN          NaN         NaN          NaN
43           5.0         3.5          NaN         NaN  Iris-setosa
44           5.1         3.8          1.9         0.4  Iris-setosa

=> List of Mean Values:
SepalLength    5.002564
SepalWidth     3.422449
PetalLength    1.467391
PetalWidth     0.237500
dtype: float64
```

```
=> Second range from 40 to 45:
      SepalLength  SepalWidth  PetalLength  PetalWidth        Name
40       5.002564    3.500000     1.300000      0.3000  Iris-setosa
41       4.500000    2.300000     1.300000      0.3000  Iris-setosa
42       4.400000    3.422449     1.467391      0.2375         NaN
43       5.000000    3.500000     1.467391      0.2375  Iris-setosa
44       5.100000    3.800000     1.900000      0.4000  Iris-setosa
=> Third range from 40 to 45:
      SepalLength  SepalWidth  PetalLength  PetalWidth        Name
40       5.002564    3.500000     1.300000      0.3000  Iris-setosa
41       4.500000    2.300000     1.300000      0.3000  Iris-setosa
42       4.400000    3.422449     1.467391      0.2375     UNKNOWN
43       5.000000    3.500000     1.467391      0.2375  Iris-setosa
44       5.100000    3.800000     1.900000      0.4000  Iris-setosa
```

SORTING DATA FRAMES IN PANDAS

Listing 3.34 displays the content of `sort_df.py` that illustrates how to sort the rows in a Pandas data frame.

LISTING 3.34: sort_df.py

```python
import pandas as pd

df = pd.read_csv("duplicates.csv")
print("Contents of data frame:")
print(df)
print()

df.sort_values(by=['fname'], inplace=True)
print("Sorted (ascending) by first name:")
print(df)
print()

df.sort_values(by=['fname'], inplace=True,ascending=False)
print("Sorted (descending) by first name:")
print(df)
print()

df.sort_values(by=['fname','lname'], inplace=True)
print("Sorted (ascending) by first name and last name:")
print(df)
print()
```

Listing 3.34 initializes the data frame `df` with the contents of the CSV file `duplicates.csv`, and then displays the contents of the data frame. The next portion of Listing 3.34 displays the rows in *ascending* order based on the first name, and the next code block displays the rows in *descending* order based on the first name. The final code block in Listing 3.34 displays the rows in ascending order based on the first name as well as the last name. Launch the code in Listing 3.34 and you will see the following output:

```
Contents of data frame:
   fname  lname  level    dept      state
0  Jane   Smith  Senior   Sales   California
1  Dave   Smith  Senior   Devel   California
2  Jane   Jones  Year1    Mrktg    Illinois
3  Jane   Jones  Year1    Mrktg    Illinois
4  Jane   Stone  Senior   Mrktg    Arizona
5  Dave   Stone  Year2    Devel    Arizona
6  Mark   Aster  Year3    BizDev    Florida
7  Jane   Jones  Year1    Mrktg    Illinois

Sorted (ascending) by first name:
   fname  lname  level    dept      state
1  Dave   Smith  Senior   Devel   California
5  Dave   Stone  Year2    Devel    Arizona
0  Jane   Smith  Senior   Sales   California
2  Jane   Jones  Year1    Mrktg    Illinois
3  Jane   Jones  Year1    Mrktg    Illinois
4  Jane   Stone  Senior   Mrktg    Arizona
7  Jane   Jones  Year1    Mrktg    Illinois
6  Mark   Aster  Year3    BizDev    Florida

Sorted (descending) by first name:
   fname  lname  level    dept      state
6  Mark   Aster  Year3    BizDev    Florida
0  Jane   Smith  Senior   Sales   California
2  Jane   Jones  Year1    Mrktg    Illinois
3  Jane   Jones  Year1    Mrktg    Illinois
4  Jane   Stone  Senior   Mrktg    Arizona
7  Jane   Jones  Year1    Mrktg    Illinois
1  Dave   Smith  Senior   Devel   California
5  Dave   Stone  Year2    Devel    Arizona

Sorted (ascending) by first name and last name:
   fname  lname  level    dept      state
1  Dave   Smith  Senior   Devel   California
5  Dave   Stone  Year2    Devel    Arizona
2  Jane   Jones  Year1    Mrktg    Illinois
3  Jane   Jones  Year1    Mrktg    Illinois
7  Jane   Jones  Year1    Mrktg    Illinois
0  Jane   Smith  Senior   Sales   California
4  Jane   Stone  Senior   Mrktg    Arizona
6  Mark   Aster  Year3    BizDev    Florida
```

WORKING WITH GROUPBY() IN PANDAS

Listing 3.35 displays the content of groupby1.py that illustrates how to invoke the Pandas groupby() method to compute the subtotals of feature values.

LISTING 3.35: groupby1.py

```
import pandas as pd

# colors and weights of balls:
data = {'color':['red','blue','blue','red','blue'],
        'weight':[40,50,20,30,90]}
df1 = pd.DataFrame(data)
print("df1:")
print(df1)
print()
print(df1.groupby('color').mean())
print()

red_filter = df1['color']=='red'
print(df1[red_filter])
print()
blue_filter = df1['color']=='blue'
print(df1[blue_filter])
print()

red_avg = df1[red_filter]['weight'].mean()
blue_avg = df1[blue_filter]['weight'].mean()
print("red_avg,blue_avg:")
print(red_avg,blue_avg)
print()

df2 = pd.DataFrame({'color':['blue','red'],'weight':[red_avg,blue_
avg]})
print("df2:")
print(df2)
print()
```

Listing 3.35 defines the variable `data` containing `color` and `weight` values, and then initializes the data frame `df` with the contents of the variable `data`. The next two code blocks define `red_filter` and `blue_filter` that match the rows whose colors are red and blue, respectively, and then prints the matching rows.

The next portion of Listing 3.35 defines the two filters `red_avg` and `blue_avg` that calculate the average weight of the red value and the blue values, respectively. The last code block in Listing 3.35 defines the data frame `df2` with a `color` column and a `weight` column, where the latter contains the average weight of the red values and the blue values. Launch the code in Listing 3.35 and you will see the following output:

```
initial data frame:
df1:
   color  weight
0    red      40
1   blue      50
2   blue      20
3    red      30
4   blue      90
```

```
          weight
color
blue    53.333333
red     35.000000


   color  weight
0    red      40
3    red      30


   color  weight
1   blue      50
2   blue      20
4   blue      90


red_avg,blue_avg:
35.0 53.333333333333336


df2:
   color    weight
0   blue  35.000000
1    red  53.333333
```

AGGREGATE OPERATIONS WITH THE TITANIC.CSV DATASET

Listing 3.36 displays the content of `aggregate2.py` that illustrates how to perform aggregate operations with columns in the CSV file `titanic.csv`.

LISTING 3.36: aggregate2.py

```python
import pandas as pd

#Loading titanic.csv in Seaborn:
#df = sns.load_dataset('titanic')
df = pd.read_csv("titanic.csv")

# convert floating point values to integers:
df['survived'] = df['survived'].astype(int)

# specify column and aggregate functions:
aggregates1 = {'embark_town': ['count', 'nunique', 'size']}

# group by 'deck' value and apply aggregate functions:
result = df.groupby(['deck']).agg(aggregates1)
print("=> Grouped by deck:")
print(result)
print()

# some details regarding count() and nunique():
# count() excludes NaN values whereas size() includes them
# nunique() excludes NaN values in the unique counts

# group by 'age' value and apply aggregate functions:
```

```
result2 = df.groupby(['age']).agg(aggregates1)
print("=> Grouped by age (before):")
print(result2)
print()


# some "age" values are missing (so drop them):
df = df.dropna()
# convert floating point values to integers:
df['age'] = df['age'].astype(int)


# group by 'age' value and apply aggregate functions:
result3 = df.groupby(['age']).agg(aggregates1)
print("=> Grouped by age (after):")
print(result3)
print()
```

Listing 3.36 initializes the data frame df with the contents of the CSV file titanic.csv. The next code snippet converts floating point values to integers, followed by defining the variable aggregates1 that specifies the functions count(), nunique(), and size() that will be invoked on the embark_town field.

The next code snippet initializes the variable result after invoking the groupby() method on the deck field, followed by invoking the agg() method.

The next code block performs the same computation to initialize the variable result2, except that the groupby() function is invoked on the age field instead of the embark_town field. Notice the comment section regarding the count() and nunique() functions: let's drop the rows with missing values via df.dropna() and investigate how that affects the calculations.

After dropping the rows with missing values, the final code block initializes the variable result3 in exactly the same way that result2 was initialized. Launch the code in Listing 3.36. The output is shown here:

```
=> Grouped by deck:
     embark_town
          count nunique size
deck
A             15       2   15
B             45       2   47
C             59       3   59
D             33       2   33
E             32       3   32
F             13       3   13
G              4       1    4


=> Grouped by age (before):
        age
      count nunique size
age
0.42      1       1    1
0.67      1       1    1
0.75      2       1    2
0.83      2       1    2
0.92      1       1    1
```

```
...         ...         ...   ...
70.00       2           1     2
70.50       1           1     1
71.00       2           1     2
74.00       1           1     1
80.00       1           1     1
[88 rows x 3 columns]
=> Grouped by age (after):
        age
      count nunique size
age
0           1           1     1
1           1           1     1
2           3           1     3
3           1           1     1
4           3           1     3
6           1           1     1
11          1           1     1
14          1           1     1
15          1           1     1
// details omitted for brevity
60          2           1     2
61          2           1     2
62          1           1     1
63          1           1     1
64          1           1     1
65          2           1     2
70          1           1     1
71          1           1     1
80          1           1     1
```

WORKING WITH APPLY() AND MAPAPPLY() IN PANDAS

Earlier in this chapter, you saw an example of the Pandas `apply()` method for modifying the categorical values of a feature in the CSV file `shirts.csv`. This section contains more examples of the `apply()` method, along with examples of the `mapappy()` method.

Listing 3.37 displays the content of `apply1.py` that illustrates how to invoke the Pandas `apply()` method to compute the sum of a set of values.

LISTING 3.37: apply1.py

```
import pandas as pd

df = pd.DataFrame({'X1': [1,2,3], 'X2': [10,20,30]})

def cube(x):
  return x * x * x

df1 = df.apply(cube)
# same result:
# df1 = df.apply(lambda x: x * x * x)
```

```
print("initial data frame:")
print(df)
print("cubed values:")
print(df1)
```

Listing 3.37 initializes the data frame df with columns X1 and X2, where the values for X2 are 10 times the corresponding values in X1. Next, the Python function cube() returns the cube of its argument. Listing 3.36 then defines the variable df1 by invoking the apply() function, which specifies the user-defined Python function cube(), and then prints the values of df as well as df1. Launch the code in Listing 3.37 and you will see the following output:

```
initial data frame:
   X1  X2
0   1  10
1   2  20
2   3  30
cubed values:
   X1      X2
0   1    1000
1   8    8000
2  27   27000
```

Listing 3.38 displays the content of apply2.py that illustrates how to invoke the Pandas apply() method to compute the sum of a set of values.

LISTING 3.38: apply2.py

```
import pandas as pd
import numpy as np

df = pd.DataFrame({'X1': [10,20,30], 'X2': [50,60,70]})

df1 = df.apply(np.sum, axis=0)
df2 = df.apply(np.sum, axis=1)

print("initial data frame:")
print(df)
print("add values (axis=0):")
print(df1)
print("add values (axis=1):")
print(df2)
```

Listing 3.38 is a variation of Listing 3.37: the variables df1 and df2 contain the column-wise sum and the row-wise sum, respectively, of the data frame df. Launch the code in Listing 3.38 and you will see the following output:

```
   X1  X2
0  10  50
1  20  60
2  30  70
add values (axis=0):
```

```
X1       60
X2      180
dtype: int64
add values (axis=1):
0        60
1        80
2       100
dtype: int64
```

Listing 3.39 displays the content of `mapapply1.py` that illustrates how to invoke the Pandas `mapapply()` method to compute the sum of a set of values.

LISTING 3.39: mapapply1.py

```
import pandas as pd
import math

df = pd.DataFrame({'X1': [1,2,3], 'X2': [10,20,30]})
df1 = df.applymap(math.sqrt)

print("initial data frame:")
print(df)
print("square root values:")
print(df1)
```

Listing 3.39 is yet another variant of Listing 3.37: in this case, the variable `df1` is defined by invoking the `applymap()` function on the variable `df`, which in turn references (but does not execute) the `math.sqrt()` function. Next, a `print()` statement displays the contents of `df`, followed by a `print()` statement that displays the contents of `df1`: it is at this point that the built-in `math.sqrt()` function is invoked to calculate the square root of the values in `df`. Launch the code in Listing 3.39 and you will see the following output:

```
initial data frame:
   X1  X2
0   1  10
1   2  20
2   3  30

square root values:
          X1        X2
0  1.000000  3.162278
1  1.414214  4.472136
2  1.732051  5.477226
```

Listing 3.40 displays the content of `mapapply2.py` that illustrates how to invoke the Pandas `mapapply()` method to convert strings to lowercase and uppercase.

LISTING 3.40: mapapply2.py

```
import pandas as pd

df = pd.DataFrame({'fname': ['Jane'], 'lname': ['Smith']},
                  {'fname': ['Dave'], 'lname': ['Jones']})
```

```
df1 = df.applymap(str.lower)
df2 = df.applymap(str.upper)
print("initial data frame:")
print(df)
print()
print("lowercase:")
print(df1)
print()
print("uppercase:")
print(df2)
print()
```

Listing 3.40 initializes the variable df with two first and last name pairs, and then defines the variables df1 and df2 by invoking the applymap() method to the variable df. The variable df1 converts its input values to lowercase, whereas the variable df2 converts its input values to uppercase. Launch the code in Listing 3.40 and you will see the following output:

```
initial data frame:
       fname  lname
fname  Jane   Smith
lname  Jane   Smith

lowercase:
       fname  lname
fname  jane   smith
lname  jane   smith

uppercase:
       fname  lname
fname  JANE   SMITH
lname  JANE   SMITH
```

USEFUL ONE-LINE COMMANDS IN PANDAS

This section contains an eclectic mix of one-line commands in Pandas (some of which you have already seen in this chapter) that are useful to know:

List the column names of a data frame:

```
df.columns
```

Drop missing data from a data frame:

```
df.dropna(axis=0, how='any')
```

Remove an unnecessary column:

```
my_dataset = my_dataset.drop(["url"],axis=1)
```

Remove columns with a single value, or columns that are missing more than 50% of their values:

```
dataset = dataset.dropna(thresh=half_count,axis=1)
```

Replace missing data in a data frame:

```
df.replace(to_replace=None, value=None)
```

Check for NANs in a data frame:

```
pd.isnull(object)
```

Drop a feature in a data frame:

```
df.drop('feature_variable_name', axis=1)
```

Convert the object type to float in a data frame:

```
pd.to_numeric(df["feature_name"], errors='coerce')
```

Convert data in a data frame to a NumPy array:

```
df.as_matrix()
```

Display the first n rows of a data frame:

```
df.head(n)
```

Get data by feature name in a data frame:

```
df.loc[feature_name]
```

Apply a function to a data frame, such as multiplying all values in the "height" column of the data frame by 3:

```
df["height"].apply(lambda height: 3 * height)
```

OR

```
def multiply(x):
    return x * 3
df["height"].apply(multiply)
```

Rename the fourth column of the data frame as height:

```
df.rename(columns = {df.columns[3]:'height'}, inplace=True)
```

Get the unique entries of the column first in a data frame:

```
df["first"].unique()
```

Create a data frame with columns first and last from an existing data frame:

```
new_df = df[["first", "last"]]
```

Sort the data in a data frame:

```
df.sort_values(ascending = False)
```

Filter the data column named size to display only values equal to 7:

```
df[df["size"] == 7]
```

Select the first row of the height column in a data frame:

```
df.loc([0], ['height'])
```

WORKING WITH JSON-BASED DATA

A JSON object consists of data represented as colon-separated name/value pairs and data objects that are separated by commas. An object is specified inside curly braces {}, and an array of objects is indicated by square brackets []. Note that character-valued data elements are inside a pair of double quotes "" (but no quotes for numeric data).

Here is a simple example of a JSON object:

```
{ "fname":"Jane", "lname":"Smith", "age":33, "city":"SF" }
```

Here is a simple example of an array of JSON objects (note the outer enclosing square brackets):

```
[
{ "fname":"Jane", "lname":"Smith", "age":33, "city":"SF" },
{ "fname":"John", "lname":"Jones", "age":34, "city":"LA" },
{ "fname":"Dave", "lname":"Stone", "age":35, "city":"NY" },
]
```

Python Dictionary and JSON

The json library enables you to work with JSON-based data in Python.

Listing 3.41 displays the content of dict2json.py that illustrates how to convert a Python dictionary to a JSON string.

LISTING 3.41: dict2json.py

```
import json

dict1 = {}
dict1["fname"] = "Jane"
dict1["lname"] = "Smith"
dict1["age"]   = 33
dict1["city"]  = "SF"

print("Python dictionary to JSON data:")
print("dict1:",dict1)
```

```
json1 = json.dumps(dict1, ensure_ascii=False)
print("json1:",json1)
print("")

# convert JSON string to Python dictionary:
json2 = '{"fname":"Dave", "lname":"Stone", "age":35, "city":"NY"}'
dict2 = json.loads(json2)
print("JSON data to Python dictionary:")
print("json2:",json2)
print("dict2:",dict2)
```

Listing 3.41 invokes the json.dumps() function to perform the conversion from a Python dictionary to a JSON string. Launch the code in Listing 3.41 and you will see the following output:

```
Python dictionary to JSON data:
dict1: {'fname': 'Jane', 'lname': 'Smith', 'age': 33, 'city': 'SF'}
json1: {"fname": "Jane", "lname": "Smith", "age": 33, "city": "SF"}

JSON data to Python dictionary:
json2: {"fname":"Dave", "lname":"Stone", "age":35, "city":"NY"}
dict2: {'fname': 'Dave', 'lname': 'Stone', 'age': 35, 'city': 'NY'}
```

Python, Pandas, and JSON

Listing 3.42 displays the content of pd_python_json.py that illustrates how to convert a Python dictionary to a Pandas data frame and then convert the data frame to a JSON string.

LISTING 3.42: pd_python_json.py

```
import json
import pandas as pd

dict1 = {}
dict1["fname"] = "Jane"
dict1["lname"] = "Smith"
dict1["age"]   = 33
dict1["city"]  = "SF"

df1 = pd.Data frame.from_dict(dict1, orient='index')
print("Pandas df1:")
print(df1)
print()

json1 = json.dumps(dict1, ensure_ascii=False)
print("Serialized to JSON1:")
print(json1)
print()

print("Data frame to JSON2:")
json2 = df1.to_json(orient='split')
print(json2)
```

Listing 3.42 initializes a Python dictionary dict1 with multiple attributes for a user (first name, last name, and so forth). Next, the data frame df1 is created from the Python dictionary dict1, and its contents are displayed.

The next portion of Listing 3.42 initializes the variable json1 by serializing the contents of dict1, and its contents are displayed. The last code block in Listing 3.42 initializes the variable json2 to the result of converting the data frame df1 to a JSON string. Launch the code in Listing 3.42 and you will see the following output:

```
dict1: {'fname': 'Jane', 'lname': 'Smith', 'age': 33, 'city': 'SF'}
Pandas df1:
            0
fname    Jane
lname   Smith
age        33
city       SF

Serialized to JSON1:
{"fname": "Jane", "lname": "Smith", "age": 33, "city": "SF"}

Data frame to JSON2:
{"columns":[0],"index":["fname","lname","age","city"],"data":[["Jane"],[
"Smith"],[33],["SF"]]}
json1: {"fname": "Jane", "lname": "Smith", "age": 33, "city": "SF"}
```

SUMMARY

This chapter introduced you to Pandas for creating labeled data frames and displaying metadata of Pandas data frames. Then you learned how to create Pandas data frames from various sources of data, such as random numbers and hard-coded data values.

You also learned how to read Excel spreadsheets and perform numeric calculations on that data, such as the minimum, mean, and maximum values in numeric columns. Then you saw how to create Pandas data frames from data stored in CSV files. In addition, you learned how to generate a scatterplot from data in a Pandas data frame.

Finally, you had a brief introduction to JSON, along with an example of converting a Python dictionary to JSON-based data (and vice versa).

## CHAPTER 4

RDBMS AND SQL

This chapter introduces you to RDBMSs, various SQL concepts, and a quick introduction to MySQL. MySQL is a robust RDBMS, and it's available as a free download from the Oracle website. Moreover, virtually everything that you learn about MySQL in this chapter transfers to other RDBMSs, such as PostgreSQL and Oracle.

This chapter describes a hypothetical website that enables users to register themselves for the purpose of purchasing various tools (such as hammers and wrenches). Although there is no code in this section, you will learn about the tables that are required, their relationships, and the structure of those tables.

WHAT IS AN RDBMS?

A Relational DataBase Management System (RDBMS) stores data in tables that contain labeled attributes (informally sometimes called *columns*) that have a specific data type. Examples of an RDBMS include MySQL, Oracle, and IBM DB2. Although relational databases usually provide a decent solution for storing data, speed and scalability might be an issue in some cases. NoSQL databases (such as MongoDB) might be more suitable for scalability.

What Relationships Do Tables Have in an RDBMS?

While an RDBMS can consist of a single table, it often comprises multiple tables that can have various types of associations with each other. For example, when you buy various items at a food store, your receipt consists of one purchase order that contains one or more "line items," where each line item indicates the details of a particular item that you purchased. This is called a *one-to-many* relationship between a purchase order (which is stored in a `pur-chase_orders` table) and the line items (stored in a `line_items` table) for each item that you purchased.

Another example involves students and courses: each student is enrolled in one or more courses, which is a one-to-many relationship from students to courses. Moreover, each course contains one or more students, so there is a one-to-many relationship from courses to students. Hence, the students and courses tables have a many-to-many relationship.

A third example is an `employees` table, where each row contains information about one employee. If each row includes the `id` of the manager of the given employee, then the `employees` table is a *self-referential* table because finding the manager of the employee involves searching the `employees` table with the manager's `id` that is stored in the given employee record. However, if the rows in an `employees` table do *not* contain information about an employee's manager, then the table is not self-referential.

In addition to table definitions, a database frequently contains indexes, primary keys, and foreign keys that facilitate searching for data in tables and also "connecting" a row in a given table with its logically related row (or rows) in another table. For example, if we have the `id` value for a particular purchase order in a `purchase_orders` table, we can find all the line items (i.e., the items that were purchased) in a `line_items` table that contain the same purchase order `id`.

Features of an RDBMS

An RDBMS provides a convenient way to store data, often associated with some type of application. For example, later you will see the details of a four-table RDBMS that keeps track of tools that are purchased via a Web-based application. From a high-level perspective, an RDBMS provides the following characteristics:

- a database contains one or more tables
- data is stored in tables
- data records have the same structure
- well-suited for vertical scaling
- support for ACID (explained below)

Another useful concept is a *logical schema*, which consists of the collection of tables and their relationships (along with indexes, views, triggers, and so forth) in an RDBMS. The schema is used for generating a physical schema, which consists of all the SQL statements that are required to create the specified tables and their relationships.

What is ACID?

ACID is an acronym for Atomicity, Consistency, Isolation, and Durability, which refers to the properties of RDBMS transactions.

- *Atomicity* means that each transaction is all-or-nothing, so if a transaction fails, the system is rolled back to its previous state.
- *Consistency* means that successful transactions always result in a valid database state.
- *Isolation* means that executing transactions concurrently or serially will result in the state.
- *Durability* means that a committed transaction will remain in the same state.

RDBMSs support ACID, whereas NoSQL databases generally do not support ACID.

WHEN DO WE NEED AN RDBMS?

The short answer is that an RDBMS is useful when we need to store one or more records of events that have occurred, which can be involve simple item purchases as well as complex multi-table financial transactions.

An RDBMS allows you to define a collection of tables that contain rows of data, where a row contains one or more attributes (informally called *fields*). A row of data is a record of an event that occurred at a specific point in time, which can involve more than one table, and can also involve some type of "transaction."

For example, consider a database that contains a single table called `events` in which a single row contains information about a single event that you created by some process (such as a Web page registration form). Although this is conceptually simple, notice that the following attributes are relevant for each row in the `events` table: `event_id`, `event_time`, `event_title`, `event_duration`, and `event_location`, and possibly additional attributes.

Now consider a money transfer scenario between two bank accounts: you need to transfer $100 from a savings account to a checking account. The process involves two steps:

1. Debiting (subtracting) the savings account by $100
2. Crediting (adding) the savings account with $100

However, if there is a system failure after Step 1 and before Step 2 can be completed, you have lost $100. Obviously, Steps 1 and 2 must be treated as an *atomic transaction*, which means that the transaction is successful only when both steps have completed successfully. If the transaction is unsuccessful, the transaction is "rolled back" so the system is returned to the state prior to transferring money between the two accounts.

As you learned earlier in this chapter, RDBMSs support ACID, which ensures that the previous transaction (i.e., transferring money between accounts) is treated as an atomic transaction.

Although atomic transactions are fundamental to financial systems, they might not be as critical for other systems. For example, the previous example involved inserting a new row in an `events` table whenever a new event is created. If this process fails, the solution might involve registering the event again when the system is online again (perhaps the database crashed).

As another example, displaying a set of pictures in a Web page might not display the pictures in the correct order (e.g., based on their creation time). However, a failure in the event creation is not as critical as a failure in a financial system, and displaying images in the wrong sequence will probably be rectified when the Web page is refreshed.

THE IMPORTANCE OF NORMALIZATION

This section contains an introduction to the concept of *normalization*; online articles provide more detailed information regarding normal forms. Splitting this topic into two sections in two chapters will facilitate an understanding of normalization in an RDBMS.

As a starting point, consider an RDBMS that stores records for the temperature of a room during a time interval (such as a day, a week, or some other time interval). We just need one device_temperature table where each row contains the temperature of a room at a specific time. In the case of the IoT (Internet of Things), the temperature is recorded during regular time intervals (such as minute-by-minute or hourly).

If you need to track only one room, the device_temperature table is probably sufficient. However, if you need to track *multiple* devices in a room, then it's convenient to create a second table called device_details that contains attributes for each device, such as device_id, device_name, device_year, device_price, and device_warranty.

However, we need to connect information from a row in the table device_temperature to its associated row in the device_details table. The two-table connection is simple: each row in the device_details table contains a device_id that uniquely identifies the given row. Moreover, the same device_id appears in any row of the device_temperature table that refers to the given device.

The preceding two-table structure is a minimalistic example of database *normalization*, which reduces data redundancy in database tables, sometimes at the expense of slower performance during the execution of some types of SQL statements (e.g., those that contain a JOIN keyword).

If you are new to the concept of database normalization, you might be thinking that normalization increases complexity and reduces performance without providing tangible benefits. While this is a valid consideration, the trade-off is worthwhile.

To convince you of the value of normalization, suppose that every record in the purchase_orders table contains all the details of the customer who made the associated purchase. As a result, we can eliminate the customers table. However, if we ever need to update the address of a particular customer, *we need to update all the rows in the* purchase_orders *table that contain that customer.* By contrast, *if we maintain a* customers *table, then updating a customer's address involves changing a* **single** *row in the* customers *table.*

Normalization enables us to avoid data duplication so that there is a single "source of truth" in the event that information (such as a customer's address) must be updated. From another perspective, data duplication means that the same data appears in two (or possibly more) locations, and if an update is not applied to all those locations, the database data is in an inconsistent state. Depending on the nature of the application, the consequences of inconsistent data can range from minor to catastrophic.

Always remember the following point: whenever you need to update the same data that resides in two different locations, you increase the risk of data inconsistency that adversely affects data integrity.

As another example, suppose that a website sells widgets online: at a minimum, the associated database needs the following four tables:

- customer_details
- purchase_orders
- po_line_items
- item_desc

The preceding scenario is explored in greater detail in the next section that specifies the attributes of each of the preceding tables.

A FOUR-TABLE RDBMS

As an introductory example, suppose that *www.mytools.com* sells tools for home use or construction (the details of which are not important). For simplicity, let's pretend that an actual Web page is available at the preceding URL, and the Web page contains the following sections:

- new user register registration
- existing user log in
- input fields for selecting items for purchase (and the quantities)

For example, the registered user `John Smith` wants to purchase one hammer, two screwdrivers, and three wrenches. The Web page needs to provide users with the ability to search for products by their type (e.g., hammer, screwdriver, and wrench) and then display a list of matching products. Each product in that list would also contain an SKU, which is an industry-standard labeling mechanism for products (just like ISBNs for identifying books).

The preceding functionality is necessary to develop a Web page that enables users to purchase products. However, the purpose of this section is to describe a set of tables (and their relationships to each other) in an RDBMS, so we will assume that the necessary Web-based features are available at our URL.

Let's describe a "use case" that contains the sequence of steps that will be performed on behalf of an existing customer John Smith (whose customer `id` is 1000), who wants to purchase 1 hammer, 2 screwdrivers, and 3 wrenches:

Step 1: Customer John Smith (with `cust_id` 1000) initiates a new purchase.
Step 2: A new purchase order is created with the value 12500 for `po_id`.
Step 3: John Smith selects 1 hammer, 2 screwdrivers, and 3 wrenches.
Step 4: The associated prices of 20.00, 16.00, and 30.00 are displayed on the screen.
Step 5: The subtotal is displayed, which is 66.00.
Step 6: The tax of 6.60 is displayed (a tax rate of 10%).
Step 7: The total cost of 72.60 displayed.

Step 8 would allow John Smith to remove an item, increase/decrease the quantity for each selected item, delete items, or cancel the purchase order. Step 9 would enable John Smith to make a payment. Once again, for the sake of simplicity, we will assume that Steps 8 and 9 are available.

Note that Step 8 involves updating several of our tables with the details of the purchase order. Step 9 creates a time stamp for the date when the purchase order was created, as well as the status of the purchase order ("paid" versus "pending"). The status of a purchase order is used to generated reports to display the customers whose payment is overdue (and perhaps also send them friendly reminders). Sometimes companies have a reward-based system whereby customers who have paid on time can collect credits that can be applied to other purchases (in other words, a discount mechanism).

DETAILED TABLE DESCRIPTIONS

If you visualize the use case described in the previous section, you can probably see that we need a table for storing customer-specific information, another table to store purchase orders (which is somehow linked to the associated customer), a table that contains the details of the items and quantity that are purchased (which are commonly called "line items"), and a table that contains information about each tool (which includes the name, the description, and the price of the tool). Hence, the RDBMS for our website requires the following tables:

```
customers
purchase_orders
line_items
item_desc
```

The following subsections describe the contents of the preceding tables, along with the relationships among these tables.

The customers Table

Although there are different ways to specify the attributes of the customers table, you need enough information to uniquely identify each customer in the table. By analogy, the following information (except for cust_id) is required to mail an envelope to a person:

```
cust_id
first_name
last_name
home_address
city
state
zip_code
```

We will create the customers table with the attributes in the preceding list. Note that the cust_id attribute is called a *key* because it uniquely identifies every customer. Although we won't discuss the topic of the role of keys in an RDBMS, it's obvious that we need a mechanism for uniquely identifying every customer.

Whenever we need to refer to the details of a particular customer, we will use the associated value of cust_id to retrieve those details from the row in the customers table that has the associated cust_id.

The preceding paragraph describes the essence of linking related tables T1 and T2 in an RDBMS: the key in T1 is stored as an attribute value in T2. If we need to access related information in table T3, then we store the key in T2 as an attribute value in T3.

Note that a customers table in a production system would contain other attributes, such as the following:

```
title (Mr, Mrs, Ms, and so forth)
shipping_address
cell_phone
```

For the sake of simplicity, we'll use the initial set of attributes to define the customers table. Later on, you can add the new attributes to the three table schema to make the system more like a real life system.

To make this table more concrete, suppose that the following information pertains to customer John Smith, who has been assigned a cust_id of 1000:

```
cust_id: 1000
first_name: John
last_name: Smith
home_address: 1000 Appian Way
city: Sunnyvale
state: California
zip_code:95959
```

Whenever `John Smith` makes a new purchase, we will use the `cust_id` value of 1000 to create a new row for this customer in the `purchase_order` table.

The purchase_orders Table

When customers visit the website, we need to create a purchase order that will be inserted as a new row in the `purchase_orders` table. While you might be tempted to place all the customers' details in the new row, we will identify the customer by the associated `cust_id` and use this value instead.

Note that we create a new row in the `customers` table whenever new users register at the website, whereas repeat customers are identified by an existing `cust_id` that must be determined by searching the `customers` table with the information that the customer types into the input fields of the main Web page.

We saw that the `customers` table contains a key attribute; similarly, the `purchase_orders` table requires an attribute that we will call `po_id` (you are free to use a different string) to identify a purchase order for a given customer.

Keep in mind the following detail: the row with a given `po_id` requires a `cust_id` attribute to also identify the customer (in the `customers` table) who is making the current purchase.

Although there are multiple ways to define a set of suitable attributes, let's use the following set of attributes for the `purchase_orders` table:

```
po_id
cust_id
purchase_date
```

For example, suppose that customer `John Smith`, whose `cust_id` is 1000, purchases some tools on December 15, 2021. There are dozens of different date formats that are supported in RDBMSs: for simplicity, we will use the **MM-DD-YYYY** format (which you can change to suit your particular needs).

Then the new row for `John Smith` in the `purchase_orders` would look something like the following:

```
po_id: 12500
cust_id: 1000
purchase_date: 12-01-2021
```

The line_items Table

As an example, suppose that customer `John Smith` requested 1 hammer, 2 screwdrivers, and 3 wrenches in his most recent purchase order. Each of these purchased items requires a row in the `line_items` table that

- is identified by a `line_id` value
- specifies the quantity of each purchased item
- contains the value for the associated `po_id` in the `purchase_orders` table
- contains the value for the associated `item_id` in the `item_desc` table

For simplicity, let's assign the values 5001, 5002, and 5003 to the `line_id` attribute for the three new rows in the `line_items` table that represent the hammer, screwdriver, and wrench items in the current purchase order. A `line_item` row might look something like this:

```
po_id: 12500
line_id: 5001
item_id: 100 <= we'll discuss this soon
item_count: 1
item_price: 20.00
item_tax:  2.00
item_subtotal: 22.00
```

Notice there is no `cust_id` in the preceding `line_item`: that's because of the top-down approach for retrieving data. Specifically, we start with a particular `cust_id` that we use to find a list of purchase orders in the `purchase_orders` table that belong to the given `cust_id`, and for each purchase order in the `purchase_orders` table, we perform a search for the associated line items in the `line_items` table. Moreover, we can repeat the preceding sequence of steps for each customer in a list of `cust_id` values.

Returning to the earlier `line_item` details: we need to reference each purchased item by its associated identifier in the `item_desc` table. Once again, we will arbitrarily assign `item_id` values of 100, 200, and 300, respectively, for the hammer, screwdriver, and wrench items. The actual values will undoubtedly be different in your application, so there is no special significance to the numbers 100, 200, and 300.

The three rows in the `line_items` table (that belong to the same purchase order) would look like this (we'll look at the corresponding SQL statements later):

```
po_id: 12500
line_id: 5001
item_id: 100
item_count: 1
item_price: 20.00
item_tax:  2.00
item_subtotal: 22.00

po_id: 12500
line_id: 5002
item_id: 200
item_count: 2
item_price: 8.00
item_tax:   1.60
item_subtotal: 17.60

po_id: 12500
line_id: 5003
item_id: 300
```

```
item_count: 3
item_price: 10.00
item_tax:    3.00
item_subtotal: 33.00
```

The item_desc Table

Recall that the `customers` table contains information about each customer, and a new row is created each time that a new customer creates an account for our Web application. In a somewhat analogous fashion, the `item_desc` table contains information about each item (product) that can be purchased from our website. If our website becomes popular, the contents of the `item_desc` table are updated more frequently than the `customers` table, typically in the following situations:

- A new tool (product) is available for purchase
- An existing tool is no longer available for purchase

Thus, the `item_desc` table contains all the details for every tool that is available for sale, and it's the "source of truth" for the tools that customers can purchase from the website. At a minimum, this table contains three fields (we'll discuss the SQL statement for creating and populating this table later):

```
SELECT *
FROM item_desc;
+---------+-------------+------------+
| item_id | item_desc   | item_price |
+---------+-------------+------------+
|     100 | hammer      |      20.00 |
|     200 | screwdriver |       8.00 |
|     300 | wrench      |      10.00 |
+---------+-------------+------------+
3 rows in set (0.001 sec)
```

There is one more important detail to discuss: if an item is no longer for sale, can we simply drop its row from the `item_desc` table? The answer is "no" because we need this row to generate reports that contain information about the items that customers purchased.

Hence, it would be a good idea to add another attribute called AVAILABLE (or something similar) that contains either 1 or 0 to indicate whether the product is available for purchase. As a result, some of the SQL queries that involve this table will also need to take into account this new attribute. Implementation of this functionality is not central to the purpose of this book, and therefore it is left as an enhancement to the reader.

WHAT IS SQL?

Structured Query Language (SQL) is used for managing data in tables in a relational database (RDBMS). In fact, SQL is a standard language for retrieving and manipulating structured databases.

In high-level terms, a SQL statement to retrieve data generally involves the following:

- what data you want (SELECT)
- the table(s) where the data resides (FROM)
- constraints (if any) on the data (WHERE)

For example, suppose that a friends table contains the attributes (database parlance for *fields*) lname and fname for the last name and first name, respectively, of a set of friends, and each row in this table contains details about one friend.

In Chapter 2, we discussed how to create database tables and how to populate those tables with data, but for now let's just pretend that those tasks have already been performed. Then the SQL statement for retrieving the first and last names of the people in the friends table looks like this:

```
SELECT lname, fname
FROM friends;
```

Suppose that the friends table also contains a height attribute, which is a number (in centimeters) for each person in the friends table. We can extend the preceding SQL statement to specify that we want the people (rows) whose height attribute is less than 180 as follows:

```
SELECT lname, fname
FROM friends
WHERE height < 180;
```

SQL provides a plethora of keywords that enable you to specify sophisticated queries for retrieving data from multiple tables. Both of the preceding SQL statements are called DML statements, which is one of the four categories of SQL statements:

- DCL (Data Control Language)
- DDL (Data Definition Language)
- DQL (Data Query Language)
- DML (Data Manipulation Language)

The following subsections provide additional information for each item in the preceding list.

DCL, DDL, DQL, DML, and TCL

Data Control Language (DCL) refers to any SQL statement that contains the keywords GRANT or REVOKE. Both of these keywords affect the permissions that are either granted or revoked for a particular user.

Data Definition Language (DDL) includes any SQL statements that specify the following: CREATE, ALTER, DROP, RENAME, TRUNCATE, or COMMENT. These SQL keywords are used in conjunction with database tables and, in many cases, with database views (discussed later).

Data Query Language (DQL) refers to any SQL statement that contains the keyword SELECT.

Data Manipulation Language (DML) refers to SQL statements that execute queries against one or more tables in a database. The SQL statements contain any of the keywords `INSERT`, `UPDATE`, `DELETE`, `MERGE`, `CALL`, `EXPLAIN PLAN`, or `LOCK TABLE`. In most cases, these keywords modify the existing values of data in one or more tables.

Transaction Control Language (TCL) includes the keywords `COMMIT`, `ROLLBACK`, `SAVEPOINT`, or `SET TRANSACTION`, all of which are advanced concepts that are not discussed in this book.

SQL Privileges

There are two types of privileges available in SQL, both of which are described briefly in this section. These privileges refer to database objects, such as database tables and indexes, that are discussed in greater detail in subsequent chapters.

System privileges involve an object of a particular type and specifies the right to perform one or more actions on the object. Such actions include the administrator giving users permission to perform tasks such as `ALTER ANY INDEX`, `ALTER ANY CACHE GROUP`, `CREATE/ALTER/DELETE TABLE`, or `CREATE/ALTER/DELETE VIEW`.

Object privileges allow users to perform actions on an object or object of another user, such as tables, views, and indexes. Additional object privileges are `EXECUTE`, `INSERT`, `UPDATE`, `DELETE`, `SELECT`, `FLUSH`, `LOAD`, `INDEX`, and `REFERENCES`.

PROPERTIES OF SQL STATEMENTS

SQL statements and functions are not case sensitive, but quoted text *is* case sensitive. Here are some examples:

```
select VERSION();
+-----------+
| VERSION() |
+-----------+
| 8.0.21    |
+-----------+
1 row in set (0.000 sec)

MySQL [mytools]> SeLeCt Version();
+-----------+
| Version() |
+-----------+
| 8.0.21    |
+-----------+
1 row in set (0.000 sec)
```

Keep in mind the following useful details regarding SQL statements:

- SQL statements are not case sensitive.
- SQL statements can be on one or more lines.
- Keywords cannot be abbreviated or split across lines.
- Clauses are usually placed on separate lines.
- Indentation is for enhancing readability.

The CREATE Keyword

In general, you will sometimes use the CREATE keyword to create a database, but more often use it to create tables, views, and indexes. However, the following list contains all the objects that you can create via the CREATE statement:

```
DATABASE
EVENT
FUNCTION
INDEX
PROCEDURE
TABLE
TRIGGER
USER
VIEW
```

Only database-specific examples are discussed, whereas online articles delve into the other topics in the preceding list.

WHAT IS MYSQL?

MySQL is an open source database that is portable and provides many features that are available in commercial databases. Oracle is the steward of the MySQL database, which you can download at the following site:

https://www.mysql.com/downloads/

MySQL also provides a GUI interface for performing database-related operations. MySQL 8 provides the following new features:

- A transactional data dictionary
- Improved support for the BLOB, TEXT, GEOMETRY, and JSON data types

As you will see in Chapter 7, MySQL supports pluggable storage engines, such as InnoDB (the most commonly used MySQL storage engine). In addition, Facebook developed an open source storage engine called MyRocks that has better compression and performance, so it might be worthwhile to explore the advantage of MyRocks over the other storage engines for MySQL.

What about MariaDB?

MySQL began as an open source project, and retained its name after the Oracle acquisition. Shortly thereafter, the MariaDB database was created, which is a "fork" of the MySQL database. Although MariaDB supports all the features of MySQL, there are important differences between MySQL and MariaDB that you can read about online:

https://mariadb.com/kb/en/mariadb-vs-mysql-compatibility/

Installing MySQL

Download the MySQL distribution for your machine and perform the installation procedure.

https://towardsdatascience.com/pandas-and-sql-together-a-premier-league-and-player-scouting-example-b41713a5dd3e

You can log into MySQL as root with the following command, which will prompt you for the root password:

```
$ m  ysql -u root -p
```

If you installed MySQL via a DMG file, then the root password is the same as the password for your machine.

DATA TYPES IN MYSQL

This section starts with a lengthy list of data types that MySQL supports, followed by some comments about several of the data types, all of which you can use in table definitions:

- The `BIT` datatype is for storing bit values in MySQL.
- The `BOOLEAN` datatype stores True/False values.
- The `CHAR` data type is for storing fixed length strings.
- The `DATE` datatype is for storing date values.
- The `DATETIME` datatype is for storing combined date and time values.
- The `DECIMAL` datatype is for storing exact values in decimal format.
- The `ENUM` datatype is a compact way to store string values.
- The `INT` datatype is for storing an integer data type.
- The `JSON` data type is for storing JSON documents.
- The `TEXT` datatype is for storing text values.
- The `TIME` datatype is for storing time values.
- The `TIMESTAMP` datatype is for a wider range of date and time values.
- The `TO_SECONDS` datatype is for converting time to seconds.
- The `VARCHAR` datatype is for variable length strings.
- The `XML` data type provides support for XML documents.

The CHAR and VARCHAR Data Types

The `CHAR` type has a fixed column length, declared while creating tables, whose length can range from 1 to 255. `CHAR` values are right padded with spaces to the specified length, and trailing spaces are removed when `CHAR` values are retrieved.

By contrast, the `VARCHAR` type indicates variable length `CHAR` values whose length can be between 1 and 2000, and it occupies the space for `NULL` values.

By contrast, the `VARCHAR2` type indicates variable length `CHAR` values whose length can be between 1 and 4000, but cannot occupy the space for `NULL` values. Hence, `VARCHAR2` has better performance that `VARCHAR`.

String-based Data Types

The previous bullet list contains various string types, and the latter have been extracted and placed in a separate list below for your convenience:

```
BLOB
CHAR
ENUM
SET
TEXT
VARCHAR
```

The ENUM datatype is string object that specifies a set of predefined values, which can be used during table creation, as shown here:

```
CREATE TABLE PIZZA(name ENUM('Small', 'Medium','Large'));
Query OK, 0 rows affected (0.021 sec)

DESC pizza;
+-------+-------------------------------+------+-----+---------+-------+
| Field | Type                          | Null | Key | Default | Extra |
+-------+-------------------------------+------+-----+---------+-------+
| name  | enum('Small','Medium','Large')| YES  |     | NULL    |       |
+-------+-------------------------------+------+-----+---------+-------+
1 row in set (0.004 sec)
```

FLOAT and DOUBLE Data Types

Numbers in the FLOAT format are stored in four bytes and have eight decimal places of accuracy. Numbers in the DOUBLE format are stored in eight bytes and have eighteen decimal places of accuracy.

BLOB and TEXT Data Types

A binary large object (BLOB) can hold a variable amount of data. There are four BLOB types whose only difference is their maximum length:

```
TINYBLOB
BLOB
MEDIUMBLOB
LONGBLOB
```

A TEXT data type is a case-insensitive BLOB, and there are four TEXT types whose difference pertains to their maximum length (all of which are non-standard data types):

```
TINYTEXT
TEXT
MEDIUMTEXT
LONGTEXT
```

Keep in mind the following difference between BLOB types and TEXT types: BLOB types involve case-sensitive sorting and comparisons, whereas these operations are case-insensitive for TEXT types.

MYSQL DATABASE OPERATIONS

There are several operations that you can perform with a MySQL database, as shown here:

- Create a database
- Export a database
- Drop a database
- Rename a database

You will see examples of how to perform each of the preceding bullet items in the following subsections.

Creating a Database

Log into MySQL and invoke the following command to create the `mytools` database:

```
MySQL [mysql]> create database mytools;
Query OK, 1 row affected (0.004 sec)
```

Select the `mytools` database with the following command:

```
MySQL [(none)]> use mytools;
Reading table information for completion of table and column names
You can turn off this feature to get a quicker startup with -A
Database changed
```

Display a List of Databases

Display the existing databases by invoking the following SQL statement:

```
mysql> SHOW DATABASES;
```

The preceding command displays the following output (the output will be different for your machine):

```
+--------------------+
| Database           |
+--------------------+
| beans              |
| information_schema |
| minimal            |
| mysql              |
| mytools            |
| performance_schema |
| sys                |
+--------------------+
9 rows in set (0.002 sec)
```

Display a List of Database Users

Display the existing users by invoking the following SQL statement:

```
mysql> select user from mysql.user;
The preceding command displays the following output:
+------------------+
| user             |
+------------------+
| mysql.infoschema |
| mysql.session    |
| mysql.sys        |
| root             |
+------------------+
4 rows in set (0.001 sec)
```

Dropping a Database

Log into MySQL and invoke the following command to create, select, and then drop the `pizza` database:

```
MySQL [(none)]> create database pizza;
Query OK, 1 row affected (0.004 sec)

MySQL [(none)]> use pizza;
Database changed
MySQL [pizza]> drop database pizza;
Query OK, 0 rows affected (0.007 sec)
```

Although performing this task with a database that does not contain any data might seem pointless, it's simple and you will already know how to perform this task if it becomes necessary to do so in the future.

EXPORTING A DATABASE

Although you currently have an empty database, it's still good to know how the steps for exporting a database, which is handy as a backup and also provides a simple way to create a copy of an existing database on another machine.

By way of illustration, let's first create the database called `minimal` in MySQL, as shown here:

```
MySQL [mytools]> create database minimal;
Query OK, 1 row affected (0.006 sec)
```

Next, invoke the `mysqldump` command to export the minimal database, as shown here:

```
mysqldump -u username -p"password" -R minimal > minimal.sql
```

Notice the following details at the preceding command. First, there are no intervening spaces between the -p flag and the password in order to bypass a command line prompt to enter the password. Second, make sure that you omit the quotation marks. Third, the `-R` flag instructs `mysqldump` to copy stored procedures and functions in addition to the database data.

At this point, you can create tables in the minimal database, and periodically export its contents. Listing 4.1 displays the content of `minimal.sql`, which is the complete description of the minimal database.

LISTING 4.1: minimal.sql

```
-- MariaDB dump 10.18  Distrib 10.5.8-MariaDB, for osx10.15 (x86_64)
--
-- Host: localhost    Database: minimal
-- ------------------------------------------------------
-- Server version       8.0.21

/*!40101 SET @OLD_CHARACTER_SET_CLIENT=@@CHARACTER_SET_CLIENT */;
/*!40101 SET @OLD_CHARACTER_SET_RESULTS=@@CHARACTER_SET_RESULTS */;
/*!40101 SET @OLD_COLLATION_CONNECTION=@@COLLATION_CONNECTION */;
/*!40101 SET NAMES utf8mb4 */;
/*!40103 SET @OLD_TIME_ZONE=@@TIME_ZONE */;
/*!40103 SET TIME_ZONE='+00:00' */;
/*!40014 SET @OLD_UNIQUE_CHECKS=@@UNIQUE_CHECKS, UNIQUE_CHECKS=0 */;
/*!40014 SET @OLD_FOREIGN_KEY_CHECKS=@@FOREIGN_KEY_CHECKS, FOREIGN_KEY_
CHECKS=0 */;
/*!40101 SET @OLD_SQL_MODE=@@SQL_MODE, SQL_MODE='NO_AUTO_VALUE_ON_ZERO' */;
/*!40111 SET @OLD_SQL_NOTES=@@SQL_NOTES, SQL_NOTES=0 */;


--
-- Dumping routines for database 'minimal'
--
/*!40103 SET TIME_ZONE=@OLD_TIME_ZONE */;

/*!40101 SET SQL_MODE=@OLD_SQL_MODE */;
/*!40014 SET FOREIGN_KEY_CHECKS=@OLD_FOREIGN_KEY_CHECKS */;
/*!40014 SET UNIQUE_CHECKS=@OLD_UNIQUE_CHECKS */;
/*!40101 SET CHARACTER_SET_CLIENT=@OLD_CHARACTER_SET_CLIENT */;
/*!40101 SET CHARACTER_SET_RESULTS=@OLD_CHARACTER_SET_RESULTS */;
/*!40101 SET COLLATION_CONNECTION=@OLD_COLLATION_CONNECTION */;
/*!40111 SET SQL_NOTES=@OLD_SQL_NOTES */;

-- Dump completed on 2022-02-03 22:44:54
```

RENAMING A DATABASE

Although you currently have an empty database, it's still good to know how to rename a database (and besides, it's faster to do so with an empty database).

Older versions of MySQL provided the `RENAME DATABASE` command to rename a database; however, newer versions of MySQL have removed this functionality to avoid security risks.

Fortunately, you can perform a three-step process involving several MySQL command line utilities to rename a MySQL database `OLD_DB` (which you need to replace with the name of the database that you want to rename) to a new database NEW_DB (replaced with the actual new database name):

Step 1: Create an exported copy of database OLD_DB.
Step 2: Create a new database called NEW_DB.
Step 3: Import data from OLD_DB into NEW_DB.

Perform Step 1 by invoking the following command (see previous section):

```
mysqldump -u username -p"password" -R OLD_DB > OLD_DB.sql
```

Perform Step 2 by invoking the following command:

```
mysqladmin -u username -p"password" create NEW_DB
```

Perform Step 3 by invoking the following command:

```
mysql -u username -p"password" newDbName < OLD_DB.sql
```

Verify that everything worked correctly by logging into MySQL and selecting the new database:

```
MySQL [mysql]> use NEW_DB;
Database changed
```

THE INFORMATION_SCHEMA TABLE

The INFORMATION_SCHEMA table enables you to retrieve information about the columns in a given table.

```
TABLE_SCHEMA
TABLE_NAME
COLUMN_NAME
ORDINAL_POSITION
COLUMN_DEFAULT
IS_NULLABLE
DATA_TYPE
CHARACTER_MAXIMUM_LENGTH
NUMERIC_PRECISION
NUMERIC_SCALE
DATETIME_PRECISION
```

For example, let's look at the structure of the weather table that is available with the companion files (see the Preface for details):

```
MySQL [mytools]> desc weather;
+-----------+-----------+------+-----+---------+-------+
| Field     | Type      | Null | Key | Default | Extra |
+-----------+-----------+------+-----+---------+-------+
| day       | date      | YES  |     | NULL    |       |
| temper    | int       | YES  |     | NULL    |       |
```

```
| wind     | int      | YES |     | NULL  |        |
| forecast | char(20) | YES |     | NULL  |        |
| city     | char(20) | YES |     | NULL  |        |
| state    | char(20) | YES |     | NULL  |        |
+----------+----------+------+-----+--------+-------+
6 rows in set (0.001 sec)
```

We can obtain additional information about the columns in the weather table with the following SQL query:

```
SELECT COLUMN_NAME, DATA_TYPE, IS_NULLABLE, COLUMN_DEFAULT
FROM INFORMATION_SCHEMA.COLUMNS
WHERE TABLE_NAME = 'weather'
AND table_schema = 'mytools';
```

The preceding SQL query generates the following output:

```
+-------------+-----------+-------------+----------------+
| COLUMN_NAME | DATA_TYPE | IS_NULLABLE | COLUMN_DEFAULT |
+-------------+-----------+-------------+----------------+
| city        | char      | YES         | NULL           |
| day         | date      | YES         | NULL           |
| forecast    | char      | YES         | NULL           |
| state       | char      | YES         | NULL           |
| temper      | int       | YES         | NULL           |
| wind        | int       | YES         | NULL           |
+-------------+-----------+-------------+----------------+
6 rows in set (0.001 sec)
```

THE PROCESSLIST TABLE

The PROCESSLIST table contains information about the status of SQL statements. This information is useful when you want to see the status of table-level or row-level locks on a table. The following SQL statement shows you an example of the contents of this table:

```
MySQL [mytools]> show processlist;
+----+-----------------+-----------+---------+---------+--------+-------
----------------+-----------------+
| Id | User            | Host      | db      | Command | Time   | State
| Info            |
+----+-----------------+-----------+---------+---------+--------+-------
----------------+-----------------+
|  5 | event_scheduler | localhost | NULL    | Daemon  | 138765 |
Waiting on empty queue | NULL           |
|  9 | root            | localhost | mytools | Query   |      0 |
starting         | show processlist |
+----+-----------------+-----------+---------+---------+--------+-------
----------------+-----------------+
2 rows in set (0.000 sec)
```

SQL FORMATTING TOOLS

As you might expect, there are various formatting styles for SQL statements, and you can peruse them to determine which style is most appealing to you. The following link is for an online SQL formatter:

https://codebeautify.org/sqlformatter

The following link contains 18 SQL formatters, some of which are commercial and some are free:

https://www.sqlshack.com/sql-formatter-tools/

The following link contains a list of SQL formatting conventions (i.e., it's not about formatting tools):

https://opendatascience.com/best-practices-sql-formatting

If you work in an environment where the SQL formatting rules have already been established, it might be interesting to compare that style with those of the SQL formatting tools in the preceding links.

If you are a SQL beginner working on your own, it's also worth exploring these links as you learn more about SQL statements throughout this book. As you gain more knowledge about writing SQL statements, you will encounter various styles in blog posts, which means you will also notice which conventions those blog posts adopt for formatting SQL statements.

SUMMARY

This chapter started with an introduction to the concept of an RDBMS, and the rationale for using an RDBMS. In particular, you saw an example of an RDBMS with a single table, two tables, and four tables (and much larger RDBMSs abound).

Then you obtained a brief introduction to the notion of database normalization, and how doing so will help you maintain data integrity ("single source of truth") in an RDBMS.

Next, you learned about the structure of the tables in a four-table database that keeps track of customer purchases of tools through a Web page. You also saw which tables have a one-to-many relationship so that you can find all the line items that belong to a given purchase order.

In addition, you had a brief introduction to SQL and some basic examples of SQL queries. You also learned about various types of SQL statements that can be classified as DCL, DDL, DQL, or DML.

## CHAPTER 5

JAVA, JSON, AND XML

This chapter is for anyone who needs to work with Java to access data that is stored in MySQL tables. Although this chapter is probably optional for all other users, it's worthwhile to peruse its contents if you anticipate working with Java and MySQL at some point in the future, or even if you are merely curious about Java code for managing data in a MySQL database.

Please keep in mind that this chapter does not contain a technical introduction to Java, XML, or JSON. However, the Java code samples perform basic functionality, such as creating database tables via Java, followed by code samples for inserting, selecting, and deleting data from a MySQL database. Consequently, a short tutorial regarding the preceding technologies might be sufficient for you to understand the Java code samples.

In condensed terms, this chapter will help you learn how to use Java to perform CRUD (Create, Replace, Update, and Delete) operations in a MySQL database via Java. The first section shows you how to use Java to create a relational database as well as a relational table. You will learn where you can download the JAR (Java ARchive) file that is needed for JDBC (Java Database Connectivity). Moreover, you will see how to compile Java classes and launch the compiled Java code. This section also contains an example of inserting data into such a table and then how to retrieve that data using Java.

The first section contains Java code samples for creating a MySQL database through Java code. You will also learn how to create a MySQL table and then populate that table with data in Java code. In addition, you will see how to drop a MySQL table (also in Java).

The second section contains Java code samples that enable you to work with JSON-based data. You will learn how to create a table for JSON data, how to insert JSON data into that table, and then how to retrieve that JSON data, all of which is performed by Java code.

The third section contains Java code samples that enable you to work with XML-based data. You will learn how to create a table for XML data, how to insert XML data into that table, and then how to retrieve that XML data, all of which is performed by Java code.

A few more details to keep in mind. First, the Java code samples show you how to create the `mytools` database and how to create tables in this database. However, if you have already imported the `mytools` database, it would be better to specify a different database, such as `mytools2` to avoid collisions with the `mytools` database. The new database name must be specified as the value of the `URL` variable.

Second, you need to specify the password for the root user in the PASS variable, which is the same as the password for your laptop if you installed MySQL from a DMG on a MacBook (the latter is a file type that is specific to Mac).

WORKING WITH JAVA AND MYSQL

Java code for working with MySQL (and other databases) requires a JAR file that contains the relevant classes to make a database connection and execute a SQL statement. The set-up steps involve downloading Java for your laptop, downloading a JDBC driver file, and updating the CLASSPATH environment variable.

Performing the Set-up Steps

The JAR file for communicating with a database through Java is called a JDBC driver, and the JAR file that works for MySQL is downloadable here:

https://dev.mysql.com/downloads/connector/j/

Step 1: Download, uncompress the driver file for your platform, and place the JAR file mysql-connector-java-8.0.24.jar in a convenient location. Note that this JAR file is contained in a subdirectory of the uncompressed driver file.

Step 2: Update the CLASSPATH environment variable, as shown here:

```
export CLASSPATH=$CLASSPATH:.:mysql-connector-java-8.0.24.jar:
```

The preceding code snippet works correctly if the JAR file and the compiled Java classes are in the same directory.

Suggestion: If you are comfortable with basic shell scripts, place the preceding export code snippet in a shell script that you can source ("dot") whenever you need to set the CLASSPATH environment variable.

CREATING A MYSQL DATABASE IN JAVA

This section contains a Java code sample for creating the mytools database. If you have already imported the mytools database, then modify the value of the URL variable in Listing 5.1 to specify a different database. The variables to update are confined to URL, USER, and PASS in the Java code samples that access a MySQL database.

Listing 5.1 displays the content of the Java file CreateDataBase.java that illustrates how to create a MySQL database in Java.

LISTING 5.1: CreateDataBase.java

```
import java.sql.Connection;
import java.sql.DriverManager;
import java.sql.SQLException;
import java.sql.Statement;

public class CreateDataBase
{
```

```java
// specify the URL and username/password to access MySQL
// the URL specifies the mytools database that already exists:
static final String URL  = "jdbc:mysql://localhost/mytools";
static final String USER = "root";
static final String PASS = "yourpassword";

public static void main(String[] args)
{
    // Open a connection
    try(Connection conn =
        DriverManager.getConnection(URL, USER, PASS);

        Statement stmt = conn.createStatement();
    ) {
        String sql = "CREATE DATABASE mytools";
        stmt.executeUpdate(sql);
        System.out.println("Database created");
    } catch (SQLException e) {
        e.printStackTrace();
    }
}
}
```

Listing 5.1 starts with several import statements that specify Java classes that are located in the JDBC JAR file, which is also included in the CLASSPATH environment variable (otherwise, the code will not compile successfully).

The next section of code initializes the string variables URL, USER, and PASS. Replace mytools with your own database (either an existing database or a new database) and also specify the correct value for PASS.

The next portion of Listing 5.1 is the main() method that contains a try/catch block in which a database connection is established, and the string variable sql is initialized to a SQL statement for creating the mytools database. If the database is successfully created, a message is printed; if an error occurs, then the catch() block displays a stack trace that describes the error that was encountered. Launch the code in Listing 5.1 and you will see the following output:

```
Database created
```

If the database mytools already exists, or you launch Listing 5.1 more than once, then you will see the following output:

```
java.sql.SQLException: Can't create database 'mytools'; database exists
```

In this situation you have two options:

1. Drop the database manually.
2. Execute a SQL statement in Java to drop the database.

You can perform option #2 by inserting the following Java code snippet in Listing 5.1 *before* the code block that creates a database:

```
String drop1 = "DROP DATABASE IF EXISTS mytools";
stmt.executeUpdate(drop1);
```

NOTE *Make sure you export the* `mytools` *database to a SQL file before you drop this database.*

CREATING A MYSQL TABLE IN JAVA

Listing 5.2 displays the content of the file `CreateTable.java` that illustrates how to create a MySQL table in Java code.

LISTING 5.2: CreateTable.java

```java
// the downloaded JAR file contains the following Java classes:
import java.sql.Connection;
import java.sql.DriverManager;
import java.sql.SQLException;
import java.sql.Statement;

public class CreateTable
{
    // specify the URL and username/password to access MySQL
    // the URL specifies the mytools database that already exists:
    static final String URL  = "jdbc:mysql://localhost/mytools";
    static final String USER = "root";
    static final String PASS = "yourpassword";

    public static void main(String[] args)
    {
        // Step 1: open a database connection:
        try(Connection conn =
               DriverManager.getConnection(URL,USER, PASS);
          Statement stmt = conn.createStatement();
        ) {
            // drop the table if it already exists: otherwise the
            // code will fail during subsequent invocations with
            // an error message that table 'friends' already exists

            // Step 2: SQL to drop the table if it exists:
            String sql1 = "DROP TABLE IF EXISTS FRIENDS ";

            // Step 3: SQL to create the table FRIENDS:
            String sql2 = "CREATE TABLE FRIENDS " +
                    "(id INTEGER not NULL, " +
                    " fname VARCHAR(100), " +
                    " lname VARCHAR(100), " +
                    " height INTEGER, " +
                    " PRIMARY KEY ( id ))";
```

```
        // Step 4: execute both SQL statements:
        stmt.executeUpdate(sql1);
        stmt.executeUpdate(sql2);
        System.out.println("Created table FRIENDS in database");
    } catch (SQLException e) {
        e.printStackTrace();
    }
  }
}
```

Listing 5.2 starts with several `import` statements that specify Java classes that are located in the JDBC JAR file, which is also included in the `CLASSPATH` environment variable (otherwise, the code will not compile successfully).

The next section of code initializes the string variables `URL`, `USER`, and `PASS`. You must replace `mytools` with your own database (either an existing database or a new database) and specify the correct value for `PASS`.

The next portion of Listing 5.2 is the `main()` method that contains a `try/catch` block in which a database connection is established, and the string variable `sql1` is initialized to a SQL statement for dropping the `friends` table if it already exists. The third step initializes the string variable `sql2` with a SQL statement for creating the `friends` table.

The fourth step executes the SQL code in the string variables `sql1` and `sql2`. If an error occurs, then the `catch()` block displays a stack trace that describes the error that was encountered. Launch the code in Listing 5.2 and you will see the following output:

```
Created table FRIENDS in database
```

Note that older versions of code in the JDBC JAR file require explicitly closing the database connection, whereas this step is now performed automatically.

INSERTING DATA INTO A MYSQL TABLE IN JAVA

Listing 5.3 displays the content of the file `InsertData.java` that illustrates how insert data into the `friends` table that you created in the previous section.

LISTING 5.3: InsertData.java

```
// the downloaded JAR file contains the following Java classes:
import java.sql.Connection;
import java.sql.DriverManager;
import java.sql.SQLException;
import java.sql.Statement;

public class InsertData
{
    // specify the URL and username/password to access MySQL
    // the URL specifies the mytools database that already exists:
    static final String URL  = "jdbc:mysql://localhost/mytools";
    static final String USER = "root";
    static final String PASS = "yourpassword";
```

```
public static void main(String[] args)
{
    String sql = "";

    // Step 1: open a database connection:
    try(Connection conn =
            DriverManager.getConnection(URL, USER, PASS);
        Statement stmt = conn.createStatement();
    ) {
        // Step 2: Execute SQL statements for inserting data
        // and you must make sure the ID values are distinct
        // otherwise you will see the following type of error:
        // Duplicate entry '100' for key 'friends.PRIMARY'
        // One solution involves deleting all the rows from
        // the FRIENDS table but you must exercise caution

        // Step 2: SQL to delete rows from FRIENDS:
        String del1 = "DELETE FROM FRIENDS";
        stmt.executeUpdate(del1);

        sql = "INSERT INTO FRIENDS VALUES(100,'Jane','Jones',170)";
        stmt.executeUpdate(sql);

        sql = "INSERT INTO FRIENDS VALUES(200,'Dave','Smith',160)";
        stmt.executeUpdate(sql);

        sql = "INSERT INTO FRIENDS VALUES(300,'Jack','Stone',180)";
        stmt.executeUpdate(sql);

        System.out.println("Inserted 3 records into FRIENDS table");
    } catch (SQLException e) {
        e.printStackTrace();
    }
}
}
```

Listing 5.3 starts with several import statements that specify Java classes that are located in the JAR file containing the java.sql classes, which is also included in the CLASSPATH environment variable (otherwise, the code will not compile successfully).

The next section of code initializes the string variables URL, USER, and PASS. You must replace mytools with your own database (either an existing database or a new database) and specify the correct value for PASS.

The next portion of Listing 5.2 is the main() method that contains a try/catch block in which a database connection is established, and the string variable del1 is initialized to a SQL statement for deleting the rows in the friends table.

The next step initializes the string variable sql with a SQL statement for inserting a row of data into the friends table. This step is executed twice more with different data values. Launch the code in Listing 5.3 and you will see the following output (the Java code is executed three times):

```
java InsertData
Inserted 3 records into FRIENDS table...
```

```
java InsertData
Inserted 3 records into FRIENDS table...

java InsertData
Inserted 3 records into FRIENDS table...
```

DELETING DATA AND DROPPING MYSQL TABLES IN JAVA

Listing 5.4 displays the content of the file `DeleteData.java` that illustrates how delete data from a table and how to drop a table via Java.

LISTING 5.4: DeleteDataDrop.java

```java
// the downloaded JAR file contains the following Java classes:
import java.sql.Connection;
import java.sql.DriverManager;
import java.sql.SQLException;
import java.sql.Statement;

public class DeleteDataDrop
{
   // specify the URL and username/password to access MySQL
   // the URL specifies the mytools database that already exists:
   static final String URL  = "jdbc:mysql://localhost/mytools";
   static final String USER = "root";
   static final String PASS = "yourpassword";

   public static void main(String[] args)
   {
      String sql = "";

      // Step 1: open a database connection:
      try(Connection conn =
             DriverManager.getConnection(URL, USER, PASS);
        Statement stmt = conn.createStatement();
      ) {
         // Step 2: delete a subset of the rows in FRIENDS:
         System.out.println("Deleting one row from FRIENDS");
         String del1 = "DELETE FROM FRIENDS WHERE id = 100";
         stmt.executeUpdate(del1);

         // Step 3: delete all the rows in FRIENDS:
         System.out.println("Deleting all rows from FRIENDS");
         String del2 = "DELETE FROM FRIENDS";
         stmt.executeUpdate(del2);

         // Step 3: truncate the table FRIENDS:
         System.out.println("Truncating table FRIENDS");
         String del3 = "TRUNCATE FRIENDS";
         stmt.executeUpdate(del3);
```

```
        // Step 4: drop the table FRIENDS:
        System.out.println("Dropping table FRIENDS");
        String del4 = "DROP TABLE FRIENDS";
        stmt.executeUpdate(del4);
      } catch (SQLException e) {
        e.printStackTrace();
      }
    }
  }
}
```

Listing 5.4 starts with several `import` statements that specify Java classes that are located in the JDBC JAR file, which is also included in the `CLASSPATH` environment variable (otherwise, the code will not compile successfully).

The next section of code initializes the string variables `URL`, `USER`, and `PASS`. You must replace `mytools` with your own database (either an existing database or a new database) and also specify the correct value for `PASS`.

The next portion of Listing 5.4 is the `main()` method that contains a `try/catch` block in which a database connection is established, and the string variable `del1` is initialized to a SQL statement for deleting the row in the `friends` table whose `id` value equals 100. The next block of code initializes the string variable `del2` with a SQL statement for deleting *all* the rows in the `friends` table.

The next block of code initializes the string variable `del3` with a SQL statement for truncating the `friends` table. Finally, the last block of code initializes the string variable `del4` with a SQL statement for dropping the `friends` table. Launch the code in Listing 5.4 and you will see the following output:

```
Deleting one row from FRIENDS
Deleting all rows from FRIENDS
Truncating table FRIENDS
Dropping table FRIENDS
```

SELECTING DATA FROM A MYSQL TABLE IN JAVA

Listing 5.5 displays the content of the file `SelectData.java` that illustrates how select data from the `friends` table via Java.

LISTING 5.5: SelectData.java

```java
// the downloaded JAR file contains the following Java classes:
import java.sql.Connection;
import java.sql.DriverManager;
import java.sql.ResultSet;
import java.sql.SQLException;
import java.sql.Statement;

public class SelectData
{
    // specify the URL and username/password to access MySQL
    // the URL specifies the mytools database that already exists:
    static final String URL  = "jdbc:mysql://localhost/mytools";
```

```
static final String USER = "root";
static final String PASS = "yourpassword";

public static void main(String[] args)
{
    String sql1,sql2 = "";

    // Step 1: open a database connection:
    try(Connection conn =
            DriverManager.getConnection(URL, USER, PASS);
        Statement stmt = conn.createStatement();
    ) {

        // Step 2: Execute SQL statement to select data:
        System.out.println("Selecting one row from FRIENDS table");
        sql1 = "SELECT * FROM FRIENDS WHERE id = 100";
        ResultSet rs1 = stmt.executeQuery(sql1);

        while(rs1.next()){
            //Display values
            System.out.print("id: " + rs1.getInt("id"));
            System.out.print(", fname: " + rs1.getString("fname"));
            System.out.print(", lname: " + rs1.getString("lname"));
            System.out.println(", height: " + rs1.getInt("height"));
        }

        // Step 3: Execute SQL statement to select data:
        System.out.print("\n");
        System.out.println("Selecting all rows from FRIENDS table");
        sql2 = "SELECT * FROM FRIENDS";
        ResultSet rs2 = stmt.executeQuery(sql2);

        while(rs2.next()){
            //Display values
            System.out.print("id: " + rs2.getInt("id"));
            System.out.print(", fname: " + rs2.getString("fname"));
            System.out.print(", lname: " + rs2.getString("lname"));
            System.out.println(", height: " + rs2.getInt("height"));
        }
    } catch (SQLException e) {
        e.printStackTrace();
    }
}
}
```

Listing 5.5 starts with several import statements that specify Java classes that are located in the JDBC JAR file, which is also included in the CLASSPATH environment variable (otherwise the code will not compile successfully).

The next section of code initializes the string variables URL, USER, and PASS. You must replace mytools with your own database (either an existing database or a new database) and also specify the correct value for PASS.

The next portion of Listing 5.2 is the main() method that contains a try/catch block in which a database connection is established, and the string variable dell is initialized to a SQL statement for deleting the rows in the `friends` table. The next step initializes the string variable `sql` with a SQL statement for inserting a row of data into the `friends` table. This step is executed twice more with different data values.

Launch the code in Listing 5.5 and you will see the following output (the Java code is executed three times):

```
Selecting one row from FRIENDS table
id: 100, fname: Jane, lname: Jones, height: 170

Selecting all rows from FRIENDS table
id: 100, fname: Jane, lname: Jones, height: 170
id: 200, fname: Dave, lname: Smith, height: 160
id: 300, fname: Jack, lname: Stone, height: 180
```

UPDATING DATA IN A MYSQL TABLE IN JAVA

Listing 5.6 displays the content of the file `UpdateData.java` that illustrates how to update data in the `friends` table via Java.

LISTING 5.6: UpdateData.java

```java
// the downloaded JAR file contains the following Java classes:
import java.sql.Connection;
import java.sql.DriverManager;
import java.sql.SQLException;
import java.sql.Statement;

public class InsertData
{
    // specify the URL and username/password to access MySQL
    // the URL specifies the mytools database that already exists:
    static final String URL  = "jdbc:mysql://localhost/mytools";
    static final String USER = "root";
    static final String PASS = "yourpassword";

    public static void main(String[] args)
    {
        // Step 1: open a database connection:
        try(Connection conn =
                DriverManager.getConnection(URL, USER, PASS);
            Statement stmt = conn.createStatement();
        ) {
            // Step 2: Execute SQL statements to update data
            String upd1 = "UPDATE FRIENDS SET lname = 'Anderson' WHERE id =
100";
            stmt.executeUpdate(upd1);
            System.out.println("Updated last name for row with id = 100");
        } catch (SQLException e) {
            e.printStackTrace();
        }
    }
}
```

Listing 5.6 starts with several `import` statements that specify Java classes that are located in the JDBC JAR file, which is also included in the `CLASSPATH` environment variable (otherwise, the code will not compile successfully).

The next section of code initializes the string variables `URL`, `USER`, and `PASS`. You must replace `mytools` with your own database (either an existing database or a new database) and also specify the correct value for `PASS`.

The next portion of Listing 5.2 is the `main()` method contains a `try/catch` block in which a database connection is established, and the string variable `del1` is initialized to a SQL statement for deleting the rows in the `friends` table. The next step initializes the string variable `sql` with a SQL statement for inserting a row of data into the `friends` table. This step is executed twice more with different data values. Launch the code in Listing 5.6 and you will see the following output:

```
Updated last name for row with id = 100
```

Launch the `SelectData` code to confirm the updated data:

```
Selecting one row from FRIENDS table
id: 100, fname: Jane, lname: Anderson, height: 170

Selecting all rows from FRIENDS table
id: 100, fname: Jane, lname: Anderson, height: 170
id: 200, fname: Dave, lname: Smith, height: 160
id: 300, fname: Jack, lname: Stone, height: 180
```

WORKING WITH JSON, MYSQL, AND JAVA

This section contains a Java code sample to insert JSON-based data into a MySQL table, and how to retrieve JSON-based data from such a table. MySQL supports the JSON data type that we'll use to define one of the attributes in a MySQL table.

In simplified terms, JSON-based data consists of name/value pairs, an example of which is shown here:

```
{"fname":"Dave", "lname":"Stone", "age":35, "city":"NY"}
```

Use an array (i.e., square brackets) to specify a set of JSON-based strings, an example of which is shown here:

```
[
{"fname":"Jane", "lname":"Smith", "age":30, "city":"NY"}
{"fname":"Dave", "lname":"Stone", "age":35, "city":"NY"}
]
```

Listing 5.7 displays the content of the file `json_table.sql` that illustrates how to create a JSON-based MySQL table directly in SQL.

LISTING 5.7: json_table.sql

```
drop table if exists json1;
CREATE TABLE json1 ( id integer, data json);
```

```
INSERT INTO json1 VALUES(100,'{"fname": "Jane", "lname": "Jones"}');
INSERT INTO json1 VALUES(200,'{"fname": "Dave", "lname": "Smith"}');
INSERT INTO json1 VALUES(300,'{"fname": "Jack", "lname": "Stone"}');
```

SELECT JSON-BASED DATA FROM A MYSQL TABLE IN JAVA

This section contains a Java code sample that selects data from a MySQL table that contains JSON-based data. In case you have not already done so, make sure that you create the MySQL table json1 in Listing 5.7 and populate that table with JSON-based data.

Listing 5.8 displays the content of the file SelectJSONTable.java that illustrates how to select data from a MySQL table that contains JSON-based data.

LISTING 5.8: SelectJSONData.java

```
// the downloaded JAR file contains the following Java classes:
import java.sql.Connection;
import java.sql.DriverManager;
import java.sql.SQLException;
import java.sql.Statement;

public class SelectSONData
{
   // specify the URL and username/password to access MySQL
   // the URL specifies the mytools database that already exists:
   static final String URL  = "jdbc:mysql://localhost/mytools";
   static final String USER = "root";
   static final String PASS = "yourpassword";

   public SelectJSONData() {}

   public static void checkJSon()
   {
      // CREATE TABLE json1 ( id integer, data json);
      try{Connection conn =
             DriverManager.getConnection(URL, USER, PASS);
         String query = "SELECT * FROM json1";
         PreparedStatement preparedStatement =
                           conn.prepareStatement(query);
         preparedStatement.execute();
         ResultSet rs = preparedStatement.executeQuery();
         while (rs.next()) {
            System.out.println(rs.getString("data"));
         }
      } catch (SQLException e) {
         e.printStackTrace();
      }
   }

   public static void main(String[] args)
   {
      checkJSon();
   }
}
```

Listing 5.8 starts with several `import` statements that specify Java classes that are located in the JDBC JAR file, which is also included in the `CLASSPATH` environment variable (otherwise, the code will not compile successfully).

The next section of code initializes the string variables `URL`, `USER`, and `PASS`. You must replace `mytools` with your own database (either an existing database or a new database) and specify the correct value for `PASS`.

The next portion of Listing 5.8 is the `main()` method that contains a `try/catch` block in which a database connection is established. The string variable `query` is initialized to a SQL statement for selecting the rows in the `json1` table that is defined in Listing 5.7 (and make sure you run that code first).

The next step initializes the variable `preparedStatement` whose `execute()` method is invoked in the following code snippet as an initialization step. Next, the variable `rs` is initialized with the result set that is returned from invoking the `executeQuery()` method of the variable `preparedStatement`. Next, a loop is executed that retrieves the contents of the data attribute and prints its value, as shown here:

```
while (rs.next()) {
    System.out.println(rs.getString("data"));
}
```

Launch the code in Listing 5.8 and you will see the following output:

```
{"fname": "Jane", "lname": "Jones"}
{"fname": "Dave", "lname": "Smith"}
{"fname": "Jack", "lname": "Stone"}
```

WORKING WITH XML, MYSQL, AND JAVA

There several approaches to working with XML in a database, some of which are listed here (only the first option is explored in this chapter):

- Read XML as a string and parse it via SAX or DOM.
- Use a CLOB data type for XML documents.
- Use JAXB (Java and XML Binding).
- Use an ORM (Object-Relational Mapper).
- Use a native XML database.

The next portion of this chapter contains Java code samples that create a string from the contents of XML documents that are stored as files and then inserts those strings in a character column of a MySQL table. Another Java code sample retrieves each XML-based string and then parses those strings to create XML documents.

In general, the typical operations involving MySQL, XML documents, and Java are as follows:

- Inserting XML documents into a MySQL table
- Reading XML documents in a MySQL table
- Deleting XML documents from a MySQL table
- Updating XML documents in a MySQL table

However, the preceding CRUD operations in Java require a deeper understanding of the Document Object Model (DOM), which is a tree-based structure that contains all the data (and metadata) in the XML document. By way of analogy, whenever you navigate to an HTML Web page in a browser session, the contents of that HTML Web page are also represented as a DOM structure in memory. If you really want to delve into the details of a DOM structure, perform an online search for additional information.

What is XML?

In simplified terms, XML-based data consists of *text* inside angle brackets that specify tag names. Here is a simple example:

```
<fname>Dave</fname>
```

The following code snippets shows you how to specify an XML tag that contains multiple tags (indentation is optional and for ease of reading):

```
<person>
  <fname>Dave</fname>
  <fname>Smith</fname>
</person>
```

Although you can specify nested XML tags that are nested arbitrarily deep, the XML documents in this chapter are only nested one level. In fact, Listing 5.9 displays the contents of the XML document friends.xml.

LISTING 5.9: friends.xml

```
<?xml version="1.0"?>
<friends>
  <friend>
    <fname>Jane</fname>
    <lname>Jones</lname>
    <height>170</height>
  </friend>
  <friend>
    <fname>Dave</fname>
    <lname>Smith</lname>
    <height>160</height>
  </friend>
  <friend>
    <fname>Jack</fname>
    <lname>Stone</lname>
    <height>180</height>
  </friend>
</friends>
```

One point to keep in mind is that XML treats everything as text, which means that XML is a text markup language, whereas JSON (discussed later) is a *data* markup format. Although a significant percentage of the contents of XML documents involves tags, one important advantage of XML is the existence of XML Schemas for validating XML documents, which is briefly discussed in the next section.

WHAT IS AN XML SCHEMA?

An XML Schema is an XML-based document that specifies the structure of XML documents that "conform" to the schema. For example, let's create an XML Schema that constrains valid "friend" XML documents to have the following structure:

- One first name (<fname> tag)
- Zero or more middle names (<mname> tag)
- One last name (<lname> tag)
- One height value (<height> tag)

As you can clearly see, the following XML-based fragment conforms to the preceding structure (one first name, zero middle names, one last name, and one height value):

```
<friend>
  <fname>Jane</fname>
  <lname>Jones</lname>
  <height>170</height>
</friend>
```

The following XML-based fragment conforms to the earlier structure (one first name, two middle names, one last name, and one height value):

```
<friend>
  <fname>Billy</fname>
  <mname>Bob</mname>
  <mname>James</mname>
  <lname>Callaway</lname>
  <height>170</height>
</friend>
```

However, the following XML-based fragment does not conform to the earlier structure because of the tag shown in bold:

```
<friend>
  <title>Mr</title>
  <fname>Billy</fname>
  <lname>Callaway</lname>
  <height>170</height>
</friend>
```

When are XML Schemas Useful?

An XML Schema is extremely valuable in situations that require transmitting a character string between applications. For example, an application that keeps track of leased equipment can contain very complex interdependencies that are tedious to perform in JavaScript in a Web-based application. However, one solution involves constructing a string by concatenating all the fields in a Web page and then passing the string to an application that converts the string into an XML document.

The next step involves validating that the dynamically constructed XML document conforms to an XML schema, after which the XML document can be sent to yet another application for additional processing steps. If necessary, it's possible to create an execution pipeline that performs the preceding sequence of steps multiple times. If an error occurs during a validation step, then the XML document in that step can be analyzed to find the cause of the error, and then resolve the error.

XML documents can be massive, and their associated XML Schema can have a very complex structure. As an example, XBRL defines an XML-based schema for business reporting documents. Moreover, XML is a vast topic, with entire books dedicated to XML. Perform an online search if you want to familiarize yourself with the rich functionality of XML.

Now that you have a cursory understanding of XML, let's see how to create a MySQL table for storing XML data, which is explained in the next section.

CREATE A MYSQL TABLE FOR XML DATA IN JAVA

This section contains a Java code sample that creates a MySQL table that will contain XML-based data. It's also possible to specify the XML data type in a MySQL table; however, the database table in this section uses attributes that you have seen in SQL statements in previous chapters.

Listing 5.10 displays the content of `CreateTableForXMLData.java` that creates a MySQL table that will be populated with data from an XML document.

LISTING 5.10: CreateTableForXMLData.java

```
import java.io.File;
import java.io.IOException;

import java.sql.Connection;
import java.sql.DriverManager;
import java.sql.SQLException;
import java.sql.Statement;

import javax.xml.parsers.DocumentBuilder;
import javax.xml.parsers.DocumentBuilderFactory;
import javax.xml.parsers.ParserConfigurationException;

import org.w3c.dom.Document;
import org.xml.sax.SAXException;

// deprecated: try { Class.forName("com.mysql.jdbc.Driver"); }

public class CreateTableForXMLData
{
    static {
      try {
        Class.forName("com.mysql.cj.jdbc.Driver");
      } catch(ClassNotFoundException ex) {
        System.err.println("Driver not found: "+ex.getMessage());
      }
    };
```

```
    // specify the URL and username/password to access MySQL
    // the URL specifies the mytools database that already exists:
    static final String URL  = "jdbc:mysql://localhost/mytools";
    static final String USER = "root";
    static final String PASS = "yourpassword";

    public CreateTableForXMLData() {}

    public static void createXMLTable()
    {
        try(Connection conn =
                DriverManager.getConnection(URL, USER, PASS);
          Statement stmt = conn.createStatement();
        ) {
          // Step 1: drop the friends table if it exists:
          conn.createStatement()
              .execute("DROP TABLE IF EXISTS friends");
          System.out.println("DROPPED TABLE friends\n");

          // Step 2: drop the friends table if it exists:
          conn.createStatement()
              .execute("CREATE TABLE friends (\n" +
                  " id INTEGER PRIMARY KEY auto_increment,\n" +
                  " fname  VARCHAR(25) NOT NULL,\n" +
                  " lname  VARCHAR(25) NOT NULL,\n" +
                  " height INTEGER)\n");
          System.out.println("CREATED TABLE friends\n");

        } catch (SQLException e) {
          e.printStackTrace();
        }
    }

    public static void main(String[] args)
    {
        createXMLTable();
    }
}
```

Listing 5.10 starts with several `import` statements that specify Java classes that are located in the JDBC JAR file, which is also included in the `CLASSPATH` environment variable (otherwise, the code will not compile successfully).

The next section of code initializes the string variables `URL,` `USER,` and `PASS.` You must replace `mytools` with your own database (either an existing database or a new database) and specify the correct value for `PASS.`

The next portion of Listing 5.10 is the `main()` method that contains a `try/catch` block in which the variable `conn` is initialized via a database connection. The next code snippet performs something called "method chaining." This technique eliminates the need for an intermediate variable. In this case, two methods are invoked sequentially to drop the `friends` table, as shown here:

```
conn.createStatement()
    .execute("DROP TABLE IF EXISTS friends");
```

The next code snippet also uses method chaining to define the structure of the `friends` table and then execute the SQL statement to actually create this table. Launch the code in Listing 5.10 and you will see the following output (the code has been launched twice):

```
DROPPED TABLE friends

CREATED TABLE friends
```

READ AN XML DOCUMENT IN JAVA

This section shows you how to read the contents of an XML document without performing any database connectivity. Listing 5.11 displays the content of the file `ReadXMLDocument.java` that illustrates how to read the contents of the XML document `friends.xml`.

LISTING 5.11: ReadXMLDocument.java

```java
import java.io.File;
import java.io.IOException;
import javax.xml.parsers.DocumentBuilder;
import javax.xml.parsers.DocumentBuilderFactory;
import javax.xml.parsers.ParserConfigurationException;
import org.w3c.dom.Document;
import org.xml.sax.SAXException;

public class ReadXMLDocument
{
    public ReadXMLDocument() {}

    public static void readXMLFile()
    {
        String fileName = "friends.xml";
        File file = new File(fileName);
        System.out.println("Reading XML file "+fileName);

        try {
            DocumentBuilderFactory factory =
                            DocumentBuilderFactory.newInstance();
            DocumentBuilder builder = factory.newDocumentBuilder();
            Document xmlDoc = builder.parse(fileName);
        } catch (SAXException e) {
            e.printStackTrace();
        } catch (ParserConfigurationException pce) {
            pce.printStackTrace();
        } catch (IOException ioe) {
            ioe.printStackTrace();
        }
    }

    public static void main(String[] args)
    {
        readXMLFile();
    }
}
```

Listing 5.11 starts with several `import` statements that specify Java classes that are necessary for manipulating XML documents. The next portion of Listing 5.11 is the `main()` method, which initializes the string variable `fileName` and then initializes the variable `file` with the contents of the `friends.xml` document.

The next step contains a `try/catch` block that involves a three-step process: instantiate a `factory` object, which is used to create a `builder` object, and the latter is used to initialize the variable `xmlDoc` as a tree-based structure that contains the contents of `friends.xml`.

Note that the code does *not* display the contents of the XML document: its purpose is merely to illustrate how to create an in-memory structure with the contents of an XML document. Launch the code in Listing 5.11 and you will see the following output:

```
Reading XML file friends.xml
```

READ AN XML DOCUMENT AS A STRING IN JAVA

Listing 5.12 displays the content of the file `ReadXMLAsString.java` that illustrates how to read an XML document into a string in Java.

LISTING 5.12: ReadXMLAsString.java

```java
import java.io.File;
import java.lang.Exception;
import java.util.Scanner;

public class ReadXMLAsString
{
    public ReadXMLAsString() {}

    public static String readXMLFile(String fileName)
    {
        String contents = "";

        try {
            File file = new File(fileName);
            System.out.println("Reading XML file "+fileName);

            Scanner scanner = new Scanner(file).useDelimiter("\\n");
            while(scanner.hasNext()) {
              contents += scanner.next();
            }
        } catch (Exception ioe) {
            ioe.printStackTrace();
        }
        return contents;
    }

    public static void main(String[] args)
    {
        String fileName = "friends.xml";
        String xmlString = readXMLFile(fileName);
        System.out.println("File contains: "+xmlString);
    }
}
```

Listing 5.12 starts with several `import` statements to read the contents of an XML document as a simple file: no DOM-related structure is required. The next portion of Listing 5.12 defines the method `readXMLFile()` that contains a `try/catch` block for reading a file from the file system. The key idea involves initializing the variable `scanner` with the contents of the file `friends.xml`. The next portion of code is a loop that iterates through the file, one line at a time, and appends each line to the string variable `contents` (initialized earlier in the code), as shown here:

```
while(scanner.hasNext()) {
  contents += scanner.next();
}
```

The final portion of Listing 5.12 is the `main()` method that initializes the variable filename as `friends.xml`, and then initializes the variable `xmlString` with the string that is returned by the method `readXMLFile()`. Launch the code in Listing 5.12 and you will see the following output:

```
Reading XML file friends.xml
File contains: <?xml version="1.0"?><friends>  <friend>      <fname>Jane</
fname>      <lname>Jones</lname>      <height>170</height>  </friend>
<friend>      <fname>Dave</fname>      <lname>Smith</lname>      <height>160</
height>  </friend>  <friend>      <fname>Jack</fname>      <lname>Stone</
lname>      <height>180</height>  </friend></friends>
```

INSERT XML-BASED DATA INTO A MYSQL TABLE IN JAVA

This section contains a Java code sample that reads an XML document into a string and then inserts that string into a MySQL table. In case you have not already done so, make sure that you create the MySQL table `friends2` in Listing 5.13.

LISTING 5.13: create_xml_string_table.sql

```
DROP TABLE IF EXISTS FRIENDS2;
CREATE TABLE FRIENDS2(id INTEGER not NULL, xml_str VARCHAR(1000),
PRIMARY KEY (id))
```

Listing 5.14 displays the content of the file `InsertXMLString.java` that illustrates how to insert XML-based data into a MySQL table.

LISTING 5.14: InsertXMLString.java

```
// the downloaded JAR file contains the following Java classes:
import java.sql.Connection;
import java.sql.DriverManager;
import java.sql.SQLException;
import java.sql.Statement;
import java.util.Scanner;
```

```java
// deprecated: try { Class.forName("com.mysql.jdbc.Driver"); }

public class InsertXMLString
{
    static {
      try {
        Class.forName("com.mysql.cj.jdbc.Driver");
      } catch(ClassNotFoundException ex) {
        System.err.println("Driver not found: "+ex.getMessage());
      }
    };

    // specify the URL and username/password to access MySQL
    // the URL specifies the mytools database that already exists:
    static final String URL  = "jdbc:mysql://localhost/mytools";
    static final String USER = "root";
    static final String PASS = "yourpassword";

    public InsertXMLString() {}

    public static String readXMLFile(String fileName)
    {
        String contents = "";

        try {
            File file = new File(fileName);
            System.out.println("Reading XML file "+fileName);

            Scanner scanner = new Scanner(file).useDelimiter("\\n");
            while(scanner.hasNext()) {
              contents += scanner.next();
            }
        } catch (Exception ioe) {
            ioe.printStackTrace();
        }
        System.out.println("File contains: "+contents);
        return contents;
    }

    public static void insertString(String xmlString)
    {
        // Step 1: open a database connection:
        try(Connection conn =
                DriverManager.getConnection(URL, USER, PASS);
            Statement stmt = conn.createStatement();
        ) {
            // Step 2: Execute SQL statements for inserting data
            // and you must make sure the ID values are distinct
            // otherwise you will see the following type of error:
            // Duplicate entry '100' for key 'friends2.PRIMARY'
            // One solution involves deleting all the rows from
            // the FRIENDS table but you must exercise caution
```

```
          // Step 2: SQL to delete rows from FRIENDS:
          String del1 = "DELETE FROM FRIENDS2 ";
          stmt.executeUpdate(del1);

          String sql = "INSERT INTO FRIENDS2 VALUES(100,"+"'"+xmlString+"')";
// System.out.println("--------------\n");
// System.out.println("===> sql:"+sql);
// System.out.println("--------------\n");

          stmt.executeUpdate(sql);
          System.out.println("Inserted XML string into FRIENDS2 table");
       } catch (SQLException e) {
          e.printStackTrace();
       }
    }

    public static void main(String[] args)
    {
       String fileName = "friends.xml";
       String xmlString = readXMLFile(fileName);
       insertString(xmlString);
    }
}
```

Listing 5.14 starts with several import statements that specify Java classes that are located in the JDBC JAR file, which is also included in the CLASSPATH environment variable (otherwise, the code will not compile successfully).

The next section of code initializes the string variables URL, USER, and PASS. You must replace mytools with your own database (either an existing database or a new database) and specify the correct value for PASS.

The next portion of Listing 5.14 consists of the three methods readXMLFile(), insert-String(), and main(). The method readXMLFile() is explained in the previous section, so there's no need to repeat those details here.

The method insertString() is mostly database-related code that you have seen in several code samples earlier in this chapter, and you can read the details in any of those code samples. The new code in insertString() initializes the variable del1 as a SQL statement that deletes all the rows from the friends2 table, after which one row is inserted into this table, as shown here:

```
String sql = "INSERT INTO FRIENDS2 VALUES(100,"+"'"+xmlString+"')";
```

As always, exercise caution whenever you delete data or drop tables in Java code, just as you would when working directly from SQL statements. Launch the code in Listing 5.14 and you will see the following output:

```
File contains: <?xml version="1.0"?><friends>  <friend>      <fname>Jane</
fname>     <lname>Jones</lname>     <height>170</height>  </friend>
<friend>     <fname>Dave</fname>      <lname>Smith</lname>      <height>160</
height>  </friend>  <friend>     <fname>Jack</fname>      <lname>Stone</
lname>     <height>180</height>  </friend></friends>
Inserted XML string into FRIENDS2 table
```

SELECT XML-BASED DATA FROM A MYSQL TABLE IN JAVA

This section contains a Java code sample that selects data from a MySQL table that contains XML-based data. In case you have not already done so, make sure that you create the MySQL table `friends2` in Listing 5.13 and populate this table with data.

Listing 5.15 displays the content of the file `SelectXMLData.java` that illustrates how to select data from a MySQL table that contains XML-based data.

LISTING 5.15: SelectXMLData.java

```
// the downloaded JAR file contains the following Java classes:
import java.sql.Connection;
import java.sql.DriverManager;
import java.sql.SQLException;
import java.sql.Statement;

public class SelectXMLData
{
    // specify the URL and username/password to access MySQL
    // the URL specifies the mytools database that already exists:
    static final String URL  = "jdbc:mysql://localhost/mytools";
    static final String USER = "root";
    static final String PASS = "yourpassword";

    public SelectXMLData() {}

    public static void selectXML()
    {
        int rowCount = 0;

        // CREATE TABLE json1 ( id integer, data json);
        try{Connection conn = DriverManager.getConnection(URL, USER, PASS);
            String query = "SELECT * FROM FRIENDS2";
            PreparedStatement preparedStatement = conn.prepareStatement(query);
            preparedStatement.execute();
            ResultSet rs = preparedStatement.executeQuery();

            while (rs.next()) {
                System.out.println("XML String:");
                System.out.println(rs.getString("xml_str"));
                System.out.println("\n");
                ++rowCount;
            }
            System.out.println("=> ROW COUNT:"+rowCount+"\n");
        } catch (SQLException e) {
            e.printStackTrace();
        }
    }

    public static void main(String[] args)
    {
        selectXML();
    }
}
```

Listing 5.15 starts with several `import` statements that specify Java classes that are located in the JDBC JAR file, which is also included in the `CLASSPATH` environment variable (otherwise, the code will not compile successfully).

The next section of code initializes the string variables `URL`, `USER`, and `PASS`. You must replace `mytools` with your own database (either an existing database or a new database) and specify the correct value for `PASS`.

The next portion of Listing 5.15 is the `main()` method that contains a `try/catch` block in which a database connection is established, and the string variable `query` is initialized to a SQL statement for selecting the rows in the `friends2` table. The next portion of code is essentially the same as the code in Listing 5.5 for iterating through a result set and then displaying the contents of the `xml_str` attribute. Launch the code in Listing 5.15 and you will see the following output:

```
XML String:
<?xml version="1.0"?><friends>  <friend>     <fname>Jane</fname>
<lname>Jones</lname>     <height>170</height>  </friend>  <friend>
<fname>Dave</fname>     <lname>Smith</lname>    <height>160</height>
</friend>  <friend>     <fname>Jack</fname>     <lname>Stone</lname>
<height>180</height>  </friend></friends>

=> ROW COUNT:1
```

PARSE XML-BASED STRING DATA FROM A MYSQL TABLE IN JAVA

This section contains a Java code sample that selects data from a MySQL table that contains XML-based data. In case you have not already done so, make sure that you create the MySQL table `friends2` in Listing 5.13 and populate this table with data.

Listing 5.16 displays the content of `ParseXMLStringInTable.java` that illustrates how to select strings of XML-based data from a MySQL table and then create an XML document based on the contents of each string.

LISTING 5.16: ParseXMLStringInTable.java

```java
import java.io.StringReader;
import java.sql.Connection;
import java.sql.DriverManager;
import java.sql.PreparedStatement;
import java.sql.ResultSet;
import java.sql.SQLException;
import java.sql.Statement;
import java.util.ArrayList;

import javax.xml.parsers.DocumentBuilder;
import javax.xml.parsers.DocumentBuilderFactory;
import javax.xml.parsers.ParserConfigurationException;

import org.w3c.dom.Document;
import org.xml.sax.SAXException;
import org.xml.sax.InputSource;
public class ParseXMLStringInTable
```

```
{
   // specify the URL and username/password to access MySQL
   // the URL specifies the mytools database that already exists:
   static final String URL  = "jdbc:mysql://localhost/mytools";
   static final String USER = "root";
   static final String PASS = "yourpassword";

   public ParseXMLStringInTable() {}

   public static void parseXMLString(ArrayList arrList)
   {
      System.out.println("=> Parsing Strings as XML");

      try {
        DocumentBuilderFactory factory =
                        DocumentBuilderFactory.newInstance();
        DocumentBuilder builder = factory.newDocumentBuilder();

        // Document xmlDoc = builder.parse(xmlString);
        // this parse(String) tries to open the URI that is specified as
        // the first line in the XML document, which causes this error:
        // java.net.MalformedURLException: no protocol: <?xml version="1.0"?>
        // Instead, use an InputStream or Reader with the string like this:

        for (int row=0; row<arrList.size(); row++)
        {
           String xml = (String)arrList.get(row);
           Document xmlDoc =
              builder.parse(new InputSource(new StringReader(xml)));
           System.out.println("Do something with this XML document...");
        }
      } catch (SAXException e) {
         e.printStackTrace();
      } catch (ParserConfigurationException pce) {
         pce.printStackTrace();
      } catch (Exception ex) {
         ex.printStackTrace();
      }
   }

   public static void selectXML()
   {
      int rowCount = 0;
      ArrayList arrList = new ArrayList();

      try{Connection conn = DriverManager.getConnection(URL, USER, PASS);
         String query = "SELECT * FROM FRIENDS2";
         PreparedStatement preparedStatement = conn.prepareStatement(query);
         preparedStatement.execute();
         ResultSet rs = preparedStatement.executeQuery();

         while (rs.next()) {
            String xmlString = rs.getString("xml_str");
            arrList.add(xmlString);
```

```
        ++rowCount;
      }

      // reconstruct each string as an XML document:
      parseXMLString(arrList);

      System.out.println("=> ROW COUNT:"+rowCount+"\n");
    } catch (SQLException e) {
      e.printStackTrace();
    }
  }

  public static void main(String[] args)
  {
    selectXML();
  }
}
```

Listing 5.16 starts with several import statements that specify Java classes that are located in the JDBC JAR file, which is also included in the CLASSPATH environment variable.

The next section of code initializes the string variables URL, USER, and PASS. You must replace mytools with your own database (either an existing database or a new database) and specify the correct value for PASS.

The rest of Listing 5.16 consists of three methods: parseXMLString(), selectXML(), and the main() method. The parseXMLString() method iterates through the contents of the variable arrList (which will contain data from the friends2 table) to construct an XML document.

The selectXML() method establishes a database connection and reads the contents of the friends2 table using familiar code. In addition, the last portion of code in the selectXML() method appends data to the arrList variable (an instance of the Java ArrayList class) in a while loop that iterates over the contents of a result set. The final code snippet invokes the method parseXMLString() with the variable arrList. Launch the code in Listing 5.16 and you will see the following output:

```
=> Parsing Strings as XML
Do something with this XML document...
=> ROW COUNT:1
```

WORKING WITH XML SCHEMAS

Earlier in this chapter, you saw some Java-based code samples that manage XML-based documents in conjunction with MySQL. Although we specified an XML document that contained multiple <friend> elements, we did not constrain the contents of the XML elements.

However, XML Schemas provide strict control over the permissible structure of the elements in XML documents, such as specifying not only their type, but their frequency and the order in which they appear in an XML element.

For example, we can define the element firstname whose type is a string with the following code snippet:

```
<xs:element name="firstname" type="xs:string"/>
```

We can define the element friend that contains two string-based elements fname and lname, as well as a numeric element called height, as shown here:

```
<?xml version="1.0"?>
<xs:element name="friend">
  <xs:complexType>
    <xs:sequence>
      <xs:element name="fname"  type="xs:string"/>
      <xs:element name="lname"  type="xs:string"/>
      <xs:element name="height" type="xs:decimal"/>
    </xs:sequence>
  </xs:complexType>
</xs:element>
```

We can modify the preceding code block to specify an optional middle name, which can occur a maximum of three times:

```
<?xml version="1.0"?>
<xs:element name="friend">
  <xs:complexType>
    <xs:sequence>
     <xs:element name="fname"  type="xs:string"/>
     <xs:element name="mname" type="xs:string" minOccurs="0" maxOccurs="3"/>
     <xs:element name="lname"  type="xs:string"/>
     <xs:element name="height" type="xs:decimal"/>
    </xs:sequence>
  </xs:complexType>
```

If you want to specify an optional middle name element that can occur an arbitrary number of times, use the following code snippet:

```
<xs:element name="mname"  type="xs:string" minOccurs="0" maxOccurs="3"/>
```

There are many features available in XML Schemas, including the ability of an XML element to reference other XML elements, and you can even specify an XML element as abstract (in the OOP sense of the word). Perform an online search for more information regarding XML Schemas.

SUMMARY

This chapter started by showing you how to write Java-based code for managing relational databases and the content of relational tables. You saw how to perform the necessary set-up steps for your laptop so that the Java code will execute correctly.

Next, you learned how to write Java code for managing JSON-based data in a MySQL database. You saw how to create a table for JSON data, how to insert data into that table, and how to retrieve that data using Java-based code.

You also learned about several Java-based technologies for working with XML documents, such as SAX-based parsers and DOM-based parsers. Finally, you saw how to write Java code for managing XML-based data in a MySQL database.

## CHAPTER 6

DATA CLEANING TASKS

This chapter discusses data cleaning tasks involving datasets that contain various types of data, such as dates, telephone numbers, and currency, all of which can have different formats. In addition, many of the code samples in this chapter reference techniques that are discussed in previous chapters of this book. This chapter provides a natural segue into Chapter 7, which discusses data wrangling in various code samples.

The first part of this chapter briefly describes data cleaning, followed by examples of data cleaning tasks for data in MySQL database table. Specifically, you will see how to replace NULL values with 0, how to replace NULL values with an average value, how to replace multiple values with a single value, how to handle mismatched attribute values, and how to convert strings to date values.

The second part of this chapter shows you how to use the sed command line utility to replace multiple delimiters in a CSV file with a single delimiter. You will also see how to use the awk command line utility to restructure a CSV file to create a file whose rows have the same number of fields.

The third part of this chapter shows you how to use the awk command line utility to process CSV files that have a variable number of columns. The awk command is a self-contained programming language, with a truly impressive capability for processing text files. If you are unfamiliar with the awk command, please read the appendix that contains an assortment of code samples that use the awk utility.

The fourth part of this chapter contains awk-based shell scripts that show you how to convert a list of phone numbers to the same format as well as a list of date formats to the same format.

This chapter assumes that you have read the data cleaning examples that are in previous chapters. Moreover, Chapter 7 also contains a section with additional code samples involving data cleaning tasks.

WHAT IS DATA CLEANING?

Data cleaning, also called data cleansing, is the task of ensuring that the contents of a dataset are complete, correct, and typically without duplicates. Hence, the focus of data cleaning is on individual files instead of combining or transforming data from two or more files. Data cleaning is often performed before any data transformation is performed. In some cases, data cleaning must also be performed after a data transformation.

For example, suppose that a CSV file contains employee-related data and a MySQL table also contains employee-related data, both of which have been cleansed of inconsistencies and duplicates have been removed. However, after exporting the table data to a CSV file that is merged with the first CSV file, it's possible that there are duplicates that must then be removed.

Incidentally, there are several techniques for determining the values to replace empty fields, and the choice of techniques can range from obvious choices to more subtle factors. Sometimes you can specify the mean or the median for missing values, but in other cases you need a more sophisticated technique. For example, suppose that a dataset with 1,000 rows consists of two types of patients: those who are healthy (the majority) as well as patients who have cancer. Obviously, you want the number of sick patients to be as low as possible, which means that the dataset is fundamentally imbalanced.

Unfortunately, machine learning algorithms can produce inaccurate results with imbalanced datasets. Moreover, generating synthetic data whose feature values are based on the mean or the median is probably risky. A better technique is called SMOTE, which generates data values that are close to values that appear in rows of the original dataset.

As another example, the format for dates, currency, and decimal numbers varies among different countries. Examples of date formats include YYYY/MM/DD, MM/DD/YYYY, and DD/MM/YYYY (as well as other possible date formats). Incidentally, YYYY/MM/DD is an ISO standard for numeric dates.

Number formats involve a comma "," for the thousands position and decimal "." for decimal values in the US (ex: $1,234.56), whereas Europe uses the opposite order for numbers (ex: 1.234,56). Depending on the dataset in question, data cleaning can also involve working with an assortment of dates, currencies, and decimal numbers to ensure that all values have the same format.

Moreover, if two CSV files contain different date formats and you need to create a single CSV file that is based on the date columns, then there will be some type of conversion process that could be one of the following:

- Convert the first date format to the second date format
- Convert the second date format to the first date format
- Convert both date formats to a third date format

In the case of financial data, you are likely to also encounter different currencies, which involves a conversion rate between a pair of currencies. Since currency conversion rates fluctuate, you need to decide the exchange rate to use for the data, which can be one of the following:

- The exchange rate during the date that the CSV files were generated
- The current currency exchange rate
- Some other mechanism

Data Cleaning for Personal Titles

Sometimes a "brute force" solution is also the simplest solution, particular when strings are involved. For example, a person's title can be misspelled in myriad ways that involves many pesky little variations, so it's good to know how to perform this task in a manner that's simple, intuitive, and easy to extend with additional cases. For example, consider how you would replace each string in the following list with the prefixes "Mr,", "Ms," or "Mrs" before you look at the solution that follows:

```
Titles = ['mr.','MR','MR.','mister','Mister','Ms','Ms.', 'Mr', 'Mr.','mr',
'MS','MS.','ms','ms.','Mis','miss','miss.','Mrs','Mrs.','mrs','mrs.',
'Madam','madam','ma"am']
```

While it's possible to solve this task with conditional logic that uses if/else code blocks, such an approach involves a lengthy code block. A simpler and easier solution involves the **in** keyword, as shown here:

```
mr_dict={}
ms_dict={}
mrs_dict={}

titles = ['mr.','MR','MR.','mister','Mister','Ms','Ms.', 'Mr', 'Mr.',
'mr','MS','MS.','ms','ms.','Mis','miss','miss.','Mrs','Mrs.','mrs','mrs.',
'Madam','madam','ma"am']

for title in ['Mr','Mr.','mr','mr.','MR','MR.','mister','Mister']:
  mr_dict[title] = "Mr"

for title in ['Ms','Ms.','MS','MS.','ms','ms.','Mis','miss','miss.']:
  ms_dict[title] = "Ms"

for title in ['Mrs','Mrs.','mrs','mrs.','Madam','madam','ma"am']:
  mrs_dict[title] = "Mrs"

print("Mr dictionary: ",mr_dict)
print()
print("Ms dictionary: ",ms_dict)
print()
print("Mrs dictionary:",mrs_dict)
```

Launch the preceding code block and you will see the following output:

```
Mr dictionary:  {'Mr': 'Mr', 'Mr.': 'Mr', 'mr': 'Mr', 'mr.': 'Mr', 'MR':
'Mr', 'MR.': 'Mr', 'mister': 'Mr', 'Mister': 'Mr'}

Ms dictionary:  {'Ms': 'Ms', 'Ms.': 'Ms', 'MS': 'Ms', 'MS.': 'Ms', 'ms':
'Ms', 'ms.': 'Ms', 'Mis': 'Ms', 'miss': 'Ms', 'miss.': 'Ms'}

Mrs dictionary: {'Mrs': 'Mrs', 'Mrs.': 'Mrs', 'mrs': 'Mrs', 'mrs.':
'Mrs', 'Madam': 'Mrs', 'madam': 'Mrs', 'ma"am': 'Mrs'}
```

The solution given here makes it very easy to maintain, debug, and extend because the only change that's required is adding a new string in the appropriate location. Moreover, the given solution does not require any additional loops or regular expressions. In the event that you need a new category, such as "Sir," define the Python dictionary `sir_dict` and then add a new code snippet, as shown here:

```
if title in ['Sir','sir','Sire','sire','Yessir','yessir']:
sir_dict[title] = "Sir"
```

DATA CLEANING IN SQL

This section contains several subsections that perform data cleaning tasks in SQL. Note that it's not mandatory to perform these tasks in SQL: another option is to read the contents of a database table into a Pandas data frame and then use Pandas methods to achieve the same result.

However, this section illustrates how to perform the following data cleaning tasks that affect an attribute of a database table:

- replace NULL with 0
- replace NULL with the average value
- replace multiple values into a single value
- handle data type mismatch
- convert a string date to a date format

Replace NULL with 0

This task is very straightforward, which you can perform with either of the following SQL statements:

```
SELECT ISNULL(column_name, 0) FROM table_name
OR
SELECT COALESCE(column_name, 0) FROM table_name
```

Replace NULL Values with Average Value

This task involves two steps: first find the average of the non-NULL values of a column in a database table, and then update the NULL values in that column with the value that you found in the first step. Listing 6.1 displays the content of the SQL file `replace_null_values.sql` that performs this pair of steps.

LISTING 6.1: replace_null_values.sql

```
USE mytools;
DROP TABLE IF EXISTS temperatures;
CREATE TABLE temperatures (temper INT, city CHAR(20));

INSERT INTO temperatures VALUES(78,'sf');
INSERT INTO temperatures VALUES(NULL,'sf');
INSERT INTO temperatures VALUES(42,NULL);
INSERT INTO temperatures VALUES(NULL,'ny');
SELECT * FROM temperatures;

SELECT @avg1 := AVG(temper) FROM temperatures;
update temperatures
set temper = @avg1
```

```
where ISNULL(temper);
SELECT * FROM temperatures;

-- initialize city1 with the most frequent city value:
SELECT @city1 := (SELECT city FROM temperatures GROUP BY city ORDER BY
COUNT(*) DESC LIMIT 1);

-- update NULL city values with the value of city1:
update temperatures
set city = @city1
where ISNULL(city);
SELECT * FROM temperatures;
```

Listing 6.1 creates and populates the table `temperatures` with several rows, and then initializes the variable `avg1` with the average temperature in the `temper` attribute of the `temperatures` table. Launch the code in Listing 6.1 and you will see the following output:

```
+--------+------+
| temper | city |
+--------+------+
|     78 | sf   |
|   NULL | sf   |
|     42 | NULL |
|   NULL | ny   |
+--------+------+
4 rows in set (0.000 sec)

+---------------------+
| @avg1 := AVG(temper) |
+---------------------+
|        60.000000000 |
+---------------------+
1 row in set, 1 warning (0.000 sec)

Query OK, 2 rows affected (0.001 sec)
Rows matched: 2  Changed: 2  Warnings: 0

+--------+------+
| temper | city |
+--------+------+
|     78 | sf   |
|     60 | sf   |
|     42 | NULL |
|     60 | ny   |
+--------+------+
4 rows in set (0.000 sec)

+----------------------------------------------------------------------+
| @city1 := (SELECT city FROM temperatures GROUP BY city ORDER BY
COUNT(*) DESC LIMIT 1) |
+----------------------------------------------------------------------+
| sf
|
+----------------------------------------------------------------------+
1 row in set, 1 warning (0.000 sec)
```

```
Query OK, 1 row affected (0.000 sec)
Rows matched: 1  Changed: 1  Warnings: 0

+--------+------+
| temper | city |
+--------+------+
|     78 | sf   |
|     60 | sf   |
|     42 | sf   |
|     60 | ny   |
+--------+------+
4 rows in set (0.000 sec)
```

REPLACE MULTIPLE VALUES WITH A SINGLE VALUE

An example of coalescing multiple values in an attribute involves replacing multiple strings for the state of New York (such as new_york, NewYork, NY, and New_York) with NY. Listing 6.2 displays the content of the SQL file reduce_values.sql that performs this pair of steps.

LISTING 6.2: reduce_values.sql

```
use mytools;
DROP TABLE IF EXISTS mytable;
CREATE TABLE mytable (str_date CHAR(15), state CHAR(20), reply
CHAR(10));

INSERT INTO mytable VALUES('20210915','New York','Yes');
INSERT INTO mytable VALUES('20211016','New York','no');
INSERT INTO mytable VALUES('20220117','Illinois','yes');
INSERT INTO mytable VALUES('20220218','New York','No');
SELECT * FROM mytable;

-- replace yes, Yes, y, Ys with Y:
update mytable
set reply = 'Y'
where upper(substr(reply,1,1)) = 'Y';
SELECT * FROM mytable;

-- replace all other values with
update mytable
set reply = 'N' where substr(reply,1,1) != 'Y';
SELECT * FROM mytable;
```

Listing 6.2 creates and populates the table mytable, and then replaces the variants of the word yes with the letter Y in the reply attribute. The final portion of Listing 6.2 replaces any string that does *not* start with the letter Y with the letter N. Launch the code in Listing 6.2 and you will see the following output:

```
+----------+----------+-------+
| str_date | state    | reply |
+----------+----------+-------+
| 20210915 | New York | Yes   |
```

```
| 20211016 | New York | no    |
| 20220117 | Illinois | yes   |
| 20220218 | New York | No    |
+----------+----------+-------+
4 rows in set (0.000 sec)


Query OK, 2 rows affected (0.001 sec)
Rows matched: 2  Changed: 2  Warnings: 0


+----------+----------+-------+
| str_date | state    | reply |
+----------+----------+-------+
| 20210915 | New York | Y     |
| 20211016 | New York | no    |
| 20220117 | Illinois | Y     |
| 20220218 | New York | No    |
+----------+----------+-------+
4 rows in set (0.000 sec)


Query OK, 2 rows affected (0.001 sec)
Rows matched: 2  Changed: 2  Warnings: 0


+----------+----------+-------+
| str_date | state    | reply |
+----------+----------+-------+
| 20210915 | New York | Y     |
| 20211016 | New York | N     |
| 20220117 | Illinois | Y     |
| 20220218 | New York | N     |
+----------+----------+-------+
4 rows in set (0.001 sec)
```

HANDLE MISMATCHED ATTRIBUTE VALUES

This task involves two steps: first find the average of the non-NULL values of a column in a database table, and then update the NULL values in that column with the value that you found in the first step. Listing 6.3 displays the content of the SQL file type_mismatch.sql that performs this pair of steps.

LISTING 6.3: type_mismatch.sql

```
USE mytools;
DROP TABLE IF EXISTS emp_details;
CREATE TABLE emp_details (emp_id CHAR(15), city CHAR(20), state
CHAR(20));

INSERT INTO emp_details VALUES('1000','Chicago','Illinois');
INSERT INTO emp_details VALUES('2000','Seattle','Washington');
INSERT INTO emp_details VALUES('3000','Santa Cruz','California');
INSERT INTO emp_details VALUES('4000','Boston','Massachusetts');
SELECT * FROM emp_details;
```

```
select emp.emp_id, emp.title, det.city, det.state
from employees emp join emp_details det
WHERE emp.emp_id = det.emp_id;

--required for earlier versions of MySQL:
--WHERE emp.emp_id = cast(det.emp_id as INT);
```

Listing 6.3 creates and populates the table emp_details, followed by a SQL JOIN statement involving the tables emp and emp_details. Although the emp_id table is defined as an INT type and a CHAR type, respectively, in the tables emp and emp_details, the code works as desired. However, in earlier versions of MySQL, you need to use the built-in CAST() function to convert a CHAR value to an INT value (or vice versa), as shown in the commented-out code snippet:

```
--WHERE emp.emp_id = cast(det.emp_id as INT);
```

Launch the code in Listing 6.3 and you will see the following output:

```
+---------+------------+----------------+
| emp_id  | city       | state          |
+---------+------------+----------------+
| 1000    | Chicago    | Illinois       |
| 2000    | Seattle    | Washington     |
| 3000    | Santa Cruz | California     |
| 4000    | Boston     | Massachusetts  |
+---------+------------+----------------+
4 rows in set (0.000 sec)
+---------+--------------------+------------+----------------+
| emp_id  | title              | city       | state          |
+---------+--------------------+------------+----------------+
|    1000 | Developer          | Chicago    | Illinois       |
|    2000 | Project Lead       | Seattle    | Washington     |
|    3000 | Dev Manager        | Santa Cruz | California     |
|    4000 | Senior Dev Manager | Boston     | Massachusetts  |
+---------+--------------------+------------+----------------+
4 rows in set (0.002 sec)
```

CONVERT STRINGS TO DATE VALUES

Listing 6.4 displays the content of str_to_date.sql that illustrates how to populate a date attribute with date values that are determined from another string-based attribute that contains strings for dates.

LISTING 6.4: str_to_date.sql

```
use mytools;
DROP TABLE IF EXISTS mytable;
CREATE TABLE mytable (str_date CHAR(15), state CHAR(20), reply
CHAR(10));
```

```
INSERT INTO mytable VALUES('20210915','New York','Yes');
INSERT INTO mytable VALUES('20211016','New York','no');)
INSERT INTO mytable VALUES('20220117','Illinois','yes');)
INSERT INTO mytable VALUES('20220218','New York','No');)

SELECT * FROM mytable;

-- 1) insert date-based feature:
ALTER TABLE mytable
ADD COLUMN (real_date DATE);
SELECT * FROM mytable;

-- 2) populate real_date from str_date:
UPDATE mytable t1
        INNER JOIN mytable t2
            ON t1.str_date = t2.str_date
SET t1.real_date = DATE(t2.str_date);
SELECT * FROM mytable;

-- 3) Remove unwanted features:
ALTER TABLE mytable
DROP COLUMN str_date;
SELECT * FROM mytable;
```

Listing 6.4 creates and populates the table `mytable` and displays the contents of this table. The remainder of Listing 6.4 consists of three SQL statements, each of which starts with a comment statement that explains its purpose.

The first SQL statement inserts a new column `real_date` of type `DATE`. The second SQL statement populates the `real_date` column with the values in the `str_date` column that have been converted to a date value via the `DATE()` function. The third SQL statement is optional: it drops the `str_date` column if you wish to do so. Launch the code in Listing 6.4 and you will see the following output:

```
+----------+----------+-------+
| str_date | state    | reply |
+----------+----------+-------+
| 20210915 | New York | Yes   |
| 20211016 | New York | no    |
| 20220117 | Illinois | yes   |
| 20220218 | New York | No    |
+----------+----------+-------+
4 rows in set (0.000 sec)

Query OK, 0 rows affected (0.007 sec)
Records: 0  Duplicates: 0  Warnings: 0

+----------+----------+-------+-----------+
| str_date | state    | reply | real_date |
+----------+----------+-------+-----------+
| 20210915 | New York | Yes   | NULL      |
| 20211016 | New York | no    | NULL      |
```

```
| 20220117 | Illinois | yes   | NULL      |
| 20220218 | New York | No    | NULL      |
+----------+----------+-------+-----------+
4 rows in set (0.002 sec)

Query OK, 4 rows affected (0.002 sec)
Rows matched: 4  Changed: 4  Warnings: 0

+----------+----------+-------+------------+
| str_date | state    | reply | real_date  |
+----------+----------+-------+------------+
| 20210915 | New York | Yes   | 2021-09-15 |
| 20211016 | New York | no    | 2021-10-16 |
| 20220117 | Illinois | yes   | 2022-01-17 |
| 20220218 | New York | No    | 2022-02-18 |
+----------+----------+-------+------------+
4 rows in set (0.000 sec)

Query OK, 0 rows affected (0.018 sec)
Records: 0  Duplicates: 0  Warnings: 0

+----------+-------+------------+
| state    | reply | real_date  |
+----------+-------+------------+
| New York | Yes   | 2021-09-15 |
| New York | no    | 2021-10-16 |
| Illinois | yes   | 2022-01-17 |
| New York | No    | 2022-02-18 |
+----------+-------+------------+
4 rows in set (0.000 sec)
```

DATA CLEANING FROM THE COMMAND LINE (OPTIONAL)

This section is marked "optional" because the solutions to tasks involve an understanding of some Unix-based utilities. If need be, you can read the appendix regarding awk and online tutorials regarding the sed utility.

This section contains several subsections that perform data cleaning tasks that involve the sed and awk utilities:

- replace multiple delimiters with a single delimiter (sed)
- restructure a dataset so all rows have the same column count (awk)

Keep in mind the following point about these examples: they must be performed from the command line before they can be processed in a Pandas data frame.

Working with the sed Utility

This section contains an example of how to use the sed command line utility to replace different delimiters with a single delimiter for the fields in a text file. You can use the same code for other file formats, such as CSV files and TSV files.

This section does not provide any details about sed beyond the code sample in this section. However, after you read the code (it's a one-liner), you will probably understand how to adapt that code snippet to your own requirements (i.e., how to specify different delimiters).

Listing 6.5 displays the content of `delimiter1.txt` and Listing 6.6 displays the content of `delimiter1.sh` that replaces all delimiters with a comma (",").

LISTING 6.5: delimiter1.txt

```
1000|Jane:Edwards^Sales
2000|Tom:Smith^Development
3000|Dave:Del Ray^Marketing
```

LISTING 6.6: delimiter1.sh

```
cat delimiter1.txt | sed -e 's/:/,/' -e 's/|/,/' -e 's/\^/,/'
```

Listing 6.6 starts with the `cat` command line utility, which sends the contents of the file `delimiter1.txt` "standard output," which is on the screen (by default). However, in this example, the output of this command becomes the input to the `sed` command because of the pipe ("|") symbol.

The `sed` command consists of three parts, all of which are connected by the `-e` switch. You can think of `-e` as indicating "there is more processing to be done" by the `sed` command. In this example, there are three occurrences of `-e`, which means that three operations will be performed by `sed`.

The first code snippet is `'s/:/,/'`, which translates into "replace each semi-colon with a comma." The result of this operation is passed to the next code snippet, which is `'s/|/,/'`. This code snippet translates into "replace each pipe symbol with a comma." The result of this operation is passed to the next code snippet, which is `'s/\^/,/'`. This code snippet translates into "replace each caret symbol ("^") with a comma." The result of this operation is sent to standard output, which can be redirected to another text file. Launch the code in Listing 6.6 and you will see the following output:

```
1000,Jane,Edwards,Sales
2000,Tom,Smith,Development
3000,Dave,Del Ray,Marketing
```

Three comments to keep in mind. First, the third snippet contains a backslash because the caret symbol ("^") is a meta character, so we need to "escape" this character. The same is true for other meta characters (such as "$" and ".").

Second, you can easily extend the `sed` command for each new delimiter that you encounter as a field separator in a text file: simply follow the pattern that you see in Listing 6.6 for each new delimiter.

Third, redirect the output of `delimiter1.sh` to the text file `delimiter2.txt` by launching the following command:

```
./delimiter1.sh > delimiter2.txt
```

If an error occurs in the preceding code snippet, make sure that `delimiter1.sh` is executable by invoking the following command:

```
chmod 755 delimiter1.sh
```

This concludes the example involving the `sed` command line utility, which is a very powerful utility for processing text files.

WORKING WITH VARIABLE COLUMN COUNTS

This section shows you how to use the `awk` command line utility in order to "pad" rows in a CSV file with `NaN` values so that all records have the same number of columns.

Listing 6.7 displays the content `variable_columns.csv` and Listing 6.8 displays the content of `variable_columns.sh` that uses the `awk` utility to pad the number of columns in a CSV file.

LISTING 6.7: variable_columns.csv

```
10,20,30
10,20,30,40
10,20,30,40,50,60
```

LISTING 6.8: variable_columns.sh

```
filename="variable_columns.csv"

cat $filename | awk -F"," '
BEGIN { colCount = 6 }
{
  printf("%s", $0)
  for(i=NF; i<colCount; i++) {
    printf(",NaN")
  }
  print ""
}
'
```

Listing 6.8 initializes the variable `filename` with the name of the CSV file for this code sample. The next snippet is an awk script that initializes `colCount` with the value 6 in the `BEGIN` block: this value is the largest number of columns in any row of the CSV file.

The next block of code displays the contents of the current line, followed by a loop that prints a comma-separated list of `NaN` values to ensure that the output line contains 6 columns. For instance, if a row has four columns, then `NaN`, will be printed twice. The `print()` statement after the loop ensures that the next line from the input file starts on a new line instead of the current output line. Launch the code in Listing 6.8 and you will see the following output:

```
10,20,30,NaN,NaN,NaN
10,20,30,40,NaN,NaN
10,20,30,40,50,60
10,20,NaN,NaN,NaN,NaN
10,20,30,40,NaN,NaN
```

One limitation of Listing 6.8 is that the maximum number of columns must be specified in the `BEGIN` block. Listing 6.9 removes this constraint by scanning the entire file to determine the maximum number of columns in the CSV file.

LISTING 6.9: *variable_columns2.sh*

```
filename="variable_columns.csv"

cat $filename | awk -F"," '
BEGIN {
  maxColCount = 0;

  ###############################################
  # maxColCount = # of fields in the longest row
  ###############################################
  while(getline line < ARGV[1]) {
    colCount = split(line,data)
    if(maxColCount < length(data)) {
       maxColCount = length(data)
    }
  }
}
{
  # print current input line:
  printf("%s", $0)

  # pad with NaN (if necessary):
  for(j=NF; j<maxColCount; j++) {
     printf(",NaN")
  }
  print ""
}
' $filename
```

Listing 6.9 initializes the variable `filename` with the name of the CSV file for this code sample. The next portion of Listing 6.9 is an `awk` script that contains a `while` loop to process the input lines from the CSV file. The variable `maxColCount` is initialized with 0 in the `BEGIN` block, and when this loop has completed, its value will be the maximum number of columns of the lines in the input file.

The next portion of Listing 6.9 is the same as the loop in Listing 6.8, which prints the lines of text and pads them with `NaN`, whenever it's necessary to do so. Launch the code in Listing 6.9 and you will see the following output:

```
10,20,30,NaN,NaN,NaN
10,20,30,40,NaN,NaN
10,20,30,40,50,60
10,20,NaN,NaN,NaN,NaN
10,20,30,40,NaN,NaN
```

TRUNCATING ROWS IN CSV FILES

The previous section showed you how to use the `awk` command line utility to "pad" rows from a CSV file with the string `NaN` so that all records have the same number of columns, whereas this section shows you how to truncate the rows in a CSV file to display only the number of columns that are in the row with the fewest number of columns.

Listing 6.10 displays the content of `variable_columns3.sh` that uses the `awk` utility to display a subset of columns in a CSV file.

LISTING 6.10: *variable_columns3.sh*

```
filename="variable_columns.csv"

cat $filename | awk -F"," '
BEGIN {
  colCount = 0; minColCount = 9999

  ##############################################
  # minColCount = # of fields in the shortest row
  ##############################################

  while(getline line < ARGV[1]) {
    colCount = split(line,data)
    if(minColCount > length(data)) {
      minColCount = length(data)
    }
  }
}
{
  # perform for each input line:
  for(j=1; j<=minColCount; j++) {
     printf("%s,",$j)
  }
  print ""
}
' $filename
```

Listing 6.10 is very similar to Listing 6.9. After initializing the variable `filename` with the name of the CSV file for this code sample, the `awk` script finds the number of columns in the row with the fewest columns from the CSV file.

The variable `minColCount` is initialized with 9999 in the `BEGIN` block, and when this loop has completed, its value will be the minimum number of columns of the lines in the input file.

The next portion of Listing 6.9 is a loop that prints the first `minColCount` columns in each line of the input file. Launch the code in Listing 6.10 and you will see the following output:

```
10,20,
10,20,
10,20,
10,20,
10,20,
```

GENERATING ROWS WITH FIXED COLUMNS WITH THE AWK UTILITY

The code sample in this section contains an `awk` script that processes a space-delimited input string CSV file and generates output in which all rows have the same number of columns (with the possible exception of the final output row). Listing 6.11 displays the content `FixedFieldCount1.sh` that illustrates how to use the `awk` utility to split a string into rows that contain three strings.

LISTING 6.11: FixedFieldCount1.sh

```
echo "=> pairs of letters:"
echo "aa bb cc dd ee ff gg hh"
echo

echo "=> split on multiple lines:"
echo "aa bb cc dd ee ff gg hh"| awk '
BEGIN { colCount = 3 }
{
  for(i=1; i<=NF; i++) {
     printf("%s ", $i)
     if(i % colCount == 0) { print "" }
  }
  print ""
}
'
```

Listing 6.11 displays the contents of a string, and then provides this string as input to the `awk` command. The main body of Listing 6.11 is a loop that iterates from 1 to NF, where NF is the number of fields in the input line, which in this example equals 8. The value of each field is represented by `$i`: `$1` is the first field, `$2` is the second field, and so forth. Note that `$0` is the content of the *entire* input line (which is used in the next code sample).

Next, if the value of `i` (which is the field *position, not* the contents of the field) is a multiple of 3, then the code prints a linefeed. Launch the code in Listing 6.11 and you will see the following output:

```
=> pairs of letters:
aa bb cc dd ee ff gg hh

=> split on multiple lines:
aa bb cc
dd ee ff
gg hh
```

Listing 6.12 displays the content of `employees.txt` and Listing 6.13 displays the content of `FixedFieldCount2.sh` that illustrates how to ensure that all the rows have the same number of columns.

LISTING 6.12: employees.txt

```
jane:jones:SF:
john:smith:LA:
dave:smith:NY:
sara:white:CHI:
>>>none:none:none<<<:
jane:jones:SF:john:
```

```
smith:LA:
dave:smith:NY:sara:white:
CHI:
```

LISTING 6.13: FixedFieldCount2.sh

```
cat employees.txt | awk -F":" '{printf("%s", $0)}' | awk -F':' '
BEGIN { colCount = 3 }
{
  for(i=1; i<=NF; i++) {
    printf("%s#", $i)
    if(i % colCount == 0) { print "" }
  }
}
'
```

Notice that the code in Listing 6.13 is almost identical to the code in Listing 6.11. The code snippet that is shown in bold removes the \n character from its input that consists of the contents of employees.txt. In case you need to be convinced, launch the following code snippet from the command line:

```
cat employees.txt | awk -F":" '{printf("%s", $0)}'
```

The output of the preceding code snippet is shown here:

```
jane:jones:SF:john:smith:LA:dave:smith:NY:sara:white:CHI:>>>none:none:no
ne<<<:jane:jones:SF:john:smith:LA:dave:smith:NY:sara:white:CHI:
```

The reason that the \n has been removed in the preceding output is because of this code snippet:

```
printf("%s", $0)
```

If you want to retain the \n linefeed character after each input line, then replace the preceding code snippet with this snippet:

```
printf("%s\n", $0)
```

We have now reduced the task in Listing 6.9 to the same task as Listing 6.7, which is why we have the same awk-based code block.

Launch the code in Listing 6.9 and you will see the following output:

```
1000,Jane,Edwards,Sales
jane#jones#SF#
john#smith#LA#
dave#smith#NY#
sara#white#CHI#
>>>none#none#none<<<#
jane#jones#SF#
john#smith#LA#
dave#smith#NY#
Sara#white#CHI#
```

CONVERTING PHONE NUMBERS

Listing 6.14 displays the content of `phone_numbers.txt` that contains (mostly fictitious) phone numbers with different formats.

LISTING 6.14: phone_numbers.txt

```
1234567890
234 4560987
234 456 0987
212 555-1212
212-555-1212
(123)5551212
(456)555-1212
(789)555 1212
1-1234567890
1 234 4560987
1-234 456 0987
1 212 555-1212
1-212-555-1212
1 (123)5551212
1-(456)555-1212
1 (789)555 1212
011-1234567890
033 234 4560987
039-234 456 0987
034 212 555-1212
081-212-555-1212
044 (123)5551212
049-(456)555-1212
052 (789)555 1212
```

Listing 6.15 displays the content of `phone_numbers.sh` that illustrates how to remove non-digit characters from the phone numbers in Listing 6.10 so that they have the same format.

LISTING 6.15: phone_numbers.sh

```
FILE="country_codes.csv"

#cat phone_numbers.txt |tr -d '()' | sed -e 's/ //g' -e 's/-//g' | awk -F" " '
cat phone_numbers.txt |sed -e 's/[()]//g' -e 's/ //g' -e 's/-//g'| awk -F" " '
{
   line_len = length($0)

   if(line_len == 10) {
     inter = ""
     area  = substr($0,0,3)
     xchng = substr($0,3,3)
     subsc = substr($0,7,4)
     printf("%s,%s,%s\n",area,xchng,subsc)
   } else if(line_len == 11) {
     inter = substr($0,0,1)
```

```
      area  = substr($0,1,3)
      xchng = substr($0,4,3)
      subsc = substr($0,8,4)
      printf("%s,%s,%s,%s\n",inter, area,xchng,subsc)
    } else if(line_len == 13) {
      inter = substr($0,0,3)
      area  = substr($0,3,3)
      xchng = substr($0,6,3)
      subsc = substr($0,10,4)
      printf("%s,%s,%s,%s\n",inter, area,xchng,subsc)
    } else {
      print "invalid format: ",$0
    }
  }
}
'
```

Listing 6.15 initializes the variable FILE with the name of the CSV file that contains the three-digit international codes for a set of countries. The next code snippet is a pipe-delimited sequence of commands that starts by redirecting the contents of the file phone_numbers.txt to the sed command that removes all left parentheses, right parentheses, hyphens (-), and multiple occurrences of a white space.

The output from the sed command is redirected to an awk script that processes input lines of length 10, 11, and 13 that contain phone numbers that lack an international code, contain a single digit international code, and a three-digit international code, respectively. Any input line that has a different length is considered invalid. Now launch the code in Listing 6.15 and you will see the following output:

```
123,345,7890
234,445,0987
234,445,0987
212,255,1212
212,255,1212
123,355,1212
456,655,1212
789,955,1212
1,112,345,7890
1,123,445,0987
1,123,445,0987
1,121,255,1212
1,121,255,1212
1,112,355,1212
1,145,655,1212
1,178,955,1212
011,112,345,7890
033,323,445,0987
039,923,445,0987
034,421,255,1212
081,121,255,1212
044,412,355,1212
049,945,655,1212
052,278,955,1212
```

CONVERTING NUMERIC DATE FORMATS

This section shows you how to convert date formats to a common format of the form MM-DD-YYYY. Before delving into the code, the following list contains sample formats for the month, day, and year of a date:

- yy: two-digit year   (ex: 22)
- yyyy: four-digit year   (ex: 2022)
- m: one-digit month   (ex: 4)
- mm: two-digit month   (ex: 04)
- mmm: three letters for month (ex: Apr)
- mmmm: month spelled in full   (ex: April)
- d: one-digit day of the month (ex: 2)
- dd: two-digit day of the month (ex: 02)
- ddd: three letter day of week (ex: Sat)
- dddd: day spelled in full   (ex: Saturday)

Listing 6.16 displays the content of dates.txt that contains fictitious dates in various formats, and the strings in bold have invalid formats.

LISTING 6.16: dates.txt

```
03/15/2021
3/15/2021
3/15/21
03/5/2021
3/5/2021
3/5/21
3/5/212
3/5/21Z
```

Listing 6.17 displays the content of dates.sh that shows how to remove non-digit characters from the dates in Listing 6.16 so that they have the same format.

LISTING 6.17: dates.sh

```
cat dates.txt | awk -F"/" '
{
   DATE_FORMAT="valid"
   # step 1: extract the month
   if($0 ~ /^[0-9]{2}/) {
     month = substr($0,1,2)
     #print "normal month: ",month
   } else if($0 ~ /^[0-9]\//) {
     month = "0" substr($0,1,1)
     #print "short month: ",month
   } else {
     DATE_FORMAT="invalid"
   }
```

```
  if(DATE_FORMAT="valid") {
    # step 2: extract the day
    if($0 ~ /^[0-9][0-9]\/[0-9][0-9]/) {
      day = substr($0,4,2)
      #print "normal day: ",day
    } else if ($0 ~ /^[0-9][0-9]\/[0-9]\//) {
      day = "0" substr($0,4,1)
      #print "short day: ",day
    } else {
      DATE_FORMAT="invalid"
    }
  }

  if(DATE_FORMAT="valid") {
    # step 3: extract the year
    if($0 ~ /^[0-9][0-9]\/[0-9][0-9]\/[0-9][0-9][0-9][0-9]$/) {
      year = substr($0,7,4)
      #print "normal year: ",year
    } else if ($0 ~ /^[0-9][0-9]\/[0-9][0-9]\/[0-9][0-9]\/$/) {
      year = "20" substr($0,7,2)
      #print "short year: ",year
    }
  } else {
    DATE_FORMAT="invalid"
  }

  if(DATE_FORMAT="valid") {
    printf("=> $0: %s MM/DD/YYYY: %s-%s-%s\n",$0,month,day,year)
  } else {
    print "invalid format: ",$0
  }
}
'
```

Listing 6.17 contains code that might seem daunting if you are unfamiliar with regular expressions. Let's try to demystify the code, starting with the regular expression [0-9] that represents any single digit. The initial caret symbol in ^[0-9]\/ indicates that a digit must appear in the left-most (i.e., first) position. In addition, the regular expression ^[0-9]\/ indicates that a "/" must follow the single digit. The backslash "\" is required to "escape" the meta character "/." This means that it will be treated as a regular character instead of a metacharacter. For instance, the string 3/ matches the regular expression, but the strings 03/, B3/, and AB/ do not match the regular expression.

Now let's examine the regular expression ^[0-9][0-9]\/, which represents any string that starts with two digits and then a "/" character. Thus, the string 03/ matches the regular expression, but the strings 3/, B3/, and AB/ do not match the regular expression.

Next, the regular expression ^[0-9][0-9]\/[0-9][0-9] represents any string that starts with two digits, followed by a "/" character, and then two more digits. Thus, the string 03/15 matches the regular expression, but the strings 3/5, 03/5, and 3/15 do not match the regular expression.

Finally, the regular expression ^[0-9][0-9]\/[0-9][0-9]\/[0-9][0-9][0-9][0-9]$ matches a string that

- starts with two digits
- is followed by a "/"
- has another two digits
- that are followed by "/"
- with four more digits
- and no additional characters

Listing 6.17 contains regular expressions that match strings containing "short" months, days, and years. Launch the code in Listing 6.17 and you will see the following output:

```
=> $0: 03/15/2021 MM/DD/YYYY: 03-15-2021
=> $0: 3/15/2021 MM/DD/YYYY: 03-15-2021
=> $0: 3/15/21 MM/DD/YYYY: 03-15-2021
=> $0: 03/5/2021 MM/DD/YYYY: 03-05-2021
=> $0: 3/5/2021 MM/DD/YYYY: 03-05-2021
=> $0: 3/5/21 MM/DD/YYYY: 03-05-2021
=> $0: 3/5/212 MM/DD/YYYY: 03-05-2021
=> $0: 3/5/21Z MM/DD/YYYY: 03-05-2021
```

Why are the preceding pair of lines (that are shown in bold) displayed as valid dates, even though the anchor meta character "$" appears in the two regular expressions for extracting the year? Unfortunately, the latter two regular expressions appear *after* the initial regular expressions that extract the day value, and those two regular expressions do *not* check for invalid year formats.

Listing 6.18 displays the content of dates2.sh that detects invalid dates, uses a short-hand notation for multiple digits, and removes extraneous print-related statements.

LISTING 6.18: dates2.sh

```
cat dates.txt | awk -F"/" '
{
   DATE_FORMAT="valid"

   # step 1: check for invalid formats
   if($0 ~ /[A-Za-z]/) {
     print "invalid characters: ",$0
     DATE_FORMAT="invalid"
   } else if($0 ~ /\/[0-9]{3}$/) {
     print "invalid format: ",$0
     DATE_FORMAT="invalid"
   }

   if(DATE_FORMAT="valid") {
     # step 2: extract the month
     if($0 ~ /^[0-9][0-9]/) {
       month = substr($0,1,2)
```

```
    } else if($0 ~ /^[0-9]\//) {
      month = "0" substr($0,1,1)
    } else {
      DATE_FORMAT="invalid"
    }
  }

  if(DATE_FORMAT="valid") {
    # step 3: extract the day
    if($0 ~ /^[0-9]{2}\/[0-9]{2}/) {
      day = substr($0,4,2)
    } else if ($0 ~ /^[0-9]{2}\/[0-9]{2}\//) {
      day = "0" substr($0,4,1)
    } else {
      DATE_FORMAT="invalid"
    }
  }

  if(DATE_FORMAT="valid") {
    # step 4: extract the year
    if($0 ~ /^[0-9]{2}\/[0-9]{2}\/[0-9]{4}$/) {
      year = substr($0,7,4)
    } else if ($0 ~ /^[0-9]{2}\/[0-9]\/[0-9]{2}\/$/) {
      year = "20" substr($0,7,2)
    }
  }

  if(DATE_FORMAT="valid") {
    printf("$0: %10s => %s-%s-%s\n",$0,month,day,year)
  } else {
    print "Date format invalid:",$0
  }
}
'
```

Listing 6.18 is very similar to contents of Listing 6.17 with some differences. The first difference is that Listing 6.18 checks for phone numbers that have alphabetic characters and reports them as having an invalid format. The second difference is the conditional code block that identifies any phone numbers that have three digits in the right-most position.

The third difference is a short-hand way to specify multiple consecutive digits: [0-9]{2} matches any pair of consecutive digits, [0-9]{3} matches any occurrence of three consecutive digits, and so forth. Launch the code in Listing 6.18 and you will see the following output:

```
$0: 03/15/2021 => 03-15-2021
$0:  3/15/2021 => 03-15-2021
$0:     3/15/21 => 03-15-2021
$0: 03/5/2021 => 03-15-2021
$0:  3/5/2021 => 03-15-2021
$0:     3/5/21 => 03-15-2021
invalid format:  3/5/212
$0:     3/5/212 => 03-15-2021
invalid characters:  3/5/21Z
$0:     3/5/21Z => 03-15-2021
```

CONVERTING ALPHABETIC DATE FORMATS

This section shows you how to convert date formats to a common format of the form DD-MON-YYYY. Listing 6.19 displays the content of `dates2.txt` that contains dates in various formats, and the strings in bold have invalid formats.

LISTING 6.19: dates2.txt

```
03/15/2021
04-SEP-2022
04-sep-  2022
04-sep-  22
05-OCT   2022
05-oct 2022
05-oct 22
06 JAN 2022
06 jan 2022
06 jnn 22
```

Listing 6.20 displays the content of `dates3.sh` that illustrates how to remove non-digit characters from the dates in Listing 6.10 so that they have the same format.

LISTING 6.20: dates3.sh

```
cat dates2.txt  | tr -s ' ' |sed -e 's/- /-/g' -e 's/ /-/g' |awk -F"-" '
BEGIN {
    months["JAN"] = "JAN"
    months["FEB"] = "FEB"
    months["MAR"] = "MAR"
    months["APR"] = "APR"
    months["MAY"] = "MAY"
    months["JUN"] = "JUN"
    months["JUL"] = "JUL"
    months["AUG"] = "AUG"
    months["SEP"] = "SEP"
    months["OCT"] = "OCT"
    months["NOV"] = "NOV"
    months["DEC"] = "DEC"
}
{
    #Valid date formats (Oracle):
    #DD-MON-YY:   04-SEP-2022
    #DD-MON-YYYY: 05-OCT-22

    $0 = toupper($0)
    DATE_FORMAT="valid"

    # step 1: extract the day:
    if($0 ~ /^[0-9]\-/) {
```

```
    day = "0" substr($0,1,1)
  } else if($0 ~ /^[0-9][0-9]\-/) {
    day = substr($0,1,2)
  } else {
    DATE_FORMAT="invalid"
  }

  if(DATE_FORMAT="valid") {
    # step 2: extract the month:
    if($0 ~ /^[0-9]{2}\-[A-Z]{3}/) {
      month = substr($0,4,3)
    } else {
      DATE_FORMAT="invalid"
    }
  }

  if(DATE_FORMAT="valid") {
    # step 3: extract the year:
    if($0 ~ /^[0-9]{2}\-[A-Z]{3}\-[0-9]{2}/) {
      year = "20" substr($0,8,2)
    } else if($0 ~ /^[0-9]{2}\-[A-Z]{3}\-[0-9]{4}/) {
      year = substr($0,8,4)
    } else {
      DATE_FORMAT="invalid"
    }
  }

  if(DATE_FORMAT="valid") {
  if(months[month] == month) {
      printf("%12s => %s-%s-%s\n",$0,month,day,year)
  } else {
      printf("Invalid month:   %s-%s-%s\n",month,day,year)
  } else {
    print "Date format invalid:",$0
  }

}
'
```

Listing 6.20 starts with a pipe-delimited sequence of commands that redirects the contents of the file dates2.txt to the tr command that removes multiple consecutive occurrences of white spaces.

Next, the output from the tr command is redirected to the sed command that removes any white spaces that follow the hyphen (-) character, and then replaces any white spaces with a hyphen (-).

The output from the sed command is redirected to an awk script that initializes an array with the three letter abbreviations of the months of the year. This array is referenced later in the code to detect any invalid month formats.

The main portion of the `awk` script is similar to the contents of Listing 6.27 for detecting various date formats to initialize the day, month (as a three-letter value), and year for each input line. Launch the code in Listing 6.20 and you will see the following output:

```
04-SEP-2022 => SEP-04-2020
04-SEP-2022 => SEP-04-2020
   04-SEP-22 => SEP-04-2022
05-OCT-2022 => OCT-05-2020
05-OCT-2022 => OCT-05-2020
   05-OCT-22 => OCT-05-2022
06-JAN-2022 => JAN-06-2020
06-JAN-2022 => JAN-06-2020
Invalid month:  JNN-06-2022
```

WORKING WITH DATE AND TIME DATE FORMATS

Now that you have seen code samples with dates of the form MM:DD:YYYY, this section handles dates of the form YYYY:MM:DD:HH:MM:SS. Although the `awk`-based code sample in this section is much longer than all other code samples in this book, it's based on techniques that you have already seen in previous date-related code samples. If you do not need to delve into the details of this code sample at this time, feel free to skip this section.

Single digit values for all fields (except the year) are considered valid, and handling all the possible combinations becomes quite tedious. However, the code sample in this section shows you a shortcut that involves dynamically modifying the input line so that it's progressively padded as the input string is processed in a left-to-right fashion.

To make sure this is clear, the string `3/15/22 5:5:44` is a valid date, and as the code checks for the validity of the individual date-related fields, the preceding string is successively modified as follows:

```
3/15/22 5:5:44
03/15/22 5:5:44
03/15/2022 5:5:44
03/15/2022 5:5:44
03/15/2022 05:5:44
03/15/2022 05:05:44
```

As you can see, the final row in the preceding list of dates is a "fully padded" date. This approach significantly reduces the number of patterns that need to be checked in order to determine whether or not a date has a valid format.

Listing 6.21 displays the content of `dates-times.txt` that contains dates, and Listing 6.22 shows you the content of `date-times-padded.sh`, which is an `awk`-based shell script that processes the dates in Listing 6.21.

LISTING 6.21: date-times.txt

```
2/30/2020 15:05:44
2/30/2020 15:05:44
3/15/22 15:5:44
```

```
4/29/23 15:5:4
5/16/24 5:05:44
6/17/25 5:5:44
7/18/26 5:5:4
8/19/24 115:05:44
```

Notice that the first and last lines in Listing 6.21 are invalid: the first row contains a value of 30 for February, which is invalid for any year, and the last row contains an invalid value for the hour.

Listing 6.22 displays the content of `date-times-padded.sh` that determines which dates in Listing 6.21 have the format `YYYY:MM:DD:HH:MM:SS`.

LISTING 6.22: date-times-padded.sh

```
cat date-times.txt | awk -F"/" '
function check_leap_year(year) {
   #########################################
   # A year is a leap year if the following:
   # 1) it is a multiple of 4 AND
   # 2) a century must be a multiple of 400
   # => 2000 is a leap year but 1900 is not.
   #########################################

   result = 0 # 0: non-leap year 1: leap year
   if((year % 4) == 0) {
     if((year % 100) == 0) {
       if((year % 400) == 0) {
         return 1 # leap year
       } else {
         return 0 # non-leap year
       }
     } else {
       return 1 # leap year
     }
   } else {
     return 0 # non-leap year
   }
}

BEGIN {
  count = 1
  for(i=0;i<12;i++) {
    months[i] = 31
  }

  # 30 days: april,june,september,november
  months[1]  = 28;
  months[3]  = 30;
  months[5]  = 30;
  months[8]  = 30;
  months[10] = 30;

  #for(i=0;i<12;i++) {
  #  print "months[",i,"]:",months[i]
```

```
   #}
}
{
   ####################################
   # valid month format:
   # [0-9], [1][0-2]
   #
   # valid day format:
   # [0-9], [1][0-9], [3][0-1]
   #
   # valid year format:
   # [0-9]{2}, [2][0-9][0-9][0-9]
   #
   # Additional comments:
   # 1) 30 versus 31 days in a month
   # 2) check february:  28 vs 29 days
   ####################################

   # sample format:
   # MM/DD/YYYY HH:MM:SS
   print "=> #" count " PROCESSING:",$0

   VALID_DATE="true"
   split($0,day_time," ")
   date_part = day_time[1]
   time_part = day_time[2]

   # step 1: extract the month
   if(date_part ~ /^[0-9]\//) {
     month = "0" substr(date_part,1,1)
     #print "short month: ",month
     # insert a "0" in the date part:
     date_part = "0" substr(date_part,1,1) substr(date_part,2)
     #print "*** new date_part:",date_part
   } else if(date_part ~ /^[0-9]{2}/) {
     month = substr(date_part,1,2)
     #print "normal month: ",month
   } else {
     print "Cannot find month"
     VALID_DATE="false"
   }

   if(VALID_DATE == "true") {
     # step 2: extract the day: #03/15/2021 15:05:44
     #print "checking for day:",date_part
     if(date_part ~ /^[0-9]{2}\/[0-9]{2}/) {
       day = substr(date_part,4,2)
       #print "1normal day: ",day
     } else if (date_part ~ /^[0-9]{2}\/[0-9]/) {
       day = "0" substr(date_part,4,1)
       #print "1short day: ",day
       date_part = substr(date_part,1,3) "0" substr(date_part,4)
       #print "*** 2new date_part:",date_part
     } else if (date_part ~ /^[0-9]{1}\/[0-9]{2}/) {
       day = substr(date_part,3,2)
```

```
      #print "2normal day: ",day
    } else if (date_part ~ /^[0-9]{1}\/[0-9]/) {
      day = "0" substr(date_part,2,1)
      #print "2short day: ",day
    } else {
      print "Cannot find day"
      VALID_DATE="false"
    }
  }

  if(VALID_DATE == "true") {
    # step 3: extract the year: #03/15/2021 15:05:44
    #print "date part:",date_part   # 03/15/2021
    #print "time part:",time_part   # 15:05:44

    if(date_part ~ /^[0-9]{2}\/[0-9]{2}\/[0-9]{4}/) {
      year = substr(date_part,7,4)
      #print "normal year: ",year
    } else if (date_part ~ /^[0-9]{2}\/[0-9]{2}\/[0-9]{2}/) {
      year = "20" substr(date_part,7,2)
      #print "1short year: ",year
      date_part = substr(date_part,1,6) "20" substr(date_part,7)
      #print "*** 3new date_part:",date_part
    } else {
      print "Cannot find year"
      VALID_DATE="false"
    }
  }

  if(VALID_DATE == "true") {
    #print "step 4 time_part:",time_part
    # step 4: extract the hours: #15:05:44
    if(time_part ~ /^[0-9]{2}:/) {
      hours = substr(time_part,1,2)
      #print "normal hours: ",hours
    } else if(time_part ~ /^[0-9]:/) {
      hours = "0" substr(time_part,1,1)
      #print "short hours: ",hours
      time_part = "0" substr(time_part,1)
      #print "*** 3new time_part:",time_part
    } else {
      print "no matching hours"
      VALID_DATE = "false"
    }
  }

  if(VALID_DATE == "true") {
    # step 5: extract the minutes: #15:5:44
    if(time_part ~ /^[0-9]{2}:[0-9]{2}/) {
      minutes = substr(time_part,4,2)
      #print "normal minutes: ",minutes
    } else if (time_part ~ /^[0-9]{2}:[0-9]:/) {
      minutes = "0" substr(time_part,4,1)
      #print "short minutes: ",minutes
      time_part = substr(time_part,1,3) "0" substr(time_part,4)
```

```
      #print "*** 4new time_part:",time_part
    } else {
      print "no matching minutes"
      VALID_DATE = "false"
    }
  }

  if(VALID_DATE == "true") {
    # step 6: extract the seconds: #15:05:44
    if(time_part ~ /^[0-9]{2}:[0-9]{2}:[0-9]{2}/) {
      seconds = substr(time_part,7,2)
      #print "normal seconds: ",seconds
    } else if(time_part ~ /^[0-9]{2}:[0-9]{2}:[0-9]{1}/) {
      seconds = "0" substr($0,7,1)
      #print "short seconds: ",seconds
      time_part = substr(time_part,1,6) "0" substr(time_part,7)
      #print "*** 5new time_part:",time_part
    } else {
      print "no matching seconds"
      VALID_DATE = "false"
    }
  }

  if(VALID_DATE == "true") {
    result = check_leap_year(year)
    if(result == 1) {
      #print "found leap year:",year
      # is day <= 29?
      if(day <= 29) {
        print "=> VALID DAY/TIME FORMAT: ",$0
      } else {
        print "*** Leap year day out of bounds:",$0
      }
    } else {
      #print "found non-leap year:",year
      # is day <= 28?
      if(day <= 28) {
        print "=> VALID DAY/TIME FORMAT: ",$0
      } else {
        print "*** Non-leap year day out of bounds:",$0
      }
    }
  } else {
    print "invalid day/time format: ",$0
  }

  print "----------------\n"
  count += 1
}
'
```

Launch the code in Listing 6.22 and you will see the following output:

```
=> #1 PROCESSING: 2/30/2020 15:05:44
*** Leap year day out of bounds: 2/30/2020 15:05:44
----------------
```

```
=> #2 PROCESSING: 3/15/22 15:5:44
=> VALID DAY/TIME FORMAT:  3/15/22 15:5:44
----------------


=> #3 PROCESSING: 4/29/23 15:5:4
*** Non-leap year day out of bounds: 4/29/23 15:5:4
----------------


=> #4 PROCESSING: 5/16/24 5:05:44
=> VALID DAY/TIME FORMAT:  5/16/24 5:05:44
----------------


=> #5 PROCESSING: 6/17/25 5:5:44
=> VALID DAY/TIME FORMAT:  6/17/25 5:5:44
----------------


=> #6 PROCESSING: 7/18/26 5:5:4
=> VALID DAY/TIME FORMAT:  7/18/26 5:5:4
----------------


=> #7 PROCESSING: 8/19/24 115:05:44
no matching hours
invalid day/time format:  8/19/24 115:05:44
----------------
```

The companion files contain `date-times-padded2.sh`, which enhances `date-times-padded.sh` to provide addition information, as shown here:

```
INVALID DATES:
8/19/24 115:05:44
2/30/2020 15:05:44
4/29/23 15:5:4
----------------
VALID DATES:
6/17/25 5:5:44
5/16/24 5:05:44
7/18/26 5:5:4
3/15/22 15:5:44


YEARS IN VALID DATES:
2022
2024
2025
2026
MONTHS IN VALID DATES:
03
05
06
07
DAYS IN VALID DATES:
15
16
17
18
```

WORKING WITH CODES, COUNTRIES, AND CITIES

This section shows you how to use the awk utility to manage CSV files that contain information about countries, cities, and telephone codes. The international telephone codes are available online:

https://www.internationalcitizens.com/international-calling-codes/

Listing 6.21 displays the content of country_codes.csv that contains the international prefix for several countries. For simplicity, the three-digit prefix has been left-padded with 0, because some countries have a two-digit prefix and other countries have a three-digit prefix.

LISTING 6.21: country_codes.csv

```
001,usa
033,france
034,spain
039,italy
044,uk
049,germany
052,mexico
081,japan
```

Listing 6.22 displays the content of add_country_codes.sh that illustrates how to increment the three-digit international prefix for a set of countries. Note that you won't need this code sample beyond this section. It's included here to show you how easily you can manipulate the numeric values in a CSV file with the awk utility. If need be, you can easily adapt this code to work with other CSV files.

LISTING 6.22: add_country_codes.sh

```
FILE="country_codes.csv"

echo "=> display code and country:"
awk -F"," '
BEGIN { code = 10000; incr = 10000 }
{
   printf("%s,%s,%d\n", $1, $2, code)
   code += incr
}
' < $FILE
echo "------------------"
echo

echo "=> increment country code:"
awk -F"," '
BEGIN { code = 1000; incr = 1000 }
{
   printf("%d,%s\n", $1 + code, $2)
   code += incr
}
' < $FILE
```

Listing 6.22 initializes the variable `FILE` with the name of the CSV file that contains country codes and abbreviations for several countries. Next, an `awk` script contains a BEGIN section with a loop that adds 10000 to each country code. For example, the following two code snippets display the "before" and "after" contains of an input line:

```
001,usa,10000
1001,usa
```

Launch the code in Listing 6.22 and you will see the following output:

```
=> display code and country:
001,usa,10000
033,france,20000
034,spain,30000
039,italy,40000
044,uk,50000
049,germany,60000
052,mexico,70000
081,japan,80000
-----------------

=> increment country code:
1001,usa
2033,france
3034,spain
4039,italy
5044,uk
6049,germany
7052,mexico
8081,japan
```

Listing 6.23 displays the content of `countries_cities.csv` in which each row consists of a country and a list of cities in that country.

LISTING 6.23: countries_cities.csv

```
italy,firenze,milano,roma,venezia
france,antibe,nice,paris,st_jeannet
germany,berlin,frankfurt
spain,barcelona,madrid
england,liverpool,london,manchester
mexico,mexico_city,tijuana
```

Listing 6.24 displays the content of `split_countries_cities.sh` that illustrates how to display a list of cities that belong to each country in `countries_cities.csv`.

LISTING 6.24: split_countries_codes.sh

```
FILE="countries_cities.csv"

awk -F"," '
{
```

```
    printf("=> CITIES in %s:\n",$1)
    for(i=2; i<=NF; i++) {
        printf("%s\n", $i)
    }
}
' < $FILE
```

Listing 6.24 initializes the variable `FILE` with the name of the CSV file that contains country codes and abbreviations for several countries. Next, an `awk` script contains a loop that adds displays the abbreviation of each city that is listed in the CSV file `countries_cities.csv`. Launch the code in Listing 6.24 and you will see the following output:

```
=> display code and country:
=> CITIES in italy:
firenze
milano
roma
venezia
=> CITIES in france:
antibe
nice
paris
st_jeannet
=> CITIES in germany:
berlin
frankfurt
=> CITIES in spain:
barcelona
madrid
=> CITIES in england:
liverpool
london
manchester
=> CITIES in mexico:
mexico_city
tijuana
```

Listing 6.25 displays the content of `countries_cities2.csv` in which each row consists of a country and a list of cities in that country.

LISTING 6.25: countries_cities2.csv

```
italy,firenze,milano,roma,venezia
france,antibe,nice,paris,st_jeannet
germany,berlin,frankfurt
spain,barcelona,madrid
england,liverpool,london,manchester
mexico,mexico_city,tijuana
usa,chicago,illinois,denver,colorado,seattle,washington,vancouver,washington
can,vancouver,bc,edmonton,calgary,hamilton,ontario
```

Listing 6.26 displays the content of `split_countries_cities2.sh` that illustrates how to display a list of cities that belong to each country in `countries_cities2.csv`.

LISTING 6.26: split_countries_codes2.sh

```
FILE="countries_cities2.csv"

awk -F"," '
BEGIN { incr = 1000 }
{
   if($1 !~ /#/) {
     printf("=> CITIES in %s:\n",$1)
     for(i=2; i<=NF; i++) {
         printf("%s\n", $i)
     }
     print("-----------\n")
   } else {
     #printf("=> CITIES in %s:\n",$1)
     printf("=> CITIES in %s:\n",substr($1,2))
     for(i=2; i<=NF; i+=2) {
         printf("%s,%s\n", $i,$(i+1))
     }
     print("-----------\n")
   }
}
' < $FILE
```

Listing 6.26 initializes the variable FILE with the name of the CSV file that contains country codes and abbreviations for several countries. Note that this CSV file differs from a similar CSV file with countries and country codes. Specifically, this CSV file contains rows that have either city/province pairs (Canada) or city/state pairs (USA).

Next, an awk script contains a BEGIN section with conditional logic and two blocks of code. The first block of code is for rows that start with a # symbol, which indicates that the row contains either city/province pairs (Canada) or city/state pairs (USA). An example of such a row is here:

```
#usa,chicago,illinois,denver,colorado,seattle,washington,vancouver,
washington
```

Note that the use of a # symbol is simply a convenient way to differentiate these rows from the rows in the second code block. One alternative is to specify one CSV file for the rows that are processed in this code block and a different CSV file for the rows that are processed in the second code block.

As you can see in Listing 6.25, the first field $1 of such rows contains the abbreviation of a country, and subsequent pairs contain the location of a city in the associated country. For example, $2 and $3 consist of a city/province pair or a city/state pair, and this is similar for $4 and $5, for $6 and $7, and so forth.

The second block of code processes rows whose countries do not have a province or state designation for each city. An example of such a row is here:

```
italy,firenze,milano,roma,venezia
```

The code in this block processes each column sequentially and displays all of them on separate output lines. Launch the code in Listing 6.26 and you will see the following output:

```
=> CITIES in italy:
firenze
milano
roma
venezia
------------

=> CITIES in france:
antibe
nice
paris
st_jeannet
------------

=> CITIES in germany:
berlin
frankfurt
------------

=> CITIES in spain:
barcelona
madrid
------------

=> CITIES in england:
liverpool
london
manchester
------------

=> CITIES in mexico:
mexico_city
tijuana
------------

=> CITIES in usa:
chicago,illinois
denver,colorado
seattle,washington
vancouver,washington
------------

=> CITIES in canada:
vancouver,bc
edmonton,calgary
hamilton,ontario
------------
```

At this point, let's summarize the files that we have examined thus far and what we have accomplished:

- `country_codes.csv`
- `add_country_codes.sh`
- `countries_cities.csv`
- `split_country_cities.sh`
- `countries_cities2.csv`
- `split_country_cities2.sh`

We have a CSV file whose rows are country code + country name combinations. We have CSV files with countries and cities that belong to those countries, one of which contains a list of cities for each country. The other CSV file contains three types of rows:

- country and list of cities
- country and a list of city/province pairs
- country and a list of city/state pairs

DATA CLEANING ON A KAGGLE DATASET

If you want to see data cleaning performed on a "real" dataset, you're in luck because this section contains an `awk` script that performs data cleaning on the following dataset:

https://www.kaggle.com/fehmifratpolat/marketing-report

The `awk` script follows most of the data cleaning steps that are performed in R that are discussed in this article:

https://towardsdatascience.com/cleaning-and-preparing-marketing-data-in-r-prior-to-machine-learning-or-analysis-ec1a12079f1

Listing 6.27 displays the content of `convert_marketing.sh` that shows you how to perform various data cleaning steps, as indicated in the comments in the code.

LISTING 6.27: convert_marketing.sh

```
# Kaggle dataset: https://www.kaggle.com/fehmifratpolat/marketing-report

# step 1: extract the 1st, 3rd, 4th, and 7th fields:
cat mark1.csv |awk -F";" '{print $1 ":" $3 ":" $4 ":" $7}' >mark2.csv

# step 2: replace Not tracked" with "direct":
# peri-Co-od;salesChannel;platformcode;marketingInvestment
# date;channel;platformcode;;spend
cat mark2.csv |awk -F":" '
{
   $3 = tolower($3)

   if($3 ~ /Not tracked/) {
      $3 = "direct"
```

```
    } else if($3 ~ /unpaid/) {
       $3 = "organic"
    } else if($3 ~ /Silverpop/) {
       $3 = "email"
    }

  if($4 ~ /,/) {
       split($4,arr1,",")
       $4 = arr1[1] "." arr1[2]
    }
    print $1 ":" $2 ":" $3 ":" $4
}
' >mark3.csv

# step 3: replace YYYYDDMM with YYYY-MM-YY format:
cat mark3.csv |awk -F":" '
{
  year  = substr($1,1,4)
  day   = substr($1,5,2)
  month = substr($1,7,2)

  printf("%s-%s-%s:%s:%s:%s\n",year,month,day,$2,$3,$4)
}
' >mark4.csv

# step 4: calculate subtotals based on $1+$2+$3:
cat mark4.csv |awk -F":" '
{
  fields=$1FS$2FS$3;subtotals[fields] += $4
}
# step 5: display values of subtotals:
END{
   total = 0
   for (i in subtotals) {
      printf("Subtotal for %44s => %-8d\n", i, subtotals[i])
      total += subtotals[i]
   }
   printf("TOTAL REVENUE: => %44d\n",total)
}
' >mark5.csv
```

Although it's not necessary to split the code into five awk scripts, it's easier to follow the code, and besides, you will also have access to the intermediate files so you can inspect their contents.

Listing 6.27 starts with Step 1 that extracts the 1st, 3rd, 4th, and 7th fields from the CSV file mark1.csv and redirects the output to the CSV file mark2.csv, as shown here:

```
cat mark1.csv |awk -F";" '{print $1 ":" $3 ":" $4 ":" $7}' >mark2.csv
```

Step 2 in Listing 6.27 replaces occurrences of the string "Not tracked" with "direct," the string "unpaid" with "organic," and the string "Silverpop" with the string email in $3. In addition, the "," that appears in $4 is replaced by a "." after which a new string is printed that contains the modifications to $3 and $4. Each output line is redirected to the CSV file mark3.csv.

Step 3 in Listing 6.27 replaces `YYYYDDMM` dates with a `YYYY-MM-YY` format, as shown here, after which the output is redirected to the CSV file `mark4.csv`:

```
year  = substr($1,1,4)
day   = substr($1,5,2)
month = substr($1,7,2)
printf("%s-%s-%s:%s:%s:%s\n",year,month,day,$2,$3,$4)
```

Step 4 in Listing 6.27 is probably the most interesting code snippet in this code sample. The concatenation of the first three fields, separated by the default field separator, form an index for the array subtotals. Each time this combination appears in `mark4.csv`, the corresponding entry in the subtotals array is incremented with the value in `$4`, as shown here:

```
fields=$1FS$2FS$3;subtotals[fields] += $4
```

After the body of this `awk` script has completed execution, an `END` block (which is labeled Step 5) displays the values in the `subtotals` array, along with the grand total, as shown here:

```
total = 0
for (i in subtotals) {
  printf("Subtotal for %44s => %-8d\n", i, subtotals[i])
  total += subtotals[i]
}
```

After the preceding code has completed execution, the output is redirected to the CSV file `mark5.csv`.

Launch the code in Listing 6.27 that generates a set of intermediate CSV files and a final CSV file named `mark5.csv`. If you want to see the first five lines from each of the intermediate files `mark1.csv, ...`, and `mark5.csv` that are generated in Listing 6.27, execute a shell script that contains the following code:

```
for f in 'ls mark*csv'
do
  echo "file: $f"
  head -5 $f
done
```

The output of the preceding code block is shown here:

```
file: mark1.csv
periodCode;reportGranularity;salesChannel;platformCode;channelCode;tagCo
des;marketingInvestment;impressions;clicks;visits;conversions;deliveries
;currencyCode;appliedAttributionModel;periodStartDate
20200102;Daily;online;Not tracked;notset;;0;0;0;0;16;14;CZK;lastTou
ch;2020-01-02T00:00:00.0000000
20200103;Daily;online;Not tracked;notset;;0;0;0;0;13;13;CZK;lastTou
ch;2020-01-03T00:00:00.0000000
20200104;Daily;online;Not tracked;notset;;0;0;0;0;6;6;CZK;lastTou
ch;2020-01-04T00:00:00.0000000
20200105;Daily;online;Not tracked;notset;;0;0;0;0;1;1;CZK;lastTou
ch;2020-01-05T00:00:00.0000000
```

```
file: mark2.csv
periodCode:salesChannel:platformCode:marketingInvestment
20200102:online:Not tracked:0
20200103:online:Not tracked:0
20200104:online:Not tracked:0
20200105:online:Not tracked:0

file: mark3.csv
periodCode:salesChannel:platformcode:marketingInvestment
20200102:online:not tracked:0
20200103:online:not tracked:0
20200104:online:not tracked:0
20200105:online:not tracked:0

file: mark4.csv
peri-Co-od:salesChannel:platformcode:marketingInvestment
2020-02-01:online:not tracked:0
2020-03-01:online:not tracked:0
2020-04-01:online:not tracked:0
2020-05-01:online:not tracked:0

file: mark5.csv
Subtotal for                    2020-12-02:online:organic => 0
Subtotal for                    2020-31-01:online:not tracked => 0
Subtotal for 2020-10-01:online:facebookbusinessadsmanager => 130
Subtotal for                    2020-06-01:online:sklik => 914
Subtotal for                    2020-24-03:online:rtbhouse => 0
TOTAL REVENUE: =>                                      1227857
```

SUMMARY

This chapter started with a brief description of data cleaning, followed by examples of replacing NULL values with numeric values, replacing multiple values with a single value, and converting strings to date values.

Next, you saw how to use the sed command line utility to replace multiple delimiters in a CSV file with a single delimiter. You also learned how to use the awk command line utility to restructure a CSV file to create a file whose rows have the same number of fields.

In addition, you saw how to perform various tasks in SQL, and then how to perform these tasks in a Pandas data frame.

## CHAPTER 7

DATA WRANGLING

This chapter is primarily about data wrangling, along with code samples that leverage technical concepts that you learned in previous chapters in this book.

The first part of this chapter briefly discusses the term "data wrangling," which means different things to different people, so it's worthwhile establishing some context for this term. Although the terminology regarding data wrangling is specific to this book and not necessarily standard terminology, the distinction can be helpful when you are involved in discussions that necessitate finer grained terminology.

The second part of this chapter contains examples of data cleaning with CSV files that contain fields that are split on two separate lines. There are several such variants that you will see, whose solutions involve Pandas or the `csv` command line utility. In this section, you will learn how to convert an ill-formatted CSV file (containing a quoted field that is split on two lines) into a proper CSV file. However, this code sample is marked as "optional" because the solution involves a rather lengthy `awk`-based shell script.

The third part of this chapter introduces a project that involves creating a CSV file that contains an event schedule for musical bands and their future concert performances. This project emulates a scenario that consists of multiple files in various formats, such as XML documents, text data, CSV files, and data in a MySQL database table. The goal is to transform the files and combine them to create a single CSV file.

WHAT IS DATA WRANGLING?

Data wrangling means different things to different people. Some online articles suggest that data wrangling involves a set of steps, and other articles suggest that data wrangling involves converting datasets from one format to a different format. The following Web page describes data wrangling as a six-step process:

https://en.wikipedia.org/wiki/Data_wrangling

In addition to the steps outlined in the preceding link, data wrangling can also involve the following tasks (performed in the code samples in Chapter 7):

• transforming datasets from one format into another format (convert)
• creating new datasets from subsets of columns in existing datasets (extract)

As you can see, the preceding steps differentiate between converting data to a different format versus extracting data from multiple datasets to create new datasets. The conversion process can be considered a data cleaning task if only the first step is performed (i.e., there is no extraction step).

In the previous chapter, you learned about data cleaning, along with a collection of Python-based code samples and Unix shell scripts to perform data cleaning tasks. By contrast, data wrangling involves multiple steps that can include transforming one or more files. The following subsection provides a more detailed distinction between data cleaning and data transformation.

Data Transformation: What Does This Mean?

In general, data cleaning involves a single data source (not necessarily in a CSV format), with some type of modification to the content of the data source (e.g., filling in missing values and changing date formats) without creating a second data source.

For example, suppose that the data source is a MySQL table called `employees` that contains employee-related information. After data cleaning tasks on the `employees` table are completed, the result will still be named the `employees` table. In database terminology, data cleaning is somewhat analogous to executing a SQL statement that involves a `SELECT` on a single table.

However, if two CSV files contain different date formats and you need to create a single CSV file that is based on the date columns, then there will be some type of conversion process that could be one of the following:

• convert the first date format to the second date format
• convert the second date format to the first date format
• convert both date formats to a third date format

In the case of financial data, you are likely to also encounter different currencies, which involves a conversion rate between a pair of currencies. Since currency conversion rates fluctuate, you need to decide the exchange rate to use for the data, which can be

• the exchange rate during the date that the CSV files were generated
• the current currency exchange rate
• some other mechanism

In addition, you might also need to convert the CSV files to XML documents, where the latter might be required to conform to an XML Schema, and perhaps also conform to XBRL, which is a requirement for business reporting purposes:

https://en.wikipedia.org/wiki/XBRL

As mentioned earlier, data transformation can involve two or more data sources to create yet another data source whose attributes are in the required format. Here are four scenarios of data transformation with just two data sources A and B, where data from A and from B are combined to create data source C, where A, B, and C can have different file formats:

- all attributes in A and all attributes in B
- all attributes in A and all attributes in B
- a subset of the attributes in A and all attributes in B
- a subset of the attributes in A and a subset of attributes in B

In database terminology, data transformation is somewhat analogous to executing a SQL statement that involves a SELECT on two or more database tables with a JOIN clause. Such SQL statements typically involve a subset of columns from each database table, which would correspond to selecting a subset of the features in the data sources.

There is also the scenario involving the concatenation of two or more data sources. If all data sources have the same attributes, then their concatenation is straightforward, but you might need to check for duplicate values. For example, if you want to load multiple CSV files into a database table that does not allow duplicates, then one solution involves concatenating the CSV files from the command line and then excluding the duplicate rows.

The preceding concatenation task can be easily performed. Suppose that you have the following set of CSV files (all of which have the same attributes) emp1.csv, emp2.csv... emp100. csv. Concatenate these files and exclude duplicate rows by creating a shell script called concat.sh with the following contents:

```
for f in `ls emp*csv`
do
  cat $f
done
```

Now make sure that the shell script is executable:

```
chmod +x concat.sh
```

Launch the shell script concat.sh that redirects its output to the sort command and then redirects its output to the uniq command, with the final output redirected to the CSV file all_emps.csv:

```
./concat.sh | sort | uniq > all_emps.csv
```

At this point you *might* be able to load the CSV file all_emps.csv into a MySQL table, provided that that table is not a "child" table of another table, with a CONSTRAINT condition on the rows of the child table. For example, a customers table typically has a one-to-many relationship with a purchase_orders table, which means that you cannot insert rows in the latter table if they do not have an associated customer row in the customers table.

When in doubt, try loading the CSV file into an appropriate table. If you encounter any errors, make the necessary corrections until the loading process is successful.

This concludes the discussion regarding the first section for data wrangling, and the next several sections contain additional data cleaning code samples, after which you will see data wrangling code samples.

CSV FILES WITH MULTI-ROW RECORDS

This section shows you how to work with CSV files that contain records that are split across two lines.

Listing 7.1 displays the content of `multi_line.csv` that will be reformatted so that each record occupies a single line: one solution involves Pandas and another solution involves the CSV library.

LISTING 7.1: multi_line.csv

```
id,fname,lname
1,donna,rhymes?
2,dave,"jones$"
3,john,van jones.#
4,stevie,"ray
vaughn#"
```

Pandas Solution (1)

Listing 7.2 displays the content of `pandas_multi_line.py` that reformats the contents of `multi_line.csv` so that each record occupies a single row.

LISTING 7.2: pandas_multi_line.py

```
import pandas as pd

filename = 'multi_line.csv'
data = pd.read_csv(filename)
print("data:")
print(data)
```

Listing 7.2 starts with an `import` statement and then initializes the variable `filename` with the name of the CSV file for this code sample. The next snippet populates the Pandas data frame `data` and then displays its contents. Launch the code in Listing 7.2 and you will see the following output:

```
data:
   id   fname        lname
0   1   donna       rhymes?
1   2    dave        jones$
2   3    john   van jones.#
3   4  stevie  ray\nvaughn#
4   5   ralph      emerson#
```

As you can see, the preceding output contains multiple metacharacters. If need be, you can create a one-line `sed` command to replace the metacharacters with one metacharacter of your choice. Check Chapter 6 for a similar task that involves the `sed` command.

Notice that the output from Listing 7.2 is not a true CSV file. However, we can generate a CSV file, as shown in the next section.

Pandas Solution (2)

Listing 7.3 displays the content of `pandas_multi_line2.py` that reformats the contents of `multi_line.csv` so that each record occupies a single row and saves the data as a CSV file.

LISTING 7.3: pandas_multi_line2.py

```
import sys

import pandas as pd

filename = 'multi_line.csv'
data = pd.read_csv(filename)

# remove the "\n" character from the data:
columns=["id","fname","lname"]
data2 = data[columns].replace('\\n',' ', regex=True)

# save to a CSV file:
data2.to_csv("multi_line2.csv",index=False)
```

Listing 7.3 starts with an `import` statement and then initializes the variable `filename` with the name of the CSV file for this code sample. The next snippet populates the Pandas data frame `data` and then initializes the Pandas data frame `data2` with the contents of data without the linefeed characters. The final code snippet saves `data2` to the CSV file `multi_line2.csv`. Launch the code in Listing 7.3 and you will see a new file `multi_line2.csv`, whose contents are displayed here:

```
id,fname,lname
1,donna,rhymes?
2,dave,jones$
3,john,van jones.#
4,stevie,ray vaughn#
5,ralph,emerson#
```

As you can see, the preceding output contains multiple meta characters that can be replaced with the same column delimiter using the same technique in the `sed`-based `delimiters1.sh` shell script.

CSV Solution

In case you have not already done so, install the CSV Python library with this command:

```
pip3 install csv
```

Listing 7.4 displays the content of `csv_multi_line.py` that reformats the contents of `multi_line.csv` so that each record occupies a single row.

LISTING 7.4: csv_multi_line.py

```
import csv

filename = 'multi_line.csv'

with open(filename, newline='', encoding='utf-8') as f:
  data = csv.reader(f, delimiter=',', quotechar='"',
                    quoting=csv.QUOTE_MINIMAL)
  for line in data:
    print("line:",line)
```

Listing 7.4 starts with an `import` statement and then initializes the variable `filename` with the name of the CSV file for this code sample. The next snippet opens the CSV file and initializes the Pandas data frame `data` with its contents. The final code block contains a loop that iterates through the rows of the data frame and prints their contents. Launch the code in Listing 7.4 and you will see the following output:

```
line: ['id', 'fname', 'lname']
line: ['1', 'donna', 'rhymes?']
line: ['2', 'dave', 'jones$']
line: ['3', 'john', 'van jones.#']
line: ['4', 'stevie', 'ray\nvaughn#']
line: ['5', 'ralph', 'emerson#']
```

CSV FILES, MULTI-ROW RECORDS, AND THE AWK COMMAND

This section shows you how to work with CSV files that contain records that are defined in multiple lines and records are separated by a blank line.

Listing 7.5 displays the content of `multi_line.csv` that will be reformatted so the each record occupies a single line: one solution involves Pandas and another solution involves the CSV library.

LISTING 7.5: multi_line_records.csv

```
nancy jones
marketing dept
san francisco

dave smith
sales dept
chicago


steve anderson
marketing dept
seattle
```

Listing 7.6 displays the content of `multi_line_records.sh` that reformats the contents of `multi_line.csv` so that each record occupies a single row.

LISTING 7.6: multi_line_records.sh

```
# Records are separated by blank lines.
input_file="multi_line_records.csv"

awk '
BEGIN { RS = "" ; FS = "\n" }
{
  printf("%s,%s,%s\n", $1, $2, $3)
}
' < $input_file
```

Listing 7.6 starts by initializing the variable `input_file` with the name of the CSV file with this code sample. The next portion of Listing 7.6 contains an `awk` script that prints the contents of each input line as a comma-separated line, which can be redirected to a CSV file. Launch the code in Listing 7.6 and you will the following output:

```
nancy jones,marketing dept,san francisco
dave smith,sales dept,chicago
steve anderson,marketing dept,seattle
```

QUOTED FIELDS SPLIT ON TWO LINES (OPTIONAL)

This section is marked "optional" primarily because it involves a custom CSV file that you might not encounter in your daily routine. Specifically, the CSV file contains multiple rows with a single field as well as a quoted field that is split on two lines. Moreover, the shell script in this section is an `awk`-based solution that is also the most complex `awk` example in this book. If you are new to the `awk` command, please read at least a portion of the appendix that contains `awk`-based code samples, which will facilitate your understanding of the code in this section.

The `awk` utility is a very powerful utility for processing text files through intricate and precise conditional logic. In particular, you can easily extract substrings of fields, perform compound conditional logic that involves adjacent fields, and also remove linefeed characters from the rows in text files.

By now you probably realize that the `awk` utility is extremely useful for data cleaning as well as wrangling that involves transforming CSV files (or general text files) with irregular structures into formats that are then easily handled through Pandas. Consider the ease with which `awk` calculated subtotals in the final example in Chapter 6: this was accomplished with a *single* line of code. For some people, `awk` is a "go to" command line utility that performs preprocessing steps on practically any type of text file or CSV file.

Portions of Listing 7.7 are quite complex and even non-intuitive, which tends to occur when you need a character-by-character analysis as well as a context dependency that involves maintaining and checking "state" information about previous characters as well as the current character, both of which occur in this code sample.

Listing 7.7 displays the content of `multi_line3.csv` and Listing 7.8 displays the content of `split_quotes.sh` that reformats the contents of `multi_line3.csv` so that each record contains exactly three fields.

LISTING 7.7: multi_line3.csv

```
id,fname,lname
1,
donna,
rhymes?
2,dave,"jones$"
3,john,van jones.#
4,stevie,"ray
vaughn#"
5,ralph,emerson#
```

LISTING 7.8: split_quotes.sh

```
# Records are separated by blank lines
# PART 1: create a single string
interfile1="temp_single_line1.csv"
interfile2="temp_single_line2.csv"
interfile3="temp_single_line3.csv"
csv_file="multi_line3.csv"

cat $csv_file | awk -F"," '
BEGIN { count = 1; colCount = 3 }
{
  printf("%s", $0)
  if( $0 !~ /,$/ ) {
     printf(",")
  } else {
    if( $0 !~ /^[0-9]/ ) {
       if( count % colCount == 0) {
         printf(",")
       }
       count += 1
    }
  }
}' > $interfile1

# id,fname,lname,1,donna,rhymes?,2,dave,"jones$",3,john,van jones.#,4,st
evie,"ray,vaughn#",5,ralph,emerson#,
# PART 2: replace patterns like "abc,def" with "abcZdef"
cat $interfile1 | awk -F"," '
{
  for(i=1; i<=NF; i++) {
    if( $i ~ /^"/ && $(i+1) ~ /"$/ ) {
       printf("%sZ",$i)
    } else {
       printf("%s,",$i)
    }
  }
}
' > $interfile2
```

```
# PART 3: ensure that each line contains three fields
cat $interfile2 | awk -F',' '
BEGIN { start_quote = 0; end_quote = 0; quote = 0; colCount = 3 }
{
  for(i=1; i<=NF; i++) {
     if($i ~ /^"/ && $i ~ /"$/ ) {
       printf("%s",$i)
     }
     else if($i !~ /^"/ && $i !~ /"$/ ) {
       printf("%s,", $i)
     }
     else {
        if($i ~ /^"/ ) {
           printf("%s,",$i)
           quote = 1
           start_quote = 1
        } else {
           if($i ~ /"$/ ) {
              printf("%s",$i)
              quote = 1
              end_quote = 1
           }
        }
     }

     if( quote == 0) {
        if(i % colCount == 0) {
          print ""
        }
     } else {
        if(start_quote == 1 && end_quote == 1) {
           quote = 0
           start_quote = 0
           end_quote = 0
        }
     }
  }
}
' > $interfile3

cat $interfile3 | sed -e 's/Z/,/' -e '/^,,/d' -e 's/,$//'
```

Listing 7.8 initializes three variables with the names of three CSV files of the form `temp_single_linex.csv`, where x is replaced with 1, 2, and 3, as well as initializing the variable `csv_file` with the CSV file `multi_line3.csv`.

Next, Listing 7.8 contains ("PART 1") an `awk` script with a `BEGIN` block that prints each input line, and then performs the following conditional logic. If the input line does *not* terminate with a ",", then a "," is printed. Otherwise, if the input line does *not* start with a digit and the value of count is a multiple of 3, then a "," is printed, as shown here:

```
if( $0 !~ /^[0-9]/ ) {
  if( count % colCount == 0) {
    printf(",")
  }
  count += 1
}
```

As you can see, the preceding code block is reminiscent of the logic in the shell script `delim-iter1.sh` in Chapter 6.

The next portion of Listing 7.8 ("PART 2") is another awk script whose purpose is to replace a nested "," with the letter z. The choice of the letter z is arbitrary, and you can replace it with another character or string that does not appear in the CSV file.

The preceding logic detects a nested "," by setting the variables `start_quote` and `end_quote` to the value 1 whenever a field contains a start quote and end quote, respectively. The code for making the preceding determination involves checking the contents of the current field with the contents of the *next* field, as shown here:

```
if( $i ~ /^"/ && $(i+1) ~ /"$/ ) {
```

As you can see, the preceding code snippet checks if field i *starts* with a quote (") and also if field (i+1) *ends* with a quote ("), in which case the letter z is printed.

The next portion of Listing 7.8 ("PART 3") is an awk script whose purpose is to print output lines that contain three fields. Fields that contain no quotes or fields that contain balanced quotes are printed as-is. Other fields are checked for start quotes and end quotes. Whenever the loop variable i is a multiple of 3, a linefeed is printed to start the next output line on a separate line. Additional conditional logic determines when to reset the variables `start_quote` and `end_quote` to 0.

The last portion of Listing 7.8 replaces the character z with a comma (","), removes initial occurrences of "," in each row, and removes any trailing "," characters, as shown here:

```
cat $interfile3 | sed -e 's/Z/,/' -e '/^,,/d' -e 's/,$//'
```

Launch the code in Listing 7.8 and you will the following output:

```
id,fname,lname
1,donna,rhymes?
2,dave,"jones$"
3,john,van jones.#
4,stevie,"ray,vaughn#"
5,ralph,emerson#
```

OVERVIEW OF THE EVENTS PROJECT

As you saw in the introduction for this chapter, this section contains a project to generate a CSV file that contains the details of the concerts (including the dates and locations) pertaining to various music bands that are scheduled to perform in different countries.

Although this project might appear to be straightforward, there are some tedious details, such as which programming language (Unix shell programming, Python, Java, or perhaps other languages) to adopt for transforming each data source into a CSV file.

Why This Project?

Before delving into the details, you might be pondering this legitimate question: why create a project that involves "excessive" complexity? The intent is to simulate a scenario in which you will be required to work with text files that are in different formats, which might be file formats that are unfamiliar to you, and perhaps even file formats that you wish could be avoided.

From another perspective, this project is *intended* to take you out of your comfort zone, for the purpose of enhancing your technical skills. As such, the nature of the project is of secondary importance. If you prefer, you could easily replace music bands with soccer clubs from countries throughout the world or chess tournaments involving chess players from various countries.

Returning to the project: the transformation from the source files to CSV files is performed via a mixture of shell scripts, Python scripts, and Java code. As you learn how to convert each source file into a CSV-based file using different technologies, you can assess their suitability for future tasks. For example, the Python code and the shell script code that solve the same task have approximately the same length, but you need to take into account the readability and maintainability of the code.

By way of comparison, the Python code for converting an XML document to a CSV file is much shorter than the corresponding Java code, which is one of several factors involved in deciding which technology to use for converting the various files to a common CSV format.

Indeed, there are multiple solutions that are possible for this project, and the "best" implementation is the one that works best for your requirements. Perhaps the central idea of this project is to illustrate a key aspect of data wrangling: how to transform data sources to create a new data source that is derived from the initial set of data sources.

For your convenience, this book contains an appendix that discusses the `awk` command line utility, which contains short code samples that illustrate how to leverage the functionality of `awk`.

Project Tasks

This project requires several CSV files to maintain information such as countries, cities, venues, and dates for concert events. Some of the tasks are

- Step 1: Populate CSV file with countries and international codes
- Step 2: Populate CSV file with list of cities per country
- Step 3: Generate city codes based on country codes
- Step 4: Generate SQL file to populate `city_code` table in MySQL
- Step 5: Convert band-related information to a CSV file
- Step 6: Convert band-related information to a CSV file
- Step 7: Generate COE (calendar of events) as a CSV file

The code samples that perform each of the preceding tasks are listed here:

- Step 1: manual process
- Step 2: manual process
- Step 3: `construct_city_codes.py` (Python)
- Step 4: `city_codes_sql.sh` (awk script)
- Step 5: `BandsToCSV.java` (Java program)
- Step 6: `generate_coe.py` (Python)
- Step 7: `generate_project.sh` (shell script)

In some cases, there is more than one code sample to perform a given task. For example, Step 5 can also be performed with the Python file `bands_to_csv.py`.

Sample data or code fragments are generated in each of the preceding steps, as well as the steps that are performed manually:

- `001,usa`
- `039,100,firenze`
- `france,antibe,nice,paris,st_jeannet`
- `INSERT INTO city_codes VALUES ( 039,100,firenze );`
- `100,The Data Wranglers,Dave Pallai`

Just to be sure it's clear: most of the steps in this project must be performed in the order that they are shown in the preceding list. The exception is Step 4, which can be at any point after Step 3.

Generate Country Codes

Among the various ways to generate a unique id for a country, a simple way to do so involves identifying each country by its international prefix for telephone numbers, which will be unique. In this project, the `country_codes.csv` is created manually by performing an online lookup for links that contain this information. For example, Listing 7.9 displays the contents of `country_codes.csv` with the country names and their corresponding international codes for this project.

LISTING 7.9: country_codes.csv

```
001,usa
033,france
034,spain
039,italy
044,uk
049,germany
052,mexico
081,japan
```

Prepare a List of Cities in Countries

Listing 7.10 displays the contents of `countries_cities.csv` with country names and a list of cities that belong to those countries.

LISTING 7.10: countries_cities.csv

```
italy,firenze,milano,roma,venezia
france,antibe,nice,paris,st_jeannet
germany,berlin,frankfurt
spain,barcelona,madrid
uk,liverpool,london,manchester
mexico,mexico_city,tijuana
```

GENERATING CITY CODES FROM COUNTRY CODES: AWK

Listing 7.11 displays the content of `construct_city_codes.sh` that illustrates how to generate a unique code for every city that belongs to a given country.

LISTING 7.11: construct_city_codes.sh

```
FILE1="country_codes.csv"
FILE2="countries_cities.csv"
rm -f city_codes.csv

awk -F"," '
BEGIN {
   FS=","; OUT_FILE="city_codes.csv";
   prev_name = ""; city_name = "";
   start_code=100; curr_code = 100;
   city_code = ""; incr_code = 100

   printf("=> BEGIN-PROCESSING: %s\n",ARGV[1])
   while(getline line < ARGV[1]){
     #format: country-code,country-name
     split(line,data)
     code = data[1]
     country = data[2]
     #printf("code: %s country: %s\n",code,country)
     country_code[country] = code
     code_country[code] = country
   }
   close(ARGV[1])
}
#########################################
# read each line from countries_cities.csv
# split each line into a list of cities
# generate a city code that contains:
# country_code, curr_code, city_name
# sample line in countries_cities.csv:
# italy,firenze,milano,roma,venezia
#########################################
{
   #sample: italy,firenze,milano,roma,venezia
   split($0,data)
   code    = data[1]
   country = data[2]

   #printf(" code = %s country = %s\n", code, country)
   #printf("=> CHECK CODE FOR: x %s x\n", country_code[code])

   if(country_code[country] == "") {
      printf("=> MAIN-CITIES in %s:\n",$0)
      curr_code = start_code
      for(i=2; i<=NF; i++) {
         city_code = country_code[$1] "_" curr_code "_" $i
         printf("=> constructed city_code:%s\n",city_code)
         print city_code >> OUT_FILE
         curr_code += incr_code
      }

      if(curr_name == "") {
        curr_name = $1
```

```
          } else {
            if(curr_name != $1) {
              # processing a different country:
              prev_name = curr_name
              curr_name = $1
              curr_code = start_code
            }
          }

          if(city_code == 0) city_code = start_code
        } else {
          #printf("=> SKIPPING INVALID LINE: %s\n",$0)
        }
      }
    }
    ' $FILE1 $FILE2
```

Listing 7.11 initializes the variables `IN_FILE1` and `IN_FILE2` with the names of two CSV files `country_codes.csv` and `countries_cities.csv`, followed by an `awk` script that initializes several string variables and numeric variables that are explained later.

Next, Listing 7.11 contains an `awk` script with a `BEGIN` block that contains a loop that reads the contents of the file `country_codes.csv` whose rows contain a country name and the associated three-digit code for the country. These pairs of values are used to populate the dictionaries `country_code` and `code_country`. The keys for the `country_code` dictionary are the names of the countries, and the values are the three-code numeric codes, whereas the keys and values for the `code_country` dictionary are reversed.

The next block of code is the main execution block of the `awk` script, which involves conditional logic and a large block of code. The reason for the conditional logic is that `awk` will process both input files that are specified at the end of the script regardless of whether they are processed in the `BEGIN` block:

```
    }
    ' $IN_FILE1 $IN_FILE2
```

Due to the nature of `awk`, Listing 7.11 processes `IN_FILE1` *twice*: once in the `BEGIN` block and again in the main execution block (is this a quirk of `awk` or just a normal feature?).

Hence, the code in the main block must *skip* the rows in `IN_FILE1` and process *only* the rows in `IN_FILE2`. The way to skip `IN_FILE1` is very simple: the rows in `IN_FILE1` are of the form `country_code,country_abbreviation` (such as `001,usa`), and the code `001` does not have an entry in the `country_code` dictionary. Consequently, only the rows in the CSV file `IN_FILE2` satisfy this condition:

```
if(country_code[country] == "") {
```

The code inside this `if` statement contains a loop that constructs a city code for each city that is listed in each row of `IN_FILE2`. The key idea is that a city code for each city is constructed by concatenating its country code, a generated number that's based on the value of `curr_code`, and the name of the city itself. For example, the following line specifies Italy (whose country code is 039) as well as four cities:

```
italy,firenze,milano,roma,venezia
```

Consequently, the city code for each of the cities in Italy in the preceding row are as follows:

```
039_100_firenze
039_200_milano
039_300_roma
039_400_venezia
```

Launch the code in Listing 7.11 and you will see the following output:

```
=> BEGIN-PROCESSING: country_codes.csv
=> MAIN-CITIES in italy,firenze,milano,roma,venezia:
=> constructed city_code:039_100_firenze
=> constructed city_code:039_200_milano
=> constructed city_code:039_300_roma
=> constructed city_code:039_400_venezia
=> MAIN-CITIES in france,antibe,nice,paris,st_jeannet:
=> constructed city_code:033_100_antibe
=> constructed city_code:033_200_nice
=> constructed city_code:033_300_paris
=> constructed city_code:033_400_st_jeannet
=> MAIN-CITIES in germany,berlin,frankfurt:
=> constructed city_code:049_100_berlin
=> constructed city_code:049_200_frankfurt
=> MAIN-CITIES in spain,barcelona,madrid:
=> constructed city_code:034_100_barcelona
=> constructed city_code:034_200_madrid
=> MAIN-CITIES in uk,liverpool,london,manchester:
=> constructed city_code:044_100_liverpool
=> constructed city_code:044_200_london
=> constructed city_code:044_300_manchester
=> MAIN-CITIES in mexico,mexico_city,tijuana:
=> constructed city_code:052_100_mexico_city
=> constructed city_code:052_200_tijuana
```

Listing 7.12 displays the content of city_codes.csv that is generated from the code in Listing 7.11.

LISTING 7.12: city_codes.csv

```
039_100_firenze
039_200_milano
039_300_roma
039_400_venezia
033_100_antibe
033_200_nice
033_300_paris
033_400_st_jeannet
049_100_berlin
049_200_frankfurt
034_100_barcelona
034_200_madrid
044_100_liverpool
044_200_london
044_300_manchester
052_100_mexico_city
052_200_tijuana
```

GENERATING CITY CODES FROM COUNTRY CODES: PYTHON

Listing 7.13 displays the content of `construct_city_codes2.py` that illustrates how to generate a unique code for every city that belongs to a given country.

LISTING 7.13: construct_city_codes2.py

```python
import csv

FILE1="country_codes.csv"
FILE2="countries_cities.csv"

OUTFILE1="python_city_codes.txt"
OUTFILE2="python_city_codes.csv"
OUTFILE3="python_city_codes.sql"

prev_name   = ""
city_name   = ""
curr_name   = ""
start_code = 100
curr_code  = 100
city_code1 = ""
city_code2 = ""
incr_code  = 100
code_country = {}
country_code = {}

# STEP 1: read file with code and country values:
print("=> BEGIN-PROCESSING:",FILE1)
with open(FILE1, mode ='r')as file:
  # reading the CSV file
  csvFile = csv.reader(file)

  # displaying the contents of the CSV file
  for line in csvFile:
    code    = line[0]
    country = line[1]
    country_code[country] = code
    code_country[code] = country

# STEP 2: read file countries and cities:
#########################################
# read each line from countries_cities.csv
# split each line into a list of cities
# generate a city code that contains:
# country_code, curr_code, city_name
# sample line in countries_cities.csv:
# italy,firenze,milano,roma,venezia
#########################################

print("=> BEGIN-PROCESSING:",FILE2)
#sample: italy,firenze,milano,roma,venezia

with open(FILE2, mode ='r')as file:
```

```
# reading the CSV file
csvFile = csv.reader(file)

# open two output files:
# create txt_writer1:
txt_writer1 = open(OUTFILE1,'w')

# create csv_writer2:
csv_writer2 = open(OUTFILE2,'w')


# create sql_writer3:
sql_writer3 = open(OUTFILE3,'w')

for line in csvFile:
  country = line[0]
  code = country_code[country]
  #print("full line:",line)
  #print(" code = ",code," country = ",country)

  #print("=> MAIN-CITIES in:",line)
  curr_code = start_code
  column_count = len(line)
  for i in range(2,column_count):
    city_code1 = str(code) + "_" +
                 str(curr_code) + "_" + str(line[i])

    city_code2 = str(code) + "," +
                 str(curr_code) + "," + str(line[i])
    print("=> constructed city_code1:",city_code1)

    # generate SQL statement from city code:
    sql_stmt = 'INSERT INTO city_codes VALUES ('
    sql_stmt += str(code)+','+str(curr_code)+',"'+line[i]+'");\n'

    # print SQL statement to SQL file:
    sql_writer3.write(sql_stmt)

    # write city code to CSV file:
    txt_writer1.write(city_code1+"\n")
    #curr_code += incr_code

    # write city code to TXT file:
    csv_writer2.write(city_code2+"\n")
    curr_code += incr_code

  if(curr_name == None):
    curr_name = line[1]
  else:
    if(curr_name != line[1]):
      # processing a different country:
      prev_name = curr_name
      curr_name = line[1]
      curr_code = start_code
```

```
    if(city_code1 == ""): city_code1 = start_code
    if(city_code2 == ""): city_code2 = start_code

# STEP 3: close the city_code file:
#city_code_file.close()
```

Listing 7.13 contains the Python-based counterpart to Listing 7.11 that contains an awk-based shell script for generating city codes. Since you are probably less familiar with shell programming than Python, Listing 7.11 contains a detailed explanation of the code, whereas a detailed explanation is omitted for the Python code. Since the flow of logic is identical, the main difference is the language-specific syntax, which you can compare in a line-by-line fashion. If you launch the code in Listing 7.13 you will see essentially the same output as Listing 7.12.

There is one significant difference between Listing 7.13 and Listing 7.12. The code snippets shown in bold in Listing 7.13 generate SQL statements for inserting a row into the city_codes table, which is not created in this listing (but you could add that code if you want to do so). Each SQL statement is appended to the file python_city_codes.sql, a portion of which is as follows:

```
INSERT INTO city_codes VALUES (039,100,"milano");
INSERT INTO city_codes VALUES (039,200,"roma");
INSERT INTO city_codes VALUES (039,300,"venezia");
INSERT INTO city_codes VALUES (033,100,"nice");
INSERT INTO city_codes VALUES (033,200,"paris");
```

Now that you have seen two solutions for generating city codes, you can use your preferred solution as a guide to help you navigate through the other solution.

GENERATING SQL STATEMENTS FOR THE CITY_CODES TABLE

Listing 7.14 displays the content of city_codes_sql.sh that creates the file city_codes.sql, which contains SQL statements for creating the table city_codes with values from the CSV file city_codes.csv.

LISTING 7.14: city_codes_sql.sh

```
OUTFILE="city_codes.sql"
rm -f OUTFILE

echo "USE mytools;" > $OUTFILE
echo "DROP TABLE IF EXISTS city_code;" >> $OUTFILE
echo "CREATE TABLE city_codes (city_code CHAR(30));" >> $OUTFILE

for line in 'cat city_codes.csv'
do
  echo "INSERT INTO city_codes VALUES ( $line );"        >> $OUTFILE
done
```

Listing 7.15 displays the content of city_codes.sql that is generated by the shell script city_codes_sql.sh.

LISTING 7.15: city_codes.sql

```
OUTFILE="city_codes.sql"
USE mytools;
DROP TABLE IF EXISTS city_code;

CREATE TABLE city_codes (city_code CHAR(30));

INSERT INTO city_codes VALUES ( 039_100_firenze );
INSERT INTO city_codes VALUES ( 039_200_milano );
INSERT INTO city_codes VALUES ( 039_300_roma );
INSERT INTO city_codes VALUES ( 039_400_venezia );
INSERT INTO city_codes VALUES ( 033_100_antibe );
INSERT INTO city_codes VALUES ( 033_200_nice );
INSERT INTO city_codes VALUES ( 033_300_paris );
INSERT INTO city_codes VALUES ( 033_400_st_jeannet );
INSERT INTO city_codes VALUES ( 049_100_berlin );
INSERT INTO city_codes VALUES ( 049_200_frankfurt );
INSERT INTO city_codes VALUES ( 034_100_barcelona );
INSERT INTO city_codes VALUES ( 034_200_madrid );
INSERT INTO city_codes VALUES ( 044_100_liverpool );
INSERT INTO city_codes VALUES ( 044_200_london );
INSERT INTO city_codes VALUES ( 044_300_manchester );
INSERT INTO city_codes VALUES ( 052_100_mexico_city );
INSERT INTO city_codes VALUES ( 052_200_tijuana );
```

GENERATING A CSV FILE FOR BAND MEMBERS (JAVA)

Listing 7.16 displays the content of `bands.xml` and Listing 7.17 displays the content of `BandsToCSV.java` that illustrates how to convert the XML file to a CSV file.

LISTING 7.16: bands.xml

```
<bands>
  <band>
    <band_id>
      100
    </band_id>
    <band_name>
      The Data Wranglers
    </band_name>
    <band_member>
      Dave Pallai
    </band_member>
    <band_member>
      Jennifer Blaney
    </band_member>
  </band>
  <band>
    <band_id>
      200
    </band_id>
```

```
    <band_name>
      The Data Cleaners
    </band_name>
    <band_member>
      Raymond Reddington
    </band_member>
    <band_member>
      Scary Joe
    </band_member>
    <band_member>
      The Smoother
    </band_member>
  </band>
</bands>
```

LISTING 7.17: BandsToCSV.java

```java
import csv
import org.w3c.dom.Document;
import org.w3c.dom.Element;
import org.w3c.dom.Node;
import org.w3c.dom.NodeList;
import org.xml.sax.SAXException;
import javax.xml.parsers.DocumentBuilder;
import javax.xml.parsers.DocumentBuilderFactory;
import javax.xml.parsers.ParserConfigurationException;
import java.io.File;
import java.io.FileWriter;
import java.io.IOException;
import java.io.InputStream;

public class BandsToCSV
{
    private static final String FILENAME = "bands.xml";

    public static void main(String[] args) {
        String filename = "bandmembers.csv";
        File outfile = null;
        FileWriter csvWriter = null;

        // 1) create a file object:
        outfile = new File(filename);

        // 2) create a FileWriter object:
        try {
          csvWriter = new FileWriter("bandmembers.csv");
        } catch (IOException e) {
          System.out.println("An error occurred:");
          e.printStackTrace();
        }

        // 3) process the XML file:
        DocumentBuilderFactory dbf =
                        DocumentBuilderFactory.newInstance();
```

```
try {
   DocumentBuilder db = dbf.newDocumentBuilder();
   Document doc = db.parse(new File(FILENAME));
   doc.getDocumentElement().normalize();
   System.out.println("ROOT: " +
                   doc.getDocumentElement().getNodeName());


   NodeList bandList = doc.getElementsByTagName("band");


   for (int idx = 0; idx < bandList.getLength(); idx++) {
      Node node = bandList.item(idx);
      if (node.getNodeType() == Node.ELEMENT_NODE) {
         Element element = (Element) node;

         // 4) the id of the band:
         String band_id = element.getElementsByTagName("band_id")
                                 .item(0).getTextContent();
         band_id = band_id.replaceAll("\\s", "");
         band_id = band_id.replaceAll("\\n", "");
         System.out.println("band_id = "+band_id);

         // 5) the name of the band:
         String band_name =
                  element.getElementsByTagName("band_name")
                        .item(0).getTextContent();

         band_name = band_name.trim();
         band_name = band_name.replaceAll("\\n", "");
         System.out.println("band_name = "+band_name);

         // 6) the band members:
         NodeList memberList =
                  element.getElementsByTagName("band_member");

         for (int idx2=0; idx2<memberList.getLength(); idx2++)
         {
            Node memberNode = memberList.item(idx2);
            if (memberNode.getNodeType() == Node.ELEMENT_NODE)
            {
               Element element2 = (Element) memberNode;
               System.out.println("Current Element: " +
                  memberNode.getNodeName());

               String band_member =
                  memberList.item(idx2).getTextContent();

               //band_member = band_member.replaceAll("\\s", "");
               band_member = band_member.trim();
               band_member = band_member.replaceAll("\\n", "");
               System.out.println("band_member = "+band_member);

               // 7) write a string to the CSV file:
               csvWriter.write(band_id+","+
```

```
                                                band_name+", "+
                                                band_member+"\n");
                        }
                    }
                }
            }
          csvWriter.close();
        } catch (ParserConfigurationException | SAXException | IOException e) {
          e.printStackTrace();
        }
    }
}
```

Listing 7.17 starts with multiple `import` statements, and then defines the Java class `BandsToCSV` that contains a `main()` method that is divided into six sections. The first section creates the file object `outfile` and the second section creates the `FileWriter` object `csvWriter`.

The third section is the longest section and also contains the fourth and fifth sections. The first portion of the third section contains a `try/catch` block in which a `Document` object `doc` is constructed, which is the root node of the XML document that contains information about the music bands.

Next, the variable `bandList` is initialized, which represents a list of nodes, and each node in the list is information about one band. The next portion of section 3 is a `for` list that iterates through the items in the variable `bandList`. If each item is of `ELEMENT_NODE`, then section 4 is executed, which involves extracting the value of the `band_id` from the current node.

At this point section 5 is executed, which extracts the value of the `band_name` in the current node, followed by section 6, which consists of a `for` loop that extracts all the other band-related information from the current node. Note that the loop in section 6 contains conditional logic: if the current element is of type `ELEMENT_NODE`, the contents of the variable `band_member` are trimmed to remove white spaces.

We have now reached section 7, which is the final section in Listing 7.17, and the location of the following code snippet that writes band-related information in CSV format:

```
csvWriter.write(band_id+", "+band_name+", "+band_member+"\n");
```

Launch the code in Listing 7.17 and you will see the following output:

```
ROOT: bands
band_id = 100
band_name = The Data Wranglers
Current Element: band_member
band_member = Dave Pallai
Current Element: band_member
band_member = Jennifer Jones
Current Element: band_member
band_member = Raymond Reddington
band_id = 200
band_name = The Data Cleaners
Current Element: band_member
band_member = Scary Joe
Current Element: band_member
band_member = The Smoother
```

Listing 7.18 displays the content of the CSV file `bandmembers.csv` that is generated by the Java code in Listing 7.17.

LISTING 7.18: bandmembers.csv

```
100,The Data Wranglers,Dave Pallai
100,The Data Wranglers,Jennifer Blaney
100,The Data Wranglers,Raymond Reddington
200,The Data Cleaners,Scary Joe
200,The Data Cleaners,The Smoother
```

GENERATING A CSV FILE FOR BAND MEMBERS (PYTHON)

Listing 7.19 displays the content of `BandsToCSV.java` that illustrates how to generate a text file as well as a CSV file from the XML document `bandmembers.csv`.

LISTING 7.19: bands_to_csv.py

```python
from xml.etree import cElementTree as ET

INFILE1="bands.xml"
OUTFILE1="python_bandmembers.txt"
OUTFILE2="python_bandmembers.csv"

# create txt_writer1:
txt_writer1 = open(OUTFILE1,'w')

# create csv_writer2:
csv_writer2 = open(OUTFILE2,'w')

band_id      = ""
band_name    = ""
band_member  = ""

xml_data = ET.parse(INFILE1).getroot()
for band in xml_data.iter('band'):
  for child in band:
    #print("child: ",child)
    print("name: ",child.tag)
    name = child.tag

    if(name == "band_id"):
      band_id = child.text
      band_id = band_id.strip()
      print("band_id =      ", band_id)
    elif(name == "band_name"):
      band_name = child.text
      band_name = band_name.strip()
      print("band_name =    ", band_name)
    elif(name == "band_member"):
      band_member = child.text
```

```
    band_member = band_member.strip()
    print("band_member = ", band_member)


    #the_member = child.text
    #the_member = the_member.strip()
    #print("the_member = ",the_member)

  if(band_id != "" and band_name != "" and band_member != ""):
    line1 = str(band_id) + "_" + band_name + "_" + band_member
    line2 = str(band_id) + "," + band_name + "," + band_member
    print("=> constructed line1:",line1)
    print("=> constructed line2:",line2)

    # write line to CSV file:
    txt_writer1.write(line1+"\n")

    # write line to TXT file:
    csv_writer2.write(line2+"\n")

    #band_id      = ""
    #band_name    = ""
    band_member  = ""
```

Listing 7.19 starts by initializing some variables for existing files and variables for output files, followed by initializing the variable `xml_data` as the root node of the `bands.xml` file that contains band-related information, as shown here:

```
xml_data = ET.parse(INFILE1).getroot()
```

The next portion of Listing 7.19 is a nested loop that iterates through the band elements, and for each band there is another loop that iterates through the elements of the current band. Next, conditional logic checks for the presence of any `band_id`, `band_name`, and `band_member` nodes, and initializes the values of corresponding variables.

The final `if` statement checks if the three variables are populated with values, and if so, constructs a CSV-based output row that written to the CSV file; similarly, another text-based output row is constructed and written to the associated text file. Launch the code in Listing 7.19 and you will see the following output:

```
name:  band_id
band_id =       100
name:  band_name
band_name =     The Data Wranglers
name:  band_member
band_member =  Dave Pallai
=> constructed line1: 100_The Data Wranglers_Dave Pallai
=> constructed line2: 100,The Data Wranglers,Dave Pallai
name:  band_member
band_member =  Jennifer Blaney
=> constructed line1: 100_The Data Wranglers_Jennifer Blaney
=> constructed line2: 100,The Data Wranglers,Jennifer Blaney
name:  band_id
band_id =       200
```

```
name:    band_name
band_name =      The Data Cleaners
name:    band_member
band_member =    Raymond Reddington
=> constructed line1: 200_The Data Cleaners_Raymond Reddington
=> constructed line2: 200,The Data Cleaners,Raymond Reddington
name:    band_member
band_member =    Scary Joe
=> constructed line1: 200_The Data Cleaners_Scary Joe
=> constructed line2: 200,The Data Cleaners,Scary Joe
name:    band_member
band_member =    The Smoother
=> constructed line1: 200_The Data Cleaners_The Smoother
=> constructed line2: 200,The Data Cleaners,The Smoother
```

Also check the directory that contains Listing 7.19 and you will see two new files:

```
python_bandmembers.txt
python_bandmembers.csv
```

GENERATING A CALENDAR OF EVENTS (COE)

Listing 7.20 displays the content of the CSV file `concert_dates.csv` that contains a short calendar of events: additional relevant details are stored in other CSV files that are created in this project.

LISTING 7.20: concert_dates.csv

```
100,039,vicenza,01/05/2022
100,039,vicenza,01/05/2022,50
100,033,paris,01/15/2022,80
100,044,london,02/02/2022,70
100,049,berlin,02/09/2022,75
100,081,tokyo,02/19/2022,100
200,039,vicenza,01/08/2022,50
200,033,paris,01/18/2022,70
200,044,london,02/05/2022,60
200,049,berlin,02/13/2022,80
200,081,tokyo,02/27/2022,100
```

Each row in Listing 7.20 contains details that have the following format:

```
band_code,country_code,city,date,price
```

The target CSV file `concert_coe.csv` will enhance the contents of `concert_dates.csv` so that each row will contain information with the following format:

```
band_code,band_name,country_code,country_name,city,date,price
```

Notice that the date format is dd/mm/yyyy and the price column is in USD (but not necessarily realistic ticket prices). The only new columns that we need to provide are the band_name and the country_name columns.

Listing 7.21 displays the content of `generate_coe.py` that show how to generate the CSV file `concert_coe.csv` by enhancing the CSV file `concert_dates.csv` with the two additional columns.

LISTING 7.21: generate_coe.py

```python
import pandas as pd
import numpy as np

# 1) read the input file concert_dates.csv
# header line: band_code,country_code,city,date,price
# sample row:   100,039,vicenza,01/05/2022,50
concert_dates_file="concert_dates.csv"

# 2) read python_bandmembers.csv (band names and members)
# sample row:100_The Data Wranglers_Dave Pallai
band_members_file="python_bandmembers.csv"

# 3) read country_codes.csv (country and code)
# sample row: 039,italy
cc_codes_file="country_codes.csv"

# 4) create the output file calendar_coe.csv:
# header line: band_code,band_name,country_code,country_
name,city,date,price
# sample row:  The Data Wranglers,italy,vicenza,01/05/2022,50
outfile1="calendar_coe.csv"

# 5) populate three data frames:
concert1_df = pd.read_csv(concert_dates_file)
band2_df = pd.read_csv(band_members_file)
cc3_df  = pd.read_csv(cc_codes_file)

# 6) add column labels:
#existing row: 100,039,vicenza,01/05/2022,50
concert1_df.columns = ['band_code','country_code','City','Concert
Date','Tickets (USD)']
band2_df.columns = ['band_code','band_name','band_members']
cc3_df.columns   = ['country_code','country_name']

# 7) extract array of unique band codes and band names:
bands_unique_codes = band2_df.band_code.unique()
bands_unique_names = band2_df.band_name.unique()

# 8) create dictionary from unique band codes and band names:
bands_codes_names_dict = {}
for code, name in zip(bands_unique_codes,bands_unique_names):
  bands_codes_names_dict[code] = name
```

```
# 9) insert a column for "Band Name":
concert1_df['Band Name'] = concert1_df['band_code'].map(bands_codes_
names_dict)

# 10) create dictionary from unique country codes and names:
country_code_to_name_dict = {}
for index, row in cc3_df.iterrows():
  country_code   = row['country_code']
  country_name   = row['country_name']
  country_code_to_name_dict[country_code] = country_name


# 11) insert a column for country names:
concert1_df['Country'] = concert1_df['country_code'].map(country_code_
to_name_dict)


# 12) remove band codes and country codes:
del concert1_df['band_code']
del concert1_df['country_code']


print("*** Concert Details ***")
print(concert1_df)
print()


# 13) save concert details to CSV file:
concert1_df.to_csv(outfile1, index=False)
```

The first three sections of Listing 7.21 specify the names of the three input files `concert_dates,csv`, `python_bandmembers.csv`, and `country_codes.csv` that we need to generate the full calendar for the concerts.

The next portion specifies `calendar-coe.csv` as the name of the output file, along with the header and sample rows in this file.

The next portion of Listing 7.21 populates three data frames with the data from the files listed in the first portion of this code sample. The next three sections add column names to the data frames, which not be necessary if the input files had a header line.

The next portion of Listing 7.21 extracts the unique band codes and their corresponding band names to create a Python dictionary with code/name pairs, which we will use later in this code sample.

In a similar fashion, the next portion of Listing 7.21 extracts the unique country codes and their corresponding names in order to create a Python dictionary with `country_code/country_name` pairs, which we will also use later in this code sample.

The next code block inserts a column into `concert1_df` with the name of the band that corresponds to the band code, for each row in `concert1_df`. Another code block inserts a column into `concert1_df` with the name of the country that corresponds to the country code, for each row in `concert1_df`.

The next pair of `del` statements drops the `band_code` and `country_code` columns from the `concert1_df` data frame (an optional step).

Finally, the contents the data frame `concert1_df` are displayed and then the contents of the data frame are saved as a CSV file. Launch the code in Listing 7.21 and you will see the following output:

```
*** Concert Details ***
         City Concert Date  Tickets (USD)           Band Name  Country
0       paris   01/15/2022             80  The Data Wranglers   france
1      london   02/02/2022             70  The Data Wranglers       uk
2      berlin   02/09/2022             75  The Data Wranglers  germany
3       tokyo   02/19/2022            100  The Data Wranglers    japan
4     vicenza   01/08/2022             50   The Data Cleaners    italy
5       paris   01/18/2022             70   The Data Cleaners   france
6      london   02/05/2022             60   The Data Cleaners       uk
7      berlin   02/13/2022             80   The Data Cleaners  germany
8       tokyo   02/27/2022            100   The Data Cleaners    japan
```

PROJECT AUTOMATION SCRIPT

Listing 7.22 displays the content of `generate_project.sh` that automates the project creation steps that are discussed earlier in this chapter.

LISTING 7.22: *generate_project.sh*

```
echo "Assigning code to countries..."
#=> manual process

echo "Assigning code to cities..."
python3 construct_city_codes.py
#=> generates city_codes.csv

echo "Generate SQL for city codes..."
./city_codes_sql.sh
#=> generates city_codes.sql

echo "Converting personnel (XLSX) to CSV..."
python3 save_xlsx_to_csv.py
#=> generates personnel.csv

echo "Converting bands_list (XML) to CSV..."
# via Java:
java BandsToCSV
# via Python:
#python3 bands_to_csv.py
#=> generates bandmembers.csv

echo "Generating CSV calendar of events (COE)..."
python3 generate_coe.py
#=> generates complete calendar

#echo "Generating SQL script for COE..."
#exercise
```

```
#echo "Inserting COE into MySQL..."
#exercise
```

Listing 7.22 contains various executable files that were discussed earlier in this chapter, and they are invoked sequentially to automate the execution of the required tasks in the correct sequence. Launch the code in Listing 7.22 and you will see the following output:

```
Assigning code to countries...
Assigning code to cities...
=> BEGIN-PROCESSING: country_codes.csv
=> BEGIN-PROCESSING: countries_cities.csv
=> constructed city_code1: 039_100_milano
=> constructed city_code1: 039_200_roma
=> constructed city_code1: 039_300_venezia
=> constructed city_code1: 033_100_nice
=> constructed city_code1: 033_200_paris
=> constructed city_code1: 033_300_st_jeannet
=> constructed city_code1: 049_100_frankfurt
=> constructed city_code1: 034_100_madrid
=> constructed city_code1: 044_100_london
=> constructed city_code1: 044_200_manchester
=> constructed city_code1: 052_100_tijuana
Generate SQL for city codes...
Contents of df1:
   Unnamed: 0 fname  lname                        Role gender  country
0           0  john  smith            VP Marketing      m      usa
1           1  jane  smith                VP Sales      f   france
2           2  jack  jones       Event Coordinator      m   france
3           3  dave  stone           Event Planner      m    italy
4           4  sara  stein  Director Public Relations  f  germany
5           5  eddy  bower     Directory of Security    m    spain
Contents of df1 after drop:
  fname  lname                        Role gender  country
0  john  smith            VP Marketing      m      usa
1  jane  smith                VP Sales      f   france
2  jack  jones       Event Coordinator      m   france
3  dave  stone           Event Planner      m    italy
4  sara  stein  Director Public Relations  f  germany
5  eddy  bower     Directory of Security    m    spain
Saving data frame to CSV file personnel.csv
Converting bands_list (XML) to CSV...
ROOT: bands
band_id = 100
band_name = The Data Wranglers
Current Element: band_member
band_member = Dave Pallai
Current Element: band_member
band_member = Jennifer Blaney
band_id = 200
band_name = The Data Cleaners
Current Element: band_member
band_member = Raymond Reddington
Current Element: band_member
band_member = Scary Joe
Current Element: band_member
band_member = The Smoother
```

```
Generating CSV calendar of events (COE)...
*** Concert Details ***
      City Concert Date  Tickets (USD)        Band Name  Country
0    paris   01/15/2022             80  The Data Wranglers   france
1   london   02/02/2022             70  The Data Wranglers       uk
2   berlin   02/09/2022             75  The Data Wranglers  germany
3    tokyo   02/19/2022            100  The Data Wranglers    japan
4  vicenza   01/08/2022             50   The Data Cleaners    italy
5    paris   01/18/2022             70   The Data Cleaners   france
6   london   02/05/2022             60   The Data Cleaners       uk
7   berlin   02/13/2022             80   The Data Cleaners  germany
8    tokyo   02/27/2022            100   The Data Cleaners    japan
```

Project Follow-up Comments

If you read the entire project up to this point in the chapter, consider it a job well done. Of course, there are variations in which you can assemble the files in this project to create the final CSV file that contains the calendar of events.

First, a general comment: the high-level description of a project is often much easier to understand than the implementation details. The latter can be tedious, and is also influenced by the technologies that you use to solve the tasks of a project. However, it's important to understand the project goals because they will assist you in maintaining a clear understanding of the purpose of the code that you write: you'll understand what needs to be done and why it needs to be done.

Second, this project attempts to strike a balance between code complexity and readability of the code (i.e., avoiding unnecessary complexity). Keep in mind that this project involves (albeit somewhat contrived) a small dataset with virtually no data cleaning requirements. In contrast, real-world projects can involve time consuming and much more tedious data cleaning tasks that will make this project seem almost trivial. Nevertheless, hopefully you can avail yourself of the data cleaning code samples in this chapter as well as the previous chapter for other tasks.

Third, this project showed you how to convert files to different formats using awk-based shell scripts, Python, Pandas, and Java. In addition, you learned how to generate new files from existing files using these same technologies. Indeed, performing the transformations with the small datasets has probably given you a sense of the complexity to expect when you work with datasets that are hundreds or thousands of times larger than those in this project.

Fourth, you probably noticed that Listing 7.21 did not use all the CSV files that were created earlier in this chapter, such as the CSV file `python_city_codes.csv` that is created by the Python script `construct_city_codes.py`. The reason is two-fold: this ensures that Listing 7.21 is only one page of code and it enables you to modify the structure of some of the CSV files that will necessitate the inclusion of the CSV file `python_city_codes.csv` in your modified solution, in case you wish to do so.

Finally, there are commented-out `print()` statements in the various files for this project. Those statements can be very helpful for debugging purposes and understanding the purpose of the code block that contain those statements. However, *too many* `print()` statements can result in an overload of details, so after you understand a particular block of code, consider commenting out those statements again when you analyze different code blocks. Moreover, you can copy/paste some of the output, as a comment block, into the files that generated the output, near the relevant code block.

SUMMARY

This chapter started with an introduction to the term data wrangling and compared it with the term data cleaning. You also saw several examples of Python scripts that performed data cleaning on malformed CSV files.

Next, you learned how to convert existing files into CSV-based files, and how to generate new CSV files based on existing files. In particular, you learned how to perform the conversion process using different tools, such as shell scripts, Python code, Java code, and Pandas-based code.

Congratulations! Whether you are a beginner or more experienced data scientist, you have probably learned some new techniques that ideally will serve you well in other projects, along with code samples to solve tasks that you might encounter in your future work.

WORKING WITH AWK

This appendix introduces you to the `awk` command, which is a highly versatile utility for manipulating data and restructuring datasets. In fact, this utility is so versatile that entire books have been written about the `awk` utility. Awk is essentially an entire programming language in a single command, which accepts standard input, gives standard output and uses regular expressions and metacharacters in the same way other Unix commands do. This lets you plug it into other expressions and do almost anything, at the cost of adding complexity to a command string that may already be doing quite a lot already. It is almost always worthwhile to add a comment when using awk. It is so versatile that it won't be clear which of the many features you are using at a glance.

The first part of this appendix provides a very brief introduction of the `awk` command. You will learn about some built-in variables for `awk`, and also how to manipulate string variables using `awk`. Note that some of these string-related examples can also be handled using other `bash` commands.

The second part of this appendix shows you conditional logic, `while` loops, and `for` loops in `awk` to manipulate the rows and columns in datasets. This section also shows you how to delete lines and merge lines in datasets, and also how to print the contents of a file as a single line of text. You will see how to "join" lines and groups of lines in datasets.

The third section contains code samples that involve metacharacters and character sets in `awk` commands. You will also see how to use conditional logic in `awk` commands to determine whether to print a line of text.

The fourth section illustrates how to "split" a text string that contains multiple "." characters as a delimiter, followed by examples of `awk` to perform numeric calculations (such as addition, subtraction, multiplication, and division) in files containing numeric data. This section shows you various numeric functions that are available in awk, and how to print text in a fixed set of columns.

The fifth section explains how to align columns in a dataset and how to align and merge columns in a dataset. You will see how to delete columns, select a subset of columns from a dataset, and work with multi-line records in datasets. This section contains some one-line `awk` commands that can be useful for manipulating the contents of datasets.

The final section of this appendix has a pair of use cases involving nested quotes and date formats in structured data sets.

THE AWK COMMAND

The awk (Aho, Weinberger, and Kernighan) command has a C-like syntax and you can use this utility to perform complex operations on numbers and text strings.

As a side comment, there is also the gawk command that is GNU awk, as well as the nawk command is "new" awk (neither command is discussed in this book). One advantage of nawk is that it allows you to set externally the value of an internal variable.

Built-in Variables That Control awk

The awk command provides variables that you can change from their default values to control how awk performs operations. Examples of such variables (and their default values) include FS (" "), RS ("\n"), OFS (" "), ORS ("\n"), SUBSEP, and IGNORECASE. The variables FS and RS specify the field separator and record separator, whereas the variables OFS and ORS specify the output field separator and the output record separator, respectively.

You can think of the field separators as delimiters/IFS we used in other commands earlier. The record separators behave in a way similar to how sed treats individual lines; for example, sed can match or delete a range of lines instead of matching or deleting something that matches a regular expression (and the default awk record separator is the newline character, so by default awk and sed have a similar ability to manipulate and reference lines in a text file).

As a simple example, you can print a blank line after each line of a file by changing the ORS, from default of one newline to two newlines, as shown here:

```
cat columns.txt | awk 'BEGIN { ORS ="\n\n" } ; { print $0 }'
```

Other built-in variables include FILENAME (the name of the file that awk is currently reading), FNR (the current record number in the current file), NF (the number of fields in the current input record), and NR (the number of input records awk has processed since the beginning of the program's execution).

Consult the online documentation for additional information regarding these (and other) arguments for the awk command.

How Does the awk Command Work?

The awk command reads the input files one record at a time (by default, one record is one line). If a record matches a pattern, then an action is performed (otherwise no action is performed). If the search pattern is not given, then awk performs the given actions for each record of the input. The default behavior if no action is given is to print all the records that match the given pattern. Finally, empty braces without any action do nothing (i.e., the program will not perform the default printing operation). Note that each statement in actions should be delimited by a semicolon.

To make the preceding paragraph more understandable, here are some simple examples involving text strings and the awk command (the results are displayed after each code snippet). The -F switch sets the field separator to whatever follows it, in this case, a space.

Switches will often provide a shortcut to an action that normally needs a command inside a
'BEGIN{} block):

```
x="a b c d e"
echo $x |awk -F" " '{print $1}'
a
echo $x |awk -F" " 'a{print NF}'
5
echo $x |awk -F" " '{print $0}'
a b c d e
echo $x |awk -F" " '{print $3, $1}'
c a
```

Let's change the FS (record separator) to an empty string to calculate the length of a string,
this time using the BEGIN{} syntax:

```
echo "abc" | awk 'BEGIN { FS = "" } ; { print NF }'
3
```

The following example illustrates several equivalent ways to specify test.txt as the input
file for an awk command:

```
awk < test.txt '{ print $1 }'
awk '{ print $1 }' < test.txt
awk '{ print $1 }' test.txt
```

Yet another way is shown here (but as we've discussed earlier, it can be inefficient, so only do
it if the cat is adding value in some way):

```
cat test.txt | awk '{ print $1 }'
```

This simple example of four ways to do the same task should illustrate why commenting awk
calls of any complexity is almost always a good idea. The next person to look at your code may
not know/remember the syntax you are using.

ALIGNING TEXT WITH THE printf() STATEMENT

Since awk is a programming language inside a single command, it also has its own way of
producing formatted output via the printf() statement.

Listing A.1 displays the content of columns2.txt and Listing A.2 displays the content of the
shell script AlignColumns1.sh that shows you how to align the columns in a text file.

LISTING A.1: columns2.txt

```
one two
three four
one two three four
five six
one two three
four five
```

LISTING A.2: AlignColumns1.sh

```
awk '
{
    # left-align  $1 on a 10-char column
    # right-align $2 on a 10-char column
    # right-align $3 on a 10-char column
    # right-align $4 on a 10-char column
    printf("%-10s*%10s*%10s*%10s*\n", $1, $2, $3, $4)
}
' columns2.txt
```

Listing A.2 contains a `printf()` statement that displays the first four fields of each row in the file `columns2.txt`, where each field is 10 characters wide.

The output from launching the code in Listing A.2 is here:

```
one        *       two*         *          *
three      *      four*         *          *
one        *       two*    three*     four*
five       *       six*         *          *
one        *       two*    three*          *
four       *      five*         *          *
```

Keep in mind that `printf` is reasonably powerful and as such has its own syntax, which is beyond the scope of this appendix. A search online can find the manual pages and also discussions of "how to do X with printf()."

CONDITIONAL LOGIC AND CONTROL STATEMENTS

Like other programming languages, `awk` provides support for conditional logic (`if/else`) and control statements (`for/while` loops). `awk` is the only way to put conditional logic inside a piped command stream without creating, installing, and adding to the path a custom executable shell script. The following code block shows you how to use `if/else` logic:

```
echo "" | awk '
BEGIN { x = 10 }
{
  if (x % 2 == 0) }
     print "x is even"
  }
  else }
     print "x is odd"
  }
}
'
```

The preceding code block initializes the variable x with the value 10 and prints "x is even" if x is divisible by 2, otherwise it prints "x is odd."

The while Statement

The following code block illustrates how to use a `while` loop in `awk`:

```
echo "" | awk '
{
  x = 0
  while(x < 4) {
    print "x:",x
    x = x + 1
  }
}
'
```

The preceding code block generates the following output:

```
x:0
x:1
x:2
x:3
```

The following code block illustrates how to use a `do while` loop in `awk`:

```
echo "" | awk '
{
  x = 0

  do {
    print "x:",x
    x = x + 1
  } while(x < 4)
}
'
```

The preceding code block generates the following output:

```
x:0
x:1
x:2
x:3
```

A for Loop in awk

Listing A.3 displays the content of `Loop.sh` that illustrates how to print a list of numbers in a loop. Note that `i++` is another way of writing "I=I+1" in `awk` (and most C-derived languages).

LISTING A.3: Loop.sh

```
awk '
BEGIN {}
{
  for(i=0; i<5; i++) {
```

```
    printf("%3d", i)
  }
}
END { print "\n" }
'
```

Listing A.3 contains a `for` loop that prints numbers on the same line via the `printf()` statement. Notice that a new line is printed only in the END block of the code. The output from Listing A.3 is here:

```
0 1 2 3 4
```

A for Loop with a break Statement

The following code block illustrates how to use a `break` statement in a `for` loop in `awk`:

```
echo "" | awk '
{
  for(x=1; x<4; x++) {
    print "x:",x
    if(x == 2) {
      break;
    }
  }
}
'
```

The preceding code block prints output only until the variable x has the value 2, after which the loop exits (because of the `break` inside the conditional logic). The following output is displayed:

```
x:1
```

The next and continue Statements

The following code snippet illustrates how to use `next` and `continue` in a `for` loop in `awk`:

```
awk '
{
   /expression1/ { var1 = 5; next }
   /expression2/ { var2 = 7; next }
   /expression3/ { continue }
   // some other code block here
' somefile
```

When the current line matches `expression1`, then `var1` is assigned the value 5 and `awk` reads the next input line: hence, `expression2` and `expression3` will not be tested. If `expression1` does not match and `expression2` *does* match, then `var2` is assigned the value 7 and `awk` will read the next input line. If only `expression3` results in a positive match, then `awk` skips the remaining block of code and processes the next input line.

DELETING ALTERNATE LINES IN DATASETS

Listing A.4 displays the content of `linepairs.csv` and Listing A.5 displays the content of `deletelines.sh` that illustrates how to print alternating lines from the dataset `linepairs.csv` that have exactly two columns.

LISTING A.4: linepairs.csv

```
a,b,c,d
e,f,g,h
1,2,3,4
5,6,7,8
```

LISTING A.5: deletelines.sh

```
inputfile="linepairs.csv"
outputfile="linepairsdeleted.csv"
awk ' NR%2 {printf "%s", $0; print ""; next}' < $inputfile > $outputfile
```

Listing A.5 checks if the current record number NR is divisible by 2, in which case it prints the current line and skips the next line in the dataset. The output is redirected to the specified output file, the contents of which are here:

```
a,b,c,d
1,2,3,4
```

A slightly more common task involves merging consecutive lines, which is the topic of the next section.

MERGING LINES IN DATASETS

Listing A.6 displays the content of `columns.txt` and Listing A.7 displays the content of `ColumnCount1.sh` that illustrates how to print the lines from the text file `columns.txt` that have exactly two columns.

LISTING A.6: columns.txt

```
one two three
one two
one two three four
one
one three
one four
```

LISTING A.7: ColumnCount1.sh

```
awk '
{
   if( NF == 2 ) { print $0 }
}
' columns.txt
```

Listing A.7 is straightforward: if the current record number is even, then the current line is printed (i.e., odd-numbered rows are skipped). The output from launching the code in Listing A.7 is here:

```
one two
one three
one four
```

If you want to display the lines that do *not* contain 2 columns, use the following code snippet:

```
if( NF != 2 ) { print $0 }
```

Printing File Contents as a Single Line

The contents of `test4.txt` are here (note the blank lines):

```
abc

def

abc

abc
```

The following code snippet illustrates how to print the contents of `test4.txt` as a single line:

```
awk '{printf("%s", $0)}' test4.txt
```

The output of the preceding code snippet is here. See if you can tell what is happening before reading the explanation in the next paragraph:

```
Abcdefabcabc
```

Explanation: `%s` here is the record separator syntax for `printf()`, and the end quote after it means the record separator is the empty field "". Our default record separator for `awk` is /n (newline), so the `printf()` statement strips out all the new lines. The blank rows will vanish entirely, as all they have is the new lines, so the result is that any actual text will be merged together with nothing between them.

Had we added a space between the `%s` and the ending quote, there would be a space between each character block, plus an extra space for each newline. Notice how the following comment improves the comprehension of the code snippet:

```
# Merging all text into a single line by removing the newlines
awk '{printf("%s", $0)}' test4.txt
```

Joining Groups of Lines in a Text File

Listing A.8 displays the content of `digits.txt` and Listing A.9 displays the content of `digits.sh` that "joins" three consecutive lines of text in the file `digits.txt`.

LISTING A.8: digits.txt

```
1
2
3
4
5
6
7
8
9
```

LISTING A.9: digits.sh

```
awk -F" " '{
  printf("%d",$0)
  if(NR % 3 == 0) { printf("\n") }
}' digits.txt
```

Listing A.9 prints three consecutive lines of text on the same line, after which a linefeed is printed. This has the effect of "joining" every three consecutive lines of text. The output from launching digits.sh is here:

```
123
456
789
```

Joining Alternate Lines in a Text File

Listing A.10 displays the content of columns2.txt and Listing A.11 displays the content of JoinLines.sh that "joins" two consecutive lines of text in the file columns2.txt.

LISTING A.10: columns2.txt

```
one two
three four
one two three four
five six
one two three
four five
```

LISTING A.11: JoinLines.sh

```
awk '
{
   printf("%s",$0)
   if( $1 !~ /one/) { print " " }
}
' columns2.txt
```

The output from launching Listing A.11 is here:

```
one two three four
one two three four five six
one two three four five
```

Notice that the code in Listing A.11 depends on the presence of the string "one" as the first field in alternating lines of text. We are merging based on matching a simple pattern, instead of tying it to record combinations.

To merge each pair of lines instead of merging based on matching a pattern, use the modified code in Listing A.12.

LISTING A.12: JoinLines2.sh

```
awk '
BEGIN { count = 0 }
{
   printf("%s",$0)
   if( ++count % 2 == 0) { print " " }
} columns2.txt
```

Yet another way to "join" consecutive lines is shown in Listing A.13, where the input file and output file refer to files that you can populate with data. This is another example of an awk command that might be a puzzle if encountered in a program without a comment. It is doing exactly the same thing as Listing A.12, but its purpose is less obvious because of the more compact syntax.

LISTING A.13: JoinLines2.sh

```
inputfile="linepairs.csv"
outputfile="linepairsjoined.csv"
awk ' NR%2 {printf "%s,", $0; next;}1' < $inputfile > $outputfile
```

MATCHING WITH META CHARACTERS AND CHARACTER SETS

If we can match a simple pattern, we can also match a regular expression. Listing A.14 displays the content of Patterns1.sh that uses metacharacters to match the beginning and the end of a line of text in the file columns2.txt.

LISTING A.14: Patterns1.sh

```
awk '
   /^f/    { print $1 }
   /two $/ { print $1 }
' columns2.txt
```

The output from launching Listing A.14 is here:

```
one
five
four
```

Listing A.15 displays the content of RemoveColumns.txt with lines that contain a different number of columns.

LISTING A.15: columns3.txt

```
123 one two
456 three four
one two three four
five 123 six
one two three
four five
```

Listing A.16 displays the content of `MatchAlpha1.sh` that matches text lines that start with alphabetic characters as well as lines that contain numeric strings in the second column.

LISTING A.16: MatchAlpha1.sh

```
awk '
{
   if( $0 ~ /^[0-9]/) { print $0 }
   if( $0 ~ /^[a-z]+ [0-9]/) { print $0 }
}
' columns3.txt
```

The output from Listing A.16 is here:

```
123 one two
456 three four
five 123 six
```

PRINTING LINES USING CONDITIONAL LOGIC

Listing A.17 displays the content of `products.txt` that contains three columns of information.

LISTING A.17: products.txt

```
MobilePhone 400   new
Tablet      300   new
Tablet      300   used
MobilePhone 200   used
MobilePhone 100   used
```

The following code snippet prints the lines of text in `products.txt` whose second column is greater than 300:

```
awk '$2 > 300' products.txt
```

The output of the preceding code snippet is here:

```
MobilePhone 400   new
```

The following code snippet prints the lines of text in `products.txt` whose product is `new`:

```
awk '($3 == "new")' products.txt
```

The output of the preceding code snippet is here:

```
MobilePhone 400   new
Tablet      300   new
```

The following code snippet prints the first and third columns of the lines of text in prod-ucts.txt whose cost equals 300:

```
awk ' $2 == 300 { print $1, $3 }' products.txt
```

The output of the preceding code snippet is here:

```
Tablet new
Tablet used
```

The following code snippet prints the first and third columns of the lines of text in prod-ucts.txt that start with the string Tablet:

```
awk '/^Tablet/ { print $1, $3 }' products.txt
```

The output of the preceding code snippet is here:

```
Tablet new
Tablet used
```

SPLITTING FILENAMES WITH AWK

Listing A.18 displays the content of SplitFilename2.sh that illustrates how to split a filename containing the "." character to increment the numeric value of one of the components of the filename. Note that this code only works for a file name with exactly the expected syntax.

LISTING A.18: SplitFilename2.sh

```
echo "05.20.144q.az.1.zip" | awk -F"." '
{
  f5=$5 + 1
  printf("%s.%s.%s.%s.%s.%s",$1,$2,$3,$4,f5,$6)
}'
```

The output from Listing A.18 is here:

```
05.20.144q.az.2.zip
```

WORKING WITH POSTFIX ARITHMETIC OPERATORS

Listing A.19 displays the content of mixednumbers.txt that contains postfix operators, which refer to numbers where the negative (and/or positive) sign appears at the end of a column value instead of the beginning of the number.

LISTING A.19: mixednumbers.txt

```
324.000-|10|983.000-
453.000-|30|298.000-
783.000-|20|347.000-
```

Listing A.20 displays the content of `AddSubtract1.sh` that illustrates how to add the rows of numbers in Listing A.19.

LISTING A.20: AddSubtract1.sh

```
myFile="mixednumbers.txt"

awk -F"|" '
BEGIN { line = 0; total = 0 }
{
    split($1, arr, "-")
    f1 = arr[1]
    if($1 ~ /-/) { f1 = -f1 }
    line += f1

    split($2, arr, "-")
    f2 = arr[1]
    if($2 ~ /-/) { f2 = -f2 }
    line += f2

    split($3, arr, "-")
    f3 = arr[1]
    if($3 ~ /-/) { f3 = -f3 }
    line += f3

    printf("f1: %d f2: %d f3: %d line: %d\n",f1,f2,f3, line)
    total += line
    line = 0
}
END { print "Total: ",total }
' $myfile
```

The output from Listing A.20 is here. See if you can work out what the code is doing before reading the explanation that follows:

```
f1: -324 f2: 10 f3: -983 line: -1297
f1: -453 f2: 30 f3: -298 line: -721
f1: -783 f2: 20 f3: -347 line: -1110
Total:  -3128
```

The code assumes we know the format of the file. The `split()` function turns each field record into a length two vector: the first position is a number and second position either an empty value or a dash, and then it captures the first position number into a variable. The `if` statement checks if the original field contains a hyphen (-). If it is present, then the numeric variable is made negative, after which the sum of the values in the line is computed.

NUMERIC FUNCTIONS IN AWK

The int(x) function returns the integer portion of a number. If the number is not already an integer, it falls between two integers. Of the two possible integers, the function will return the one closest to zero. This is different from a rounding function, which chooses the closer integer.

For example, int(3) is 3, int(3.9) is 3, int(-3.9) is -3, and int(-3) is -3, as well. An example of the int(x) function in an awk command is here:

```
awk 'BEGIN {
    print int(3.534);
    print int(4);
    print int(-5.223);
    print int(-5);
}'
```

The output is here:

```
3
4
-5
-5
```

The exp(x) function gives you the exponential of x, or reports an error if x is out of range. The range of values x can have depends on your machine's floating point representation.

```
awk 'BEGIN{
    print exp(123434346);
    print exp(0);
    print exp(-12);
}'
```

The output is here:

```
inf
1
6.14421e-06
```

The log(x) function gives you the natural logarithm of x, if x is positive; otherwise, it reports an error (inf means infinity and nan in output means "not a number").

```
awk 'BEGIN{
    print log(12);
    print log(0);
    print log(1);
    print log(-1);
}'
```

The output is here:

```
2.48491
-inf
0
nan
```

The `sin(x)` function gives you the sine of `x` and `cos(x)` gives you the cosine of `x`, with `x` in radians:

```
awk 'BEGIN {
   print cos(90);
   print cos(45);
}'
```

The output is here:

```
-0.448074
0.525322
```

The `rand()` function gives you a random number. The values of `rand()` are uniformly-distributed between 0 and 1: the value is never 0 and never 1.

Often, you want random integers instead. Here is a user-defined function you can use to obtain a random nonnegative integer less than `n`:

```
function randint(n) {
    return int(n * rand())
}
```

The product generates a random real number greater than 0 and less than `n`. We then make it an integer (using int) between 0 and n - 1.

Here is an example where a similar function is used to produce random integers between 1 and n:

```
awk '
# Function to roll a simulated die.
function roll(n) { return 1 + int(rand() * n) }
# Roll 3 six-sided dice and print total number of points.
{
    printf("%d points\n", roll(6)+roll(6)+roll(6))
}'
```

Note that `rand()` starts generating numbers from the same point (or "seed") each time awk is invoked. Hence, a program will produce the same results each time it is launched. If you want a program to do different things each time it is used, you must change the seed to a value that will be different in each run.

Use the `srand(x)` function to set the starting point, or seed, for generating random numbers to the value `x`. Each seed value leads to a particular sequence of "random" numbers. Thus, if you set the seed to the same value a second time, you will get the same sequence of "random" numbers again. If you omit the argument x, as in `srand()`, then the current date and time of day are used for a seed. This is how to obtain random numbers that are truly unpredictable. The return value of `srand()` is the previous seed. This makes it easy to keep track of the seeds for use in consistently reproducing sequences of random numbers.

The `time()` function (not in all versions of awk) returns the current time in seconds since January 1, 1970. The function `ctime()` (not in all versions of awk) takes a numeric argument in seconds and returns a string representing the corresponding date, suitable for printing or further processing.

The sqrt(x) function gives you the positive square root of x. It reports an error if x is negative. Thus, sqrt(4) is 2.

```
awk 'BEGIN{
    print sqrt(16);
    print sqrt(0);
    print sqrt(-12);
}'
```

The output is here:

```
4
0
nan
```

ONE-LINE AWK COMMANDS

The code snippets in this section reference the text file short1.txt, which you can populate with any data of your choice.

The following code snippet prints each line preceded by the number of fields in each line:

```
awk '{print NF ":" $0}' short1.txt
```

Print the right-most field in each line:

```
awk '{print $NF}' short1.txt
```

Print the lines that contain more than 2 fields:

```
awk '{if(NF > 2) print }' short1.txt
```

Print the value of the right-most field if the current line contains more than 2 fields:

```
awk '{if(NF > 2) print $NF }' short1.txt
```

Remove leading and trailing whitespaces:

```
echo " a b c " | awk '{gsub(/^[ \t]+|[ \t]+$/,"");print}'
```

Print the first and third fields in reverse order for the lines that contain at least 3 fields:

```
awk '{if(NF > 2) print $3, $1}' short1.txt
```

Print the lines that contain the string one:

```
awk '{if(/one/) print }' *txt
```

As you can see from the preceding code snippets, it's easy to extract information or subsets of rows and columns from text files using simple conditional logic and built-in variables in the awk command.

USEFUL SHORT AWK SCRIPTS

This section contains a set of short awk-based scripts for performing various operations. Some of these scripts can also be used in other shell scripts to perform more complex operations. Listing A.21 displays the content of the file data.txt that is used in various code samples in this section.

LISTING A.21: *data.txt*

```
this is line one that contains more than 40 characters
this is line two
this is line three that also contains more than 40 characters
four

this is line six and the preceding line is empty

line eight and the preceding line is also empty
```

The following code snippet prints every line that is longer than 40 characters:

```
awk 'length($0) > 40' data.txt
```

Now print the length of the longest line in data.txt:

```
awk '{ if (x < length()) x = length() }
END { print "maximum line length is " x }' < data.txt
```

The input is processed by the expand utility to change tabs into spaces, so the widths compared are actually the right-margin columns.

Print every line that has at least one field:

```
awk 'NF > 0' data.txt
```

The preceding code snippet illustrates an easy way to delete blank lines from a file (or rather, to create a new file similar to the old file but from which the blank lines have been removed).

Print seven random numbers from 0 to 100, inclusive:

```
awk 'BEGIN { for (i = 1; i <= 7; i++)
print int(101 * rand()) }'
```

Count the lines in a file:

```
awk 'END { print NR }' < data.txt
```

Print the even-numbered lines in the data file:

```
awk 'NR % 2 == 0' data.txt
```

If you use the expression 'NR % 2 == 1' in the previous code snippet, the program would print the odd-numbered lines.

Insert a duplicate of every line in a text file:

```
awk '{print $0, '\n', $0}' < data.txt
```

Insert a duplicate of every line in a text file and remove blank lines:

```
awk '{print $0, "\n", $0}' < data.txt | awk 'NF > 0'
```

Insert a blank line after every line in a text file:

```
awk '{print $0, "\n"}' < data.txt
```

PRINTING THE WORDS IN A TEXT STRING IN AWK

Listing A.22 displays the content of `Fields2.sh` that illustrates how to print the words in a text string using the `awk` command.

LISTING A.22: Fields2.sh

```
echo "a b c d e"| awk '
{
  for(i=1; i<=NF; i++) {
    print "Field ",i,":",$i
  }
}
'
```

The output from Listing A.22 is here:

```
Field  1 : a
Field  2 : b
Field  3 : c
Field  4 : d
Field  5 : e
```

COUNT OCCURRENCES OF A STRING IN SPECIFIC ROWS

Listing A.23 and Listing A.24 display the contents `data1.csv` and `data2.csv`, respectively, and Listing A.25 displays the content of `checkrows.sh` that illustrates how to count the number of occurrences of the string "past" in column 3 in rows 2, 5, and 7.

LISTING A.23: data1.csv

```
in,the,past,or,the,present
for,the,past,or,the,present
in,the,past,or,the,present
for,the,paste,or,the,future
in,the,past,or,the,present
completely,unrelated,line1
```

```
in,the,past,or,the,present
completely,unrelated,line2
```

LISTING A.24: data2.csv

```
in,the,past,or,the,present
completely,unrelated,line1
for,the,past,or,the,present
completely,unrelated,line2
for,the,paste,or,the,future
in,the,past,or,the,present
in,the,past,or,the,present
completely,unrelated,line3
```

LISTING A.25: checkrows.sh

```
files="'ls data*.csv| tr '\n' ' ''"
echo "List of files: $files"

awk -F"," '
( FNR==2 || FNR==5 || FNR==7 ) {
    if ( $3 ~ "past" ) { count++ }
}
END {
    printf "past: matched %d times (INEXACT) ", count
    printf "in field 3 in lines 2/5/7\n"
}' data*.csv
```

Listing A.25 looks for occurrences in the string past in columns 2, 5, and 7 because of the following code snippet:

```
( FNR==2 || FNR==5 || FNR==7 ) {
    if ( $3 ~ "past" ) { count++ }
}
```

If a match occurs, then the value of count is incremented. The END block reports the number of times that the string past was found in columns 2, 5, and 7. Note that strings such as paste and pasted will match the string past. The output from Listing A.25 is here:

```
List of files: data1.csv data2.csv
past: matched 5 times (INEXACT) in field 3 in lines 2/5/7
```

The shell script checkrows2.sh replaces the term $3 ~ "past" with the term $3 == "past" in checkrows.sh in order to check for exact matches, which produces the following output:

```
List of files: data1.csv data2.csv
past: matched 4 times (EXACT) in field 3 in lines 2/5/7
```

PRINTING A STRING IN A FIXED NUMBER OF COLUMNS

Listing A.26 displays the content of `FixedFieldCount1.sh` that illustrates how to print the words in a text string using the `awk` command.

LISTING A.26: FixedFieldCount1.sh

```
echo "aa bb cc dd ee ff gg hh"| awk '
BEGIN { colCount = 3 }
{

  for(i=1; i<=NF; i++) {
     printf("%s ", $i)
     if(i % colCount == 0) {
        print " "
     }
  }
}
'
```

The output from Listing A.26 is here:

```
aa bb cc
dd ee ff
gg hh
```

PRINTING A DATASET IN A FIXED NUMBER OF COLUMNS

Listing A.27 displays the content of `VariableColumns.txt` with lines of text that contain a different number of columns.

LISTING A.27: VariableColumns.txt

```
this is line one
this is line number one
this is the third and final line
```

Listing A.28 displays the content of `Fields3.sh` that illustrates how to print the words in a text string using the `awk` command.

LISTING A.28: Fields3.sh

```
awk '{printf("%s ", $0)}' | awk '
BEGIN { columnCount = 3 }
{
  for(i=1; i<=NF; i++) {
     printf("%s ", $i)
     if( i % columnCount == 0 )
        print " "
  }
}
' VariableColumns.txt
```

The output from Listing A.28 is here:

```
this is line
one this is
line number one
this is the
third and final
line
```

ALIGNING COLUMNS IN DATASETS

If you have read the preceding two examples, the code sample in this section is easy to understand: you will see how to realign columns of data that are correct in terms of their content, but have been placed in different rows (and therefore are misaligned). Listing A.29 displays the content of `mixed-data.csv` with misaligned data values. In addition, the first line and final line in Listing A.28 are empty lines, which will be removed by the shell script in this section.

LISTING A.29: mixed-data.csv

```
Sara, Jones, 1000, CA, Sally, Smith, 2000, IL,
Dave, Jones, 3000, FL, John, Jones,
4000, CA,
Dave, Jones, 5000, NY, Mike,
Jones, 6000, NY, Tony, Jones, 7000, WA
```

Listing A.30 displays the content of `mixed-data.sh` that illustrates how to realign the dataset in Listing A.29.

LISTING A.30: mixed-data.sh

```
#----------------------------------------
# 1) remove blank lines
# 2) remove line feeds
# 3) print a LF after every fourth field
# 4) remove trailing ',' from each row
#----------------------------------------

inputfile="mixed-data.csv"

grep -v "^$" $inputfile |awk -F"," '{printf("%s",$0)}' | awk '
BEGIN { columnCount = 4 }
{
   for(i=1; i<=NF; i++) {
     printf("%s ", $i)
     if( i % columnCount  == 0) { print "" }
   }
}' > temp-columns

# 4) remove trailing ',' from output:
cat temp-columns | sed 's/, $//' | sed 's/ $//' > $outputfile
```

Listing A.30 starts with a `grep` command (online tutorials about `grep` are available) that removes blank lines, followed by an `awk` command that prints the rows of the dataset as a single line of text. The second `awk` command initializes the `columnCount` variable with the value 4 in the `BEGIN` block, followed by a loop that iterates through the input fields. After four fields are printed on the same output line, a linefeed is printed, which has the effect of realigning the input dataset as an output dataset consisting of rows that have four fields. The output from Listing A.30 is here:

```
Sara, Jones, 1000, CA
Sally, Smith, 2000, IL
Dave, Jones, 3000, FL
John, Jones, 4000, CA
Dave, Jones, 5000, NY
Mike, Jones, 6000, NY
Tony, Jones, 7000, WA
```

ALIGNING COLUMNS AND MULTIPLE ROWS IN DATASETS

The preceding section showed you how to re-align a dataset so that each row contains the same number of columns and also represents a single data record. The code sample in this section illustrates how to realign columns of data that are correct in terms of their content and place two records in each line of the new dataset. Listing A.31 displays the content of mixed-data2.csv with misaligned data values, followed by Listing A.32, which displays the content of aligned-data2.csv with the correctly formatted dataset.

LISTING A.31: mixed-data2.csv

```
Sara, Jones, 1000, CA, Sally, Smith, 2000, IL,
Dave, Jones, 3000, FL, John, Jones,
4000, CA,
Dave, Jones, 5000, NY, Mike,
Jones, 6000, NY, Tony, Jones, 7000, WA
```

LISTING A.32: aligned-data2.csv

```
Sara, Jones, 1000, CA, Sally, Smith, 2000, IL
Dave, Jones, 3000, FL, John, Jones, 4000, CA
Dave, Jones, 5000, NY, Mike, Jones, 6000, NY
Tony, Jones, 7000, WA
```

Listing A.33 displays the content of `mixed-data2.sh` that illustrates how to realign the dataset in Listing A.31.

LISTING A.33: mixed-data2.sh

```
#-----------------------------------------
# 1) remove blank lines
# 2) remove line feeds
# 3) print a LF after every 8 fields
# 4) remove trailing ',' from each row
```

```
#----------------------------------------
inputfile="mixed-data2.txt"
outputfile="aligned-data2.txt"

grep -v "^$" $inputfile |awk -F"," '{printf("%s",$0)}' | awk '
BEGIN { columnCount = 4; rowCount = 2; currRow = 0 }
{
    for(i=1; i<=NF; i++) {
      printf("%s ", $i)
      if( i % columnCount == 0) { ++currRow }
      if(currRow > 0 && currRow % rowCount == 0) {currRow = 0; print ""}
    }
}' > temp-columns

# 4) remove trailing ',' from output:
cat temp-columns | sed 's/, $//' | sed 's/ $//' > $outputfile
```

Listing A.33 is very similar to Listing A.30. The key idea is to print a linefeed character after a pair of "normal" records has been processed, which is implemented via the code that is shown in bold in Listing A.33.

Now you can generalize Listing A.33 very easily by changing the initial value of the row-Count variable to any other positive integer, and the code will work correctly without any further modification. For example, if you initialize rowCount to the value 5, then every row in the new dataset (with the possible exception of the final output row) will contain 5 "normal" data records.

REMOVING A COLUMN FROM A TEXT FILE

Listing A.34 displays the content of VariableColumns.txt with lines of text that contain a different number of columns.

LISTING A.34: VariableColumns.txt

```
this is line one
this is line number one
this is the third and final line
```

Listing A.35 displays the content of RemoveColumn.sh that removes the first column from a text file.

LISTING A.35: RemoveColumn.sh

```
awk '{ for (i=2; i<=NF; i++) printf "%s ", $i; printf "\n"; }'
VariableColumns.txt
```

The loop is between 2 and NF, which iterates over all the fields except for the first field. In addition, printf explicitly adds newlines. The output of the preceding code snippet is here:

```
is line one
is line number one
is the third and final line
```

SUBSETS OF COLUMN-ALIGNED ROWS IN DATASETS

Listing A.35 shows you how to align the rows of a dataset, and the code sample in this section illustrates how to extract a subset of the existing columns and a subset of the rows. Listing A.36 displays the content of sub-rows-cols.txt of the desired dataset that contains two columns from every even row of the file aligned-data.txt.

LISTING A.36: sub-rows-cols.txt

```
Sara,  1000
Dave,  3000
Dave,  5000
Tony,  7000
```

Listing A.37 displays the content of sub-rows-cols.sh that illustrates how to generate the dataset in Listing A.36. Most of the code is the same as Listing A.33, with the new code shown in bold.

LISTING A.37: sub-rows-cols.sh

```
#----------------------------------------
# 1) remove blank lines
# 2) remove line feeds
# 3) print a LF after every fourth field
# 4) remove trailing ',' from each row
#----------------------------------------

inputfile="mixed-data.txt"

grep -v "^$" $inputfile |awk -F"," '{printf("%s",$0)}' | awk '
BEGIN { columnCount = 4 }
{
   for(i=1; i<=NF; i++) {
     printf("%s ", $i)
     if( i % columnCount  == 0) { print "" }
   }
}' > temp-columns

# 4) remove trailing ',' from output:
cat temp-columns | sed 's/, $//' | sed 's/$//' > temp-columns2

cat temp-columns2 | awk '
BEGIN { rowCount = 2; currRow = 0 }
{
   if(currRow % rowCount == 0) { print $1, $3 }
   ++currRow
}' > temp-columns3

cat temp-columns3 | sed 's/,$//' | sed 's/ $//' > $outputfile
```

Listing A.37 contains a new block of code that redirects the output of Step #4 to a temporary file temp-columns2 whose contents are processed by another awk command in the last section of Listing A.37. Notice that that awk command contains a BEGIN block that initializes the variables rowCount and currRow with the values 2 and 0, respectively.

The main block prints columns 1 and 3 of the current line if the current row number is even, and then the value of currRow is then incremented. The output of this awk command is redirected to yet another temporary file that is the input to the final code snippet, which uses the cat command and two occurrences of the sed command to remove a trailing "," and a trailing space, as shown here:

```
cat temp-columns3 | sed 's/,$//' | sed 's/ $//' > $outputfile
```

There are other ways to perform the functionality in Listing A.37, and the main purpose is to show you different techniques for combining various bash commands.

COUNTING WORD FREQUENCY IN DATASETS

Listing A.38 displays the content of WordCounts1.sh that illustrates how to count the frequency of words in a file.

LISTING A.38: WordCounts1.sh

```
awk '
# Print list of word frequencies
{
    for (i = 1; i <= NF; i++)
        freq[$i]++
}
END {
    for (word in freq)
        printf "%s\t%d\n", word, freq[word]
}
' columns2.txt
```

Listing A.38 contains a block of code that processes the lines in columns2.txt. Each time that a word (of a line) is encountered, the code increments the number of occurrences of that word in the hash table freq. The END block contains a for loop that displays the number of occurrences of each word in columns2.txt.

The output from Listing A.38 is here:

```
two      3
one      3
three    3
six      1
four     3
five     2
```

Listing A.39 displays the content of WordCounts2.sh that performs a case insensitive word count.

LISTING A.39: WordCounts2.sh

```
awk '
{
    # convert everything to lower case
    $0 = tolower($0)

    # remove punctuation
    #gsub(/[^[:alnum:]_[:blank:]]/, "", $0)

    for(i=1; i<=NF; i++) {
       freq[$i]++
    }
}
END {
    for(word in freq) {
        printf "%s\t%d\n", word, freq[word]
    }
}
' columns4.txt
```

Listing A.39 contains almost identical code to that in Listing A.38, with the addition of the following code snippet that converts the text in each input line to lowercase letters, as shown here:

```
$0 = tolower($0)
```

Listing A.40 displays the contents of columns4.txt.

LISTING A.40: columns4.txt

```
123 ONE TWO
456 three four
ONE TWO THREE FOUR
five 123 six
one two three
four five
```

The output from launching Listing A.39 with columns4.txt is here:

```
456       1
two       3
one       3
three     3
six       1
123       2
four      3
five      2
```

DISPLAYING ONLY "PURE" WORDS IN A DATASET

For simplicity, let's work with a text string and that way we can see the intermediate results as we work toward the solution.

Listing A.41 displays the content of onlywords.sh that contains three awk commands for displaying the words, integers, and alphanumeric strings, respectively, in a text string.

LISTING A.41: onlywords.sh

```
x="ghi abc Ghi 123 #def5 123z"

echo "Only words:"
echo $x |tr -s ' ' '\n' | awk -F" " '
{
   if($0 ~ /^[a-zA-Z]+$/) { print $0 }
}
' | sort | uniq
echo

echo "Only integers:"
echo $x |tr -s ' ' '\n' | awk -F" " '
{
   if($0 ~ /^[0-9]+$/) { print $0 }
}
' | sort | uniq
echo

echo "Only alphanumeric words:"
echo $x |tr -s ' ' '\n' | awk -F" " '
{
   if($0 ~ /^[0-9a-zA-Z]+$/) { print $0 }
}
' | sort | uniq
echo
```

Listing A.41 starts by initializing the variable x:

```
x="ghi abc Ghi 123 #def5 123z"
```

The next step is to split x into words:

```
echo $x |tr -s ' ' '\n'
```

The output is here:

```
ghi
abc
Ghi
123
#def5
123z
```

The third step is to invoke awk and check for words that match the regular expression `^[a-zA-Z]+`, which matches any string consisting of one or more uppercase and/or lowercase letters (and nothing else):

```
if($0 ~ /^[a-zA-Z]+$/) { print $0 }
```

The output is here:

```
ghi
abc
Ghi
```

Finally, if you also want to sort the output and print only the unique words, redirect the output from the `awk` command to the `sort` command and the `uniq` command.

The second `awk` command uses the regular expression `^[0-9]+` to check for integers and the third `awk` command uses the regular expression `^[0-9a-zA-Z]+` to check for alphanumeric words. The output from launching Listing A.37 is here:

```
Only words:
Ghi
abc
ghi

Only integers:
123

Only alphanumeric words:
123
123z
Ghi
abc
ghi
```

You can replace the variable x with a dataset to retrieve only alphabetic strings from that dataset.

WORKING WITH MULTI-LINE RECORDS IN AWK

Listing A.42 displays the content of `employee.txt` and Listing A.43 displays the content of `Employees.sh` that illustrates how to concatenate text lines in a file.

LISTING A.42: employees.txt

```
Name:  Jane Edwards
EmpId: 12345
Address: 123 Main Street Chicago Illinois

Name:  John Smith
EmpId: 23456
Address: 432 Lombard Avenue SF California
```

LISTING A.43: employees.sh

```
inputfile="employees.txt"
outputfile="employees2.txt"

awk '
```

```
{
  if($0 ~ /^Name:/) {
    x = substr($0,8) ","
    next
  }

  if( $0 ~ /^Empid:/) {
   #skip the Empid data row
   #x = x substr($0,7) ","
    next
  }

  if($0 ~ /^Address:/) {
    x = x substr($0,9)
    print x
  }
}
' < $inputfile > $outputfile
```

The output from launching the code in Listing A.43 is here:

```
Jane Edwards, 123 Main Street Chicago Illinois
John Smith, 432 Lombard Avenue SF California
```

Now that you have seen a plethora of `awk` code snippets and shell scripts containing the `awk` command that illustrate various type of tasks that you can perform on files and datasets, you are ready for some uses cases. The next section (which is the first use case) shows you how to replace multiple field delimiters with a single delimiter, and the second use case shows you how to manipulate date strings.

A SIMPLE USE CASE

The code sample in this section shows you how to use the `awk` command to split the comma-separated fields in the rows of a dataset, where fields can contain nested quotes of arbitrary depth.

Listing A.44 displays the content of the file `quotes3.csv` that contains a "," delimiter and multiple quoted fields.

LISTING A.44: quotes3.csv

```
field5,field4,field3,"field2,foo,bar",field1,field6,field7,"fieldZ"
fname1,"fname2,other,stuff",fname3,"fname4,foo,bar",fname5
"lname1,a,b","lname2,c,d","lname3,e,f","lname4,foo,bar",lname5
```

Listing A.45 displays the contents of the file `delim1.sh` that illustrates how to replace the delimiters in `delim1.csv` with a "," character.

LISTING A.45 delim1.sh

```
#inputfile="quotes1.csv"
#inputfile="quotes2.csv"
inputfile="quotes3.csv"
```

```
grep -v "^$" $inputfile |   awk '
{
   print "LINE #" NR ": " $0
   printf ("------------------------\n")
   for (i = 0; ++i <= NF;)
     printf "field #%d : %s\n", i, $i
   printf ("\n")
}' FPAT='([^,]+)|("[^"]+")' < $inputfile
```

The output from launching the shell script in Listing A.44 is here:

```
LINE #1: field5,field4,field3,"field2,foo,bar",field1,field6,field7,
"fieldZ"
------------------------
field #1 : field5
field #2 : field4
field #3 : field3
field #4 : "field2,foo,bar"
field #5 : field1
field #6 : field6
field #7 : field7
field #8 : "fieldZ"


LINE #2: fname1,"fname2,other,stuff",fname3,"fname4,foo,bar",fname5
------------------------
field #1 : fname1
field #2 : "fname2,other,stuff"
field #3 : fname3
field #4 : "fname4,foo,bar"
field #5 : fname5


LINE #3: "lname1,a,b","lname2,c,d","lname3,e,f","lname4,foo,bar",lname5
------------------------
field #1 : "lname1,a,b"
field #2 : "lname2,c,d"
field #3 : "lname3,e,f"
field #4 : "lname4,foo,bar"
field #5 : lname5


LINE #4: "Outer1 "Inner "Inner "Inner C" B" A" Outer1","XYZ1,c,d","XYZ21
name3,e,f"
------------------------
field #1 : "Outer1 "Inner "Inner "Inner C" B" A" Outer1"
field #2 : "XYZ1,c,d"
field #3 : "XYZ21name3,e,f"


LINE #5:
------------------------
```

As you can see, the task in this section is very easily solved via the awk command.

ANOTHER USE CASE

The code sample in this section shows you how to use the awk command to reformat the date field in a dataset and change the order of the fields in the new dataset. For example, given the following input line in the original dataset:

```
Jane,Smith,20140805234658
```

The reformatted line in the output dataset has this format:

```
2014-08-05 23:46:58,Jane,Smith
```

Listing A.46 displays the content of the file dates2.csv that contains a "," delimiter and three fields.

LISTING A.46 dates2.csv

```
Jane,Smith,20140805234658
Jack,Jones,20170805234652
Dave,Stone,20160805234655
John,Smith,20130805234646
Jean,Davis,20140805234649
Thad,Smith,20150805234637
Jack,Pruit,20160805234638
```

Listing A.47 displays the content of string2date2.sh that converts the date field to a new format and shifts the new date to the first field.

LISTING A.47: string2date2.sh

```
inputfile="dates2.csv"
outputfile="formatteddates2.csv"

rm -f $outputfile; touch $outputfile

for line in 'cat $inputfile'
do
   fname='echo $line |cut -d"," -f1'
   lname='echo $line |cut -d"," -f2'
   date1='echo $line |cut -d"," -f3'

   # convert to new date format
   newdate='echo $date1 | awk '{ print substr($0,1,4)"-"substr($0,5,2)"-
"substr($0,7,2)" "substr($0,9,2)":"substr($0,11,2)":"substr($0,13,2)}''

   # append newly formatted row to output file
   echo "${newdate},${fname},${lname}" >> $outputfile
done
```

The contents of the new dataset are here:

```
2014-08-05 23:46:58,Jane,Smith
2017-08-05 23:46:52,Jack,Jones
2016-08-05 23:46:55,Dave,Stone
2013-08-05 23:46:46,John,Smith
```

```
2014-08-05 23:46:49,Jean,Davis
2015-08-05 23:46:37,Thad,Smith
2016-08-05 23:46:38,Jack,Pruit
```

SUMMARY

This appendix introduced the `awk` command, which is essentially an entire programming language packaged into a single Unix command.

We explored some of its built-in variables as well as conditional logic, `while` loops, and `for` loops in `awk` in order to manipulate the rows and columns in datasets. You then saw how to delete lines and merge lines in datasets, and also how to print the contents of a file as a single line of text.

Next you learned how to use meta characters and character sets in `awk` commands. You learned how to perform numeric calculations (such as addition, subtraction, multiplication, and division) in files containing numeric data, and also some numeric functions that are available in `awk`.

In addition, you saw how to align columns in a dataset, delete columns, select a subset of columns from a dataset, and work with multi-line records in datasets. Finally, you saw a couple of simple use cases involving nested quotes and date formats in a structured dataset.

At this point, you have all the tools necessary to do quite sophisticated data cleansing and processing, and you are strongly encouraged to apply them to some task or problem of interest. The final step of the learning process is doing something real.

INDEX